HOLY WARRIORS:
ISLAM AND THE DEMISE OF
CLASSICAL CIVILIZATION

D1609929

John J. O'Ne

3N 13: 9780980994896
N 10:   0980994896

Felibri publications are distributed by Ingram Books Group

TABLE OF CONTENTS

INTRODUCTION

I t should not have been necessary to write the first two or perhaps three chapters of the present book, chapters dealing with the end of the Roman Empire and the demise of Classical civilization. We're all familiar with the story; one that has been told in various forms for very many years. After the Germanic and Asiatic Invasions of the fifth century, the peoples of Western Europe, we are told, reverted to living in thatched, wattle-and-daub huts. Cities were destroyed and abandoned, the art of writing virtually lost, and the mass of the population kept in a state of ignorance by an obscurantist and fanatical Church, which effectively completed the destructive work of the Barbarians. Into this darkened stage, the Arabs arrived in the seventh and eighth centuries like a ray of light. Tolerant and learned, they brought knowledge of the science of antiquity back into Europe and, under their influence, the Westerners began the long journey back to civilization.

That, in a nutshell, is the story told in an enormous number of scholarly treatises and academic textbooks. It is a story implicitly accepted by a large majority of professional historians, both in Europe and North America – among them Bernard Lewis, the doyen of Middle Eastern studies in the English-speaking world; and yet it is a version of the past that is completely and utterly

1

INTRODUCTION

false. Indeed, it would be difficult to imagine a narrative further removed from what actually happened. And, shocking as it may seem, historians have known this for several generations. Why this knowledge has never been fully disseminated or integrated into academic thought is a moot point, but the fact that textbooks designed for schoolchildren and students of higher education can still be printed promoting the above version of events should be a cause of deep concern. For the truth is that when the Arabs reached southern Italy and Spain they found not a bunch of primitive savages, but a highly sophisticated Latin civilization, a civilization rich in cities, agriculture, art and literature, and presided over by completely Romanized Gothic kings. How do we know this? Well, the Arabs themselves said so; and their testimony has been proven categorically by both documentary and archaeological evidence. This has demonstrated, beyond the shadow of a doubt, that the Barbarian rulers who occupied Italy and the Western Empire during the fifth century, far from destroying Roman culture and civilization, rapidly became Romanized themselves, and presided over a veritable renaissance of Classical civilization. The arts and the sciences flourished under them, and their enormous wealth was employed in the construction of brilliantly decorated residences and churches. By 500 AD, virtually all of the damage that had been done during the Invasions of the fifth century had been repaired, and cities flourished as they had under the old Imperial administration. Indeed, the "Barbarian" kings of Italy, from the very beginning, actively imitated the Court in Constantinople, and all of them regarded themselves as not only allies, but functionaries and officers of the Empire. The gold coins they issued were stamped with the image of the Byzantine Emperor, and they dwelt in the palatial villas erected by earlier Roman procurators and princes. Some of these were extended, and all were regularly renovated. Yet, having said all that, it is true that by the end of the seventh century, or at the very latest by the start of the eighth, this flowering Classical civilization came, rather suddenly, to an end; and the medieval world we are all familiar with took shape: cities and towns declined and were sometimes abandoned, trade diminished, life became more rural, the arts declined, illiteracy prevailed, and the feudal system, which fragmented the kingdoms of Western Europe, took shape. In the years which followed, the Church became the sole vehicle of learning and administration, and a barter economy largely replaced the monetary system in place shortly before. What

2

coins were issued, were minted in silver, rather than the gold used till the start of the seventh century. The Middle Ages had begun.

Who or what had produced this situation?

As early as the 1920s Belgian medievalist Henri Pirenne located the proverbial smoking gun. But it was not in the hands of the Goths or Vandals, or the Christian Church: it was in the hands of those people whom it had, even then, become fashionable to credit with *saving* Western Civilization: the Arabs. The evidence, as Pirenne was at pains to show in his posthumously published *Mohammed and Charlemagne*, was incontrovertible. From the mid-seventh century the Mediterranean had been blockaded by the Arabs. Trade with the great centers of population and culture in the Levant, a trade which had been the mainstay of Western Europe's prosperity, was terminated. The flow of all the luxury items which Pirenne found in the records of the Spanish Visigoths and the Merovingians of Gaul, came to an abrupt end, as Arab pirates scoured the seas. The flow of gold to the West dried up. Gold coinage disappeared, and the great cities of Italy, Gaul and Spain, especially the ports, which owed their wealth to the Mediterranean trade, became mere ghost towns. Worst of all, perhaps, from the perspective of culture and learning, the importation of papyrus from Egypt ceased. This material, which had been shipped into Western Europe in vast quantities since the time of the Roman Republic, was absolutely essential for a thousand purposes in a literate and mercantile civilization; and the ending of the supply had an immediate and catastrophic effect on levels of literacy. These dropped, almost overnight, to levels perhaps equivalent to those in pre-Roman times.

The first three chapters of the present work are devoted to a fairly detailed examination of the evidence for the above assertions. In these chapters I rely heavily on Pirenne, for his research is first class and in many ways not to be surpassed. As I said, by rights it should not have been necessary for me to go over this material, for it should already be part of received wisdom. But it is not. Year after year popular and scholarly works on the history of the Mediterranean and of Islam's interaction with Christianity continue to be published – especially in the English-speaking world – without mentioning Pirenne's name, far less taking on board his findings. This was the case, for example, with John Julius Norwich's history of the Mediterranean (*The Middle Sea*), published in 2006. The same is true of the latest offering of Bernard Lewis, the grand old man of

INTRODUCTION

Middle Eastern studies at Princeton, whose 2008 book *God's Crucible: Islam and the Making of Europe, 570 – 1215,* not only ignores Pirenne and his ideas, but comes to conclusions reminiscent of those taught before the appearance of *Mohammed and Charlemagne.* So for example in the above volume Lewis contrasted the cultural sophistication of the eighth century Islamic invaders of Spain with what he describes as the almost Neolithic culture and economy of the Visigoths and Franks whom they encountered. For Lewis, the "Dark Age" was still brought about by the Germanic Invaders of the fifth century, and the Arab blockade of the Mediterranean in the seventh and eighth centuries had no effect upon Europe. For him, the Arabs were still, evidently, the saviors of Europe from barbarism.

How to explain this? Without doubt, political correctness has played a part. The spirit of the age dictates that non-European civilizations (such as the Islamic) should never be criticized, or even critically examined. Such an attitude, which essentially places ideology above evidence, is most disturbing, and needs to be combated at every opportunity.

There is however another factor: Pirenne, along with almost all historians of his age, assumed that Byzantium, which had not been overrun by the Barbarians, never experienced a Dark Age or a Medieval period. This view was prompted, in part at least, by Byzantine propaganda, which always advertised the Empire as the Second Rome and the inheritor of Rome's mantle. As recently as 1953, for example, Sidney Painter could write that, "from 716 to 1057 came [for Byzantium] slightly more than three centuries of glory. The Byzantine Empire was the richest state of Europe, the strongest military power, and by far the most cultivated. During these three centuries while Western Europe was a land of partly tamed barbarians, the Byzantine Empire was a highly civilized state where a most felicitous merger of Christianity and Hellenism produced a fascinating culture." (*A History of the Middle Ages, 284-1500*). To this day, popular literature tells us how, after the taking of Constantinople by the Turks in 1453, Greek scholars and philosophers, fleeing to the West, helped "kick-start" the Renaissance in Italy. But if Byzantine civilization was not destroyed by the Arabs, why should anyone believe they destroyed classical civilization in the West? This was a point Pirenne did not address: He was perhaps unaware of its importance. Yet developments in Byzantine archaeology since the Second World War have now come dramatically to the support of Pirenne: For it has

4

been shown, much to the surprise of everyone, that from the mid-seventh century onwards, the Eastern Empire suffered its own Dark Age: Byzantium experienced three centuries during which – in complete contrast to the opinion expressed above – almost all her cities were abandoned, populations plummeted and high culture came to an end. So great was the destruction that even bronze coinage, the everyday lubricant of commercial life, disappeared. And when archaeology again appears, in the middle of the tenth century, the civilization it reveals has been radically altered: The old Byzantium of Late Antiquity is gone, and we find an impoverished and semi-literate rump; a Medieval Byzantium strikingly like the Medieval France, Germany and Italy with which it was contemporary.

The disappearance of all archaeology during the late seventh, eighth, ninth and early tenth centuries, highlighted by writers such as Cyril Mango, is so complete that it makes us wonder whether something else is involved, such as a chronological error: For the archaeological hiatus is not confined to the territory of the Eastern Empire, but occurs also in the West and elsewhere, in some very surprising places indeed. What all this might mean is a question addressed near the end of the present volume. But however we view the three Dark Age centuries, there is no doubt that, by the tenth century, Byzantium became "Medieval", and this medievalism was a precise counterpart of the medievalism of the West. Here we find too a barter or semi-barter economy; a decline in population and literacy; and an intolerant and theocratic state. And the break-off point in Byzantium, as in the West, is the first half of the seventh century – precisely corresponding to the arrival on the scene of the Arabs and of Islam.

The evidence from the East, which has, regrettably, not yet become "common knowledge" even in the world of academia, weighs decisively in favor of Pirenne. The debate is essentially over – though the knowledge of that fact has yet to percolate through to the history faculties of our universities. Classical civilization, just as Pirenne said all those years ago, did not end in the fifth century; it ended in the seventh; and it was terminated by the Arabs.

In this spirit then, and to emphasize the point, the first two chapters examine European society during the fifth and sixth centuries, when the "Barbarian" Kingdoms were established in Western Europe. We find, as did Pirenne, that there was no "Dark Age" at this time, and that Classical

INTRODUCTION

civilization continued, after a short period of disruption in the early and mid-fifth century, to flourish. Indeed, as time passed these "Barbarians" rapidly became more and more Romanized, or should we say, Byzantinized; and by the sixth century the influence of Constantinople was felt everywhere in the West – even in distant Britain, where the kings interred at Sutton Hoo were laid to rest with a great hoard of Byzantine silverware. Europe, the whole of Europe, was becoming a cultural colony of Constantinople.

This all came to an abrupt end in the seventh century. The arrival of Islam, as we see in the third chapter, effectively isolated Europe, all of Europe, East and West, both intellectually and economically. The resulting impoverishment produced what is now known as the Dark Ages, or more correctly, the Middle Ages. Society rapidly became more rural, as the great cities which depended on the Mediterranean trade declined. Illiteracy became rampant, as the Egyptian papyrus, which had fueled the economic and cultural life of Europe for centuries, became unavailable. Kings lost much of their power, as the taxable sources of their wealth dried up, and powerful local potentates, who were to become the feudal barons of the Middle Ages, began to flex their muscles. And with this economic paralysis came war: the Muslim conquests were to unleash a torrent of violence against Europe. As a direct result of the Arab advance, by the seventh and eighth centuries, Christendom, the area within which Christianity was the dominant religion, diminished almost to vanishing-point. This catastrophic loss of territory – everything from northern Syria to the Pyrenees – took place in a space of two or three generations. In Western Europe there remained only a nucleus of Christian territory, comprising France, Western Germany, the Upper Danube and Italy (as well as Ireland and parts of Britain); and these regions felt themselves threatened also with imminent extinction: For the surviving Christian territories were besieged and under sustained attack from the north and east, as well as the south. As the Arabs sent army after army to plunder, destroy and occupy, they encouraged and, in some ways directed, further attacks on the core areas of Europe from other directions. Thus even the Viking onslaught, which devastated huge areas of the British Isles, France and northern Germany, was elicited by the Muslim demand for slaves. The latter is a fact not yet widely known, though well-accepted by professional historians: the Vikings, essentially, were piratical slave-traders, and their notorious expeditions across the seas to the west and

6

along the great rivers of Russia to the east were elicited first and foremost by the Muslim demand for white-skinned concubines and eunuchs. Without Islam, there would almost certainly have been no Vikings. As it was, this trading-alliance between the barbarians of the North and the Muslims of Spain and North Africa was to bring Christian Europe to the brink of collapse.

As if all that were not enough, the attempt to control the inroads of Muslims and Vikings opened Europe to the depredations of other predatory peoples, most especially from the steppe lands of central Asia, and one of these in particular, the Magyars, or Hungarians, were to prove a real threat, for a time, to the continued existence of a Christian Germany.

As the Appendix at the end will explain, the present author has serious doubts about the chronology of this so-called "dark age", and there is much evidence to indicate that the Viking and Hungarian attacks against the West began simultaneously with the main thrust of the Islamic onslaught – around the middle of the seventh century. Certainly the weight of evidence, as noted above, suggests that the Viking raids were elicited by the wealth to be had in supplying the Muslim slave-markets of North Africa, Syria and Spain. If this is the case, it means that for up to a century the west suffered a concerted attack on all fronts, an attack that threatened to extinguish Christian civilization.

In Chapter 4 we pause to take a detailed look at the culture and ideology responsible for the above events. We are all aware that in our own age of an influential body of opinion which sees Islam as a "religion of peace" and which views it is a source of much that is valuable in the modern world. This opinion, which had its roots in the nineteenth century, became predominant in the twentieth; and is now more or less the default position in academia. Convinced by the notion that the Arabs of the seventh and eighth centuries encountered a Europe enveloped in Germanic barbarism, historians wax lyrical of early Islam. Some have gone so far as to credit the Arabs with laying the foundations of modern science. That this is not a new opinion is confirmed by a look at what historians, from at least the latter years of the nineteenth century, were saying. Consider for example the words of historian and social anthropologist Robert Briffault, writing in 1917 (*The Making of Humanity*): "The incorruptible treasures and delights of intellectual culture were accounted by the princes of Baghdad, Shiraz and Cordova, the truest and proudest pomps of their courts. But it was not as a mere appendage to their princely vanity that the wonderful

INTRODUCTION

growth of Islamic science and learning was fostered by their patronage. They pursued culture with the personal ardour of an overmastering craving. Never before and never since, on such a scale, has the spectacle been witnessed of the ruling classes throughout the length and breadth of a vast empire given over entirely to a frenzied passion for the acquirement of knowledge. Learning seemed to have become with them the chief business of life. ... caravans laden with manuscripts and botanical specimens plied from Bokhara to the Tigris, from Egypt to Andalusia. ... To every mosque was attached a school; wazirs vied with their masters in establishing public libraries, endowing colleges, founding bursaries for impecunious students. ... It was under the influence of the Arabian and Moorish revival of culture, and not in the fifteenth century, that the real Renaissance took place. Spain, not Italy, was the cradle of the rebirth of Europe. After steadily sinking lower and lower into barbarism, it had reached the darkest depths of ignorance and degradation when the cities of the Saracenic world, Baghdad, Cairo, Cordova, Toledo, were growing centres of civilization and intellectual activity. It was there the new life arose which was to grow into a new phase of human evolution. From the time when the influence of their culture made itself felt, began the stirring of a new life." And so on.

Such sentiments were perhaps excusable in the years before Pirenne's revelations – though even then, it must be said, they could be held only by a very selective view of the evidence. Just how enlightened is a culture that holds (as we shall see), as a central doctrine of the faith, the existence of a perpetual war between itself and non-believers; a culture which prescribes the death-penalty for all apostates; which views slave-trading and slave-raiding as perfectly legitimate occupations, and which keeps women in a state of abject subjugation? In the years after Pirenne, there was certainly no excuse for the survival of Briffault's rose-tinted fantasy. Yet survive it did, and does, to this day.

The truth, however, is that early Islam was neither tolerant, nor enlightened: Its impact was just the opposite of that imagined by Briffault. It was an ideology and a movement that left what can only be described as a corrosive legacy whose consequences have reverberated through the generations and centuries. It was a system that, among other things, breathed new life into the institution of slavery and introduced into Europe, for the first time, a virulent and lethal form of anti-Semitism. And this is a fact not widely known: The first

8

HOLY WARRIORS

Jews to be killed in Europe for their religion were killed in Spain. They were not however killed by Christians, but by Muslims. The story of how Arab attitudes to the Jews, as well as to heretics and apostates, came to be adopted in Medieval Europe, is one of the great untold stories of history; and it is a topic of fundamental importance in our study.

Chapter 4 introduces us to the origins of these attitudes in Islam. We find too that, far from being a force for enlightenment, Islam was, from almost the beginning, hostile to the very concept of science and learning. And to describe the science that existed throughout the Middle and Near East in the seventh and eighth centuries as "Arabic" or "Islamic" is quite ridiculous. The Arabs themselves who, by the middle of the seventh century had come to control all the great and ancient centers of culture in the region – including Egypt, Syria, Mesopotamia, and Persia – were illiterate or semi-literate nomads, who had little or no understanding of the learning of the peoples of those regions. But they did not, to begin with at least, destroy it. They merely installed their religion and with it their language in the corridors of power. The result was that by the eighth century, many or most of the alchemists, mathematicians, astronomers and physicians based in those regions were known by Arab names. But they were not Arabs, nor were they, in most cases, even Muslims. The vast majority were Christians, Jews and Zoroastrians, who continued to practice their own faiths, though they now labored under an Islamic regime and Arab masters, and were compelled to publish their findings in the Arabic language. Nor should it be forgotten that virtually all of the scientific and technical innovations which Europeans have traditionally described as "Arab", actually originated in China and India, and made their way westwards to the Near East via Persia. Such, for example, was the case with the compass, paper, and the use of the zero in mathematics. It is possible, even probable, that several of these had already reached Sassanid Persia by the reign of Chosroes II, ie. just before the Islamic takeover, and the Arabs simply used ideas and technologies already in place. This was admitted even by such writers as Briffault.

With or without the Arabs, these things would have made their way to Europe. The only Arab contribution was to impede this process. Having closed the Mediterranean to their trade, thus impoverishing Europeans materially, the Arabs also prevented the rapid adoption of the new Chinese and Indian inventions by the besieged westerners. And they would not long suffer the spirit

9

INTRODUCTION

of rationalism and scientific enquiry to survive even in their own lands. Within a short time – a very short time indeed – Muslim theologians were declaring that all scientific and philosophical enquiry was contrary to Allah's will, and the flourishing sciences which the Arabs found in Egypt, Syria, Mesopotamia and Persia, were crushed under the weight of a totalitarian theocracy. Thus by the twelfth century at the latest, Europe – without the aid of paper and with limited and very late access to the ideas and technologies which reached the Near East from China and India much earlier – had taken the lead, a lead that was never to be relinquished. Thus we find that when the Turks besieged Constantinople in the fourteenth and fifteenth centuries they were compelled to find European armorers who could cast for them the cannons to breach the walls of the city – this in spite of the fact that both gunpowder and firearms were Asiatic inventions which reached the West much later than they had reached the Arab world.

Having examined Islam and the nature of Muslim culture, we return to Europe and an examination of the West's response. This was, in fact, multi-faceted, both in material and ideological terms. Perhaps the most obvious, and certainly the most controversial, European response was military: the Crusades. The average non-academic, influenced by a politically-correct popular media, now imagines the Crusades to be an almost incomprehensible adventure launched by the aggressive warrior-aristocracy of Europe against a quiescent and cultured Islamic Middle East. But this is far from being the case. The Crusades were in fact a European response to Islamic conquest, and they began not in Palestine at all, but in Spain and Sicily. In fact, the Spanish and southern Italian crusades were ongoing from the first arrival of Islamic armies on European soil, and there never was a time when this war ended or even paused. Fighting was not always intense, but it was incessant. By the end of the tenth century the war for Spain had reached a crucial stage, and early in the eleventh century the monks of Cluny in southern France called upon the kings of Europe to intervene. From this point onwards a continual stream of French, German and Burgundian knights made their way across the Pyrenees to engage the Moors, and the tide of battle turned. Yet just as Islam began to lose ground in the west, it gained spectacular new victories in the east; and it was these that eventually led to the launching of what is known as the First Crusade.

HOLY WARRIORS

By the middle of the eleventh century the newly-Islamicized Turks of Central Asia had seized control of Persia and much of the Middle East, and in 1071 their sultan, Alp Arslan, won a great victory over the Byzantines at Manzikert. This was to prove a decisive moment. Within two or three years the whole of Anatolia and Asia Minor, with the exception of a tiny portion of land close to Constantinople, had been lost to the Turks. The capital of the Eastern Empire itself was now threatened, and Emperor Alexius Comnenus appealed to the Pope for help. Thus was launched the First Crusade.

It is perfectly clear from this that the Crusades were not launched by an aggressive and expansionist Christendom against a peaceful and inoffensive Muslim world. They were, as commonsense in any case suggests, defensive actions against an aggressive and relentless foe. Having said that, it does seem strange that Christendom should wait almost four centuries after the initial Muslim expansion, which saw the loss of all the Christian lands of the Middle East and North Africa, before producing anything like an organized and full-scale response. So, here again, we must mention an apparent chronological inconsistency; and the same anomaly is encountered when we consider the most important political consequence of Islam's appearance: the re-establishment of the Western Empire.

With Byzantium fighting for her survival in the East, the Germanic kings of the West now, finally, in the tenth century, took the step they had never previously dared to: they re-established the Western Empire, with a Germanic king as Emperor. In this they obtained the full support of the Papacy. The whole of Western Europe now detached itself politically, culturally and religiously, from the East. Yet once again the problem of chronology raises its head. Commonsense alone would suggest that the break between West and East would occur within a few decades of the appearance of Islam. We know that by the middle of the seventh century, Constantinople had lost all her territories in Syria and large parts of North Africa, and the Muslims were poised to strike at the capital itself, which was besieged on more than one occasion. The Empire was now helpless. Why did no Germanic king at this point claim the crown of the Western Empire; and why would no Germanic king do so until the tenth century (leaving aside the entirely ephemeral actions of Charlemagne at the beginning of the ninth)?

INTRODUCTION

Here again then we find a mysterious gap of three centuries in the historical narrative.

The final chapter remains focused on Europe and examines the broader ideological and philosophical impact of Islam. This, as we shall see, was profound and far more important than has hitherto been realized.

Until the closing of the Mediterranean in the seventh century, the predominant cultural influence upon Europe was from the East: from Byzantium and from the ancient Hellenistic centers in the Near East, especially Egypt and Syria. With the closing of the Mediterranean, the West was isolated, and the centre of gravity moved, as Pirenne stressed, to the North; to northern Gaul, Germany and Britain. Yet the influence of the East did not come to an end. There was continuity. But now the East meant Islam. And in the centuries after the first Arab conquests, the influence of Islam became profound: It was this influence that would definitively terminate Classical civilization and give birth to the theocracy we now call "Medieval Europe".

The first and most obvious Islamic idea to be adopted by Europeans was that of Holy War. Before the seventh century, Christianity had been largely true to its pacifist roots. Even after becoming the official religion of the Empire, Christians tended to eschew the army as a career and the taking of any human life, even in war, continued to be frowned upon. In the words of Gibbon – no friend of Christianity – by the fifth century; "The clergy successfully preached the doctrines of patience and pusillanimity; the active virtues of society were discouraged, and the last remains of the military spirit [of Rome] were buried in the cloister; a large portion of public and private wealth was consecrated to the specious demands of charity and devotion; and the soldiers' pay was lavished on the useless multitudes of both sexes, who could only plead the merits of abstinence and charity." (*Decline and Fall*, Chapter 38). This may go part of the way to explain the recruitment into the army of great numbers of Barbarians from the fourth century onwards. Actually, by the late fourth and certainly by the fifth century the words "barbarian" and "soldier" became virtually synonymous.

The Gothic and Vandal kings who supplanted the Roman Emperors in the West were, to begin with, not exactly pacifists. Whilst readily accepting Christianity, the new faith had to find a place alongside the ancient warlike cults of Woden and Thor. Nonetheless, by the end of the sixth century, even the

12

warlike nature of the Teutonic rulers began to dissipate. Gibbon notes that, under the spell of Christianity, the Goths and Vandals soon lost their martial traditions: so much so that by the seventh and eighth centuries the Germanic kings of North Africa and Spain were utterly unable to stem the Islamic advance in those regions.

What a contrast this Christianity appears when we compare it with the muscular and militant faith of the Middle Ages, the faith of the Crusaders, Inquisitors and Conquistadors.

This new Christianity was a direct consequence of the clash with Islam, for it did not appear until after the arrival of Islam. In one respect, the change came quite simply because it had to: Surrounded by aggressors bent on its destruction, aggressors with whom it was impossible to make peace, Christians had to take up arms. This was as true among the Christians of the North, threatened by the Vikings and Hungarians, as it was among the Christians of the South, threatened by the Muslims. But the change was elicited by ideology as well as simple necessity. Europeans began to be profoundly influenced by Muslim ideas – ideas on war, interpretation of Scriptures, heresy, the Jews, etc. This was a purely "Medieval" outlook: indeed, it was the very epitome of what we now mean by "Medieval.".

Historians are familiar with the influence of Islamic philosophy upon the West at this time, and they quote, generally with approval, the study by Europeans of the Persian Muslim Avicenna and the Spanish Muslim Averroes. But not everything that came from Islam was so benevolent. It is widely known, for example, that the Byzantine doctrine of iconoclasm, the destruction of sacred religious images, was directly attributable to the influence of Islam. But many Islamic ideas, some of them the polar opposite of those found in early Christianity, now began to find resonance in the thinking of Europeans at almost every level. How could it have been otherwise, when impoverished Christian travelers viewed with astonishment the wealth, luxury and sophistication of Muslim cities in Spain, Sicily, and further east? That this wealth and luxury was debarred to them by the very Muslim Emirs and Caliphs whose opulence they so much admired, was beside the point. Europeans could only be impressed, and influenced. And influenced they were. From the Muslims they learned "Holy War"; from them they learned too that the Jews were an accursed race and the enemies of God. The consequences of these Islamic notions about the Jews were to be as long-lasting as they were tragic.

Islamic fatalism, founded on the conviction that Allah could not be bound by any kind of natural or scientific laws, was lethal to the rationalism of Greece and Rome, which now began to die. Parallel with this development, there appeared, first in Islamic Spain and then throughout Europe, that obsession with sorcery and witchcraft which was to be one of the hallmarks of the Middle Ages. From Islam too the Europeans breathed the essence of fanaticism. Islamic law decreed death to be the only fit punishment for a heretic or an apostate. No such idea had ever existed among Christians. True there had always been fierce doctrinal and theological disputes among Christians which even, at times, turned violent. But such violence as occurred was mainly verbal and rarely involved physical attack. By the end of the eleventh century, Christian Europe, under the influence of Islam both in Europe and in the Middle East, was beginning to think in a very different way; and within a hundred years the Popes had defined and published their new doctrine of capital punishment for dissenters. Torture too, absolutely normal in Islamic lands, began, for the first time, to be applied judicially in Europe.

We end with an examination of the vexed question of the Dark Age. As the reader will discover, this involves a radical questioning of the chronology of the period. The decision to include this topic was not an easy one, involving as it does the proposition that a large chunk of the Early Middle Ages never existed, and that several centuries of "phantom time" have been added to the calendar. These centuries, roughly from the first quarter of the seventh to the first quarter of the tenth, are virtually devoid of archaeology, and are the very core of what we call the Dark Age. In the early 1990s, German writer Heribert Illig suggested that this archaeological hiatus, which appears not only in the Christian West, but in the Byzantine East and the Islamic world (neither of which were invaded by Barbarian tribes and therefore should have no "dark age"), is explained by the fact that these centuries never existed at all, but were inserted into the calendar during the reign of German Emperor Otto III.

I could not be oblivious to the danger that including this subject might have caused an already controversial work to be branded as sensationalist. In the end, however, I felt that inclusion could not be avoided. There were several reasons for this, the most important of which was the preservation of the logic and continuity of the historical narrative. As things stand – as noted above – the early Middle Ages present the historian with several seemingly insoluble conundrums: Why, for example, is it that the ideological impact of Islam on Europe is not felt until the tenth and eleventh centuries, whereas the economic impact, as Pirenne stressed, is felt in the seventh and eighth? Again, if the Crusades were the European response to the Islamic expansion, why did that response not materialize in the eighth century? Why did it have to wait till the eleventh century? This is a problem that generations of historians have never been able to fathom. And it is the unnatural separation of these two events that has cast the Crusaders in the role of aggressors: the three-and-a-half-centuries-wide separation of them from the earlier Muslim conquests makes it appear that the Westerners, for no apparent reason, attacked a long-established and peaceful Islamic world. Yet these "Holy Wars", which actually began in Spain, were clearly part of an ongoing effort on the part of Christendom to stem an Islamic tide which had not yet begun to ebb. We see clues to this everywhere. Thus for example the Spanish *Reconquista* is said to have begun with the victory of Don Pelayo at Covadonga around 720; though the "real" *Reconquista* only got going in the 1020s and 1030s, three hundred years later. Remove three centuries from the later dates, and the two separated episodes are again "joined-up".

This war for possession of the Iberian Peninsula was to grow into a real "clash of civilizations", with both Muslims and Christians calling on the support of co-religionists from far and wide. Some of the most important Christian victories were won by knights from Normandy, France and Burgundy; and these men, who learned the idea of "Holy War" from their Muslim opponents, would form the backbone of the warriors of the First Crusade.

The profound transformation that occurred in Christian thinking at this time can best be understood if the timescales are revised. If, as Illig's chronology suggests, Western Europe was simultaneously attacked by Muslims, Vikings and Magyars, who threatened to wipe Christendom off the earth, then the radical transformation of Christianity from the pacifist cult which Gibbon blamed for destroying the military spirit of Rome, into the muscular, militant, and at times brutal religion of the Crusaders, becomes far easier to understand.

INTRODUCTION

It goes without saying that a study of this type cannot be regarded as the last word. I have been compelled to examine, in a fundamental way, several areas of human history separated from each other by substantial periods of time. All of these already possess an enormous literature; and it would be impossible to do justice to even a fraction of the work that has been done on these areas – mainly Late Antiquity and the Early Middle Ages – even in the past fifty years. The sheer quantity of material makes a comprehensive overview well-nigh impossible, and I have tried instead to provide a reasonably representative sample. In various places I have referred also to sources such as the *Encyclopaedia Britannica* and even internet sites, such as Wikipedia. This is not because I regard these as especially reliable or appropriate for use in this way, but because they tend to give a good idea of how certain things are seen in popular culture. Such knowledge is important in a topic of this type, where polemic and propaganda have given rise to numerous myths whilst simultaneously obscuring the facts.

As well as the voluminous literature of the past century or two, there exists from this supposed Dark Age a much more limited quantity of primary material – though much of this, particularly from the seventh to ninth centuries – is of questionable authenticity: An increasing number of Dark Age documents have lately been exposed as forgeries, some of them produced as recently as the nineteenth century (this is the case, for example, of several of the documents purporting to come from the Langobard era)

To these written sources must be added the important evidence of archaeology. Indeed archaeology, a science barely two centuries old, has begun to transform our understanding of Late Antiquity and the Early Middle Ages. As well as bringing to light the material conditions of the period in question, the spade of the excavator have thrown up a number of surprising, even astonishing, facts. One of the strangest is that virtually nothing from the seventh, eighth and ninth centuries has been found either in Western Europe, the Byzantine East, or the Islamic world. And this disappearing act is so complete that even the artifacts of everyday life are absent. Thus the Anglo-Saxons of England, for example, apparently stopped producing pottery for some three hundred years!

The meaning of this remarkable anomaly is examined in the Appendix.

CHAPTER 1

THE MEDIEVAL PROBLEM

Classical and Medieval

he term "medieval" means "of the middle age" and is used very broadly to describe the centuries between the end of the Roman epoch and the beginning of the modern age, which is generally reckoned to have commenced with the Renaissance, say in the mid-fifteenth century. A portion of this "Middle" age is termed "dark", or the "Dark Age". Indeed, at one time the whole period between the collapse of the Western Roman Empire and the beginning of the Renaissance was known as the Dark Age, but this usage has now been dropped, and the term confined to the seventh, eighth, ninth, and (sometimes) tenth centuries.

The era after the collapse of Rome was originally described as medieval, or dark, because so little seemed to be known of it in comparison with the period of the Roman Empire and Classical antiquity; epochs of the past which appeared much richer in documentation and monuments. Although these terms did not originally have negative connotations, that quickly changed after the Reformation. Protestant propagandists of the sixteenth and seventeenth centuries began to use the term "medieval" in an increasingly negative light; and this tendency was accentuated by the writers of the Enlightenment. Indeed, examination of the history of the Middle Ages could easily lead to the conclusion that this was a barbarous and ignorant epoch; and that is certainly the view which now prevails in popular culture. Whether or not the Middle Ages were culturally inferior or barbarous is a question of great complexity, but it is not one that concerns us at this point. For now, we content ourselves with noting that these "medieval" centuries were characterized by some features which were inferior (and I refer here to the fields of the arts, sciences, and political organization), to the world of classical antiquity. Thus, among other things, the medieval world was a time of: (a) Decline in urban life; (b) A (possible) decline in population; (c) Decline in trade and general prosperity; (d) Political fragmentation and feudalism; (e) Decline in literacy and learning; (f) A fundamentalist or literalist interpretation of Sacred Scriptures; and (g) An intolerant and narrow view of other faiths and cultures.

One of the great questions that have exercised the minds of historians over the past two or three centuries has been: How did this lamentable situation arise? How was it that the advanced and sophisticated civilization of ancient Rome, which seems much more familiar to the modern mind than does the much closer medieval world, collapsed and gave rise to this apparently primitive and ignorant age?

In the search for the authors of the collapse of Rome, there have been a number of suspects, but the usual suspects are the ones we must deal with first; and deal with at some length: namely the barbarians and the Christians.

The idea that Roman civilization, and with it all the learning of the classical world, was overthrown by the barbarian tribes of Germany and Scythia, has a long and illustrious history. Indeed, shortly after Alaric and his Goths sacked Rome in 406 AD, writers of the time were talking of the collapse of civilization. This idea was never really challenged, and it gained new currency with the revival of classical learning during the fourteenth and fifteenth centuries. By the sixteenth century, however, a new suspect was added to the list: the Christian, or, more accurately, the Catholic Christian, Church. During the sixteenth and seventeenth centuries Protestant historians began to suggest that classical civilization had been overthrown as much by the brutal and obscurantist "Roman" Catholic Church, as by the barbarians themselves. And this view was taken up again by the anti-Christian writers of the Enlightenment. Thus by 1788, Gibbon could write that, in describing the fall of the Roman Empire, he was describing "the triumph of barbarism and religion." The religion he had in mind, of course, was the Christian one.

HOLY WARRIORS

Whilst an anti-Christian such as Gibbon could reasonably be expected to compare the Christians with the Goths and Huns, the reader might wonder why Protestant writers should hold a similar view. The answer is simple: For them, the Christian hierarchy and leadership had been irredeemably corrupted when Constantine and his successors made it the official faith of the Roman Empire. With that act, they believed, the true, simple, and pure doctrine of Christ was lost; and a powerful and corrupt priesthood, in cahoots with the Imperial authorities, systematically degraded the faith of Christ, and (simultaneously) destroyed classical civilization. For them, then, it was not Christianity as such which was incompatible with learning and civilized life, but Roman Christianity.

The above view is still widely held, on both sides of the Atlantic, and is frequently given expression in popular culture. Whether or not it is correct, there is no question that by the high Middle Ages (admittedly well after the time of Constantine), Catholic Christianity had changed dramatically from the simple faith of the early centuries. A church which can torture and burn people for alleged heresy, as the medieval church did, has certainly travelled a long way from the teachings of Christ. And this brings us to another aspect of the conundrum, intimately tied to the question of what caused the Dark Age is that of the church's transformation: How did Christianity change from the pacifist and humane doctrine taught by Jesus of Nazareth, into the militant, intolerant, and frequently violent faith of the Crusaders, Inquisitors and Conquistadores?

If the big change in Christianity really did take place in the time of Constantine, and if the newly powerful Catholic hierarchy really did destroy classical learning simply to keep the people ignorant and under their control – as the Protestants and the Enlightenment thinkers believed – then there is no puzzle, and the question of the Dark Ages is answered. If however the Christian church remained essentially true to its mission after the time of Constantine, and if classical civilization did not come to an end either with the Christianization of the Empire or with the Barbarian Invasions – if neither Christians nor barbarians caused the Dark Age – then there is a real mystery; and it is a mystery that needs answering.

The evidence in fact shows that neither Christians nor barbarians were responsible for the destruction of classical culture.

THE MEDIEVAL PROBLEM

Impact of the Barbarians on Classical Civilization

It has always been known that the Germanic tribes which crossed the Roman frontiers in the fourth and fifth centuries came not to destroy Rome and her civilization, but to share in its benefits. This is commonsense. A tribesman in the forests and bogs of Germany, living with the perpetual danger of violence and starvation, would naturally prefer the peace and security of life in the Empire, where he might even aspire to living in a Roman city in a luxurious villa. In short, "The Germans did not want to overthrow the Roman Empire. They simply wanted to share its obvious wealth."[1] The latter comment was made by a popular historian writing mainly for students in the 1960s. It is a truth so obvious that it shouldn't need repeating, yet sadly it must be, given the gross misconceptions that have prevailed for such a long time. As an example of the latter, consider the words of Anglo-French historian and social anthropologist Robert Briffault, who touched on the subject in the early 20th century.

"From the fifth to the tenth century Europe lay sunk in a night of barbarism which grew darker and darker. It was a barbarism far more awful and horrible than that of the primitive savage, for it was the decomposing body of what had been a great civilization. The features and impress of that civilization were all but completely effaced. Where its development had been fullest, in Italy and in Gaul, all was ruin, squalor, desolation. The land had dropped out of cultivation; trees and shrubs rapidly encroached upon the once cultivated land, rivers overflowed their broken and neglected banks; the forest and the malarial swamp regained their sway over vast tracts of country which had been covered with prosperous farms and waving fields. The word *eremus,* wilderness, recurs with significant frequency in mediaeval land charts. Cities had practically disappeared. Where there is no trade there can be no cities. They were pulled down and used as quarries, and only the central part walled in when a bishop or a baron established himself there who could afford some protection. In Nimes, for instance, the remains of the population dwelled in huts built completely among the ruins of the amphitheatre. Others were completely abandoned. ... The Germans who regarded walled cities as a badge of servitude, hastened to pull them down. Of all the prosperous cities built by the Romans on the banks of

---

[1] Sidney Painter, *A History of the Middle Ages, 284-1500* (Macmillan, 1953) p. 24

the Rhine not one remained in the ninth century. The ruins and the scattered settlements were visited by herds of prowling wolves, boars, and even bears. The *atria* of the Roman villas, when not converted into cloisters, were filled with hovels and dunghills, the surrounding living-rooms serving as quarries and ramparts. Clad in the skins of beasts and in coarse, sack-shaped woolen garments, the enormously reduced population lived in thatched wooden huts, huddled for protection at the foot of the barons' lairs, or round monasteries. Every such little group manufactured its own materials and clothing, and supported its miserable existence by scanty cultivation of small patches of ground round their hovels. They did not dare to go further afield for fear of wild beasts and of marauders. Famines and plagues were chronic. … Cases of cannibalism were not uncommon. … It was impossible to venture abroad without a strong armed escort. … Anarchy was absolute and unchecked …"[2]

And so on. The savages responsible for this lamentable state of affairs were, says Briffault, the Germanic hordes who had crossed the Roman frontiers *en masse* in the fourth and fifth centuries. He decries attempts that had been made to rehabilitate these peoples as "panegyric twaddle" and "racial-historical mendacity" and goes on to list the violent and degenerate character of the tribesmen. "To libel them," he says, "is not possible," and to "sound the full measure of their infamy is revolting." "Gluttonous, riotous orgies, to shout, heated with strong drink, was their ideal of enjoyment. Slaughter, cruelty, obscene violence, were the natural outlets of their energies."[3]

There is no question that Briffault, who wrote these words just a year after the end of World War 1, was clearly influenced by contemporary events, and was reacting against the racist "Germanism" or "Teutonism" which had gained much popularity throughout Europe during the latter years of the nineteenth century. It is true also that the opinions expressed above are now generally rejected by historians. Nevertheless, they continue to have resonance in the popular imagination, and just two years ago English politician Boris Johnson, in his *Dream of Rome*, a book to accompany his television series of the same name, spoke of the "catastrophe" of the Germanic invasions, and of the terrible savagery that had prevailed following their entry into the Western Empire.

---

[2] Robert Briffault, *The Making of Humanity* (London, 1919) pp. 164-5.
[3] Ibid., p. 167

THE MEDIEVAL PROBLEM

Be that as it may, the progress of historical studies has now firmly found against this viewpoint. Indeed, not only did the German tribesmen fail to destroy Roman civilization, they did everything in their power to preserve it. This was a point stressed repeatedly by Hugh Trevor-Roper, formerly the dean of Medieval studies at Oxford. He notes, for example, that "The barbarians do not destroy the empire; they did not think of destroying it; they continue it ..."[4] And, "In fact, it is clear .... In some respects we may say that the barbarians preserved rather than destroyed the Empire."[5]

With the exception of the Anglo-Saxons and the Vandals, all the other Germanic groups who settled within the Empire were actually invited in by the Roman government itself: they were brought in as a ready source of new recruits for the Roman army. All of these peoples were well acquainted with Roman civilization before they entered Imperial territory. They had been recruited by the Romans in this capacity since at least the second and third centuries. Those who arrived in the fourth and fifth centuries, who are blamed for terminating the Western Roman Empire, were already Christian. Arian heretics, it is true, but Christians nevertheless. It is undeniable that these peoples did, on occasion, cause much damage and destruction; but it should not be forgotten that they were numerically tiny in comparison with the settled inhabitants of the Empire, and they had little cultural impact upon the Roman world. This was true even of the territory of the Western Empire, which was formally brought to an end in the late fifth century. And the Germanic kingdoms which supplanted the Western Empire always regarded themselves as citizens of the Empire, only then the Emperor sat in Constantinople.

The knowledge that the barbarians were not to blame for the destruction of Roman (or, more accurately, Classical) civilization was a long time in coming, though as early as the eighteenth century Gibbon, who spoke of the "innocent barbarians," showed signs of a dawning awareness of the truth. But the realization that they were wholly innocent came only in the twentieth century, with the work of Austrian medievalist Alfons Dopsch and Belgian historian Henri Pirenne. In his *Wirtschaftliche und soziale Grundlagen der europäischen Kulturentwicklung* ("The Economic and Social Foundations of

---

[4] Hugh Trevor-Roper, *The Rise of Christian Europe* (Thames and Hudson, London, 1966) p. 67
[5] Ibid.

HOLY WARRIORS

European Civilization") (Vienna, 1918-1920), Alfons Dopsch, influenced by the evidence of archaeology, stressed the surprising continuity of Roman institutions during the fifth and sixth centuries. Roman cities and imperial demesnes survived and flourished under the Germanic kings; and the villas of Late Antiquity demonstrably developed into the manors of medieval times. Although Dopsch argued for the Romanization of the Germanic kings and stressed their attempts to preserve classical civilization, he still held by the conventional notion that their epoch saw the gradual deterioration of that civilization. This was not the conclusion reached by Henri Pirenne. While agreeing with Dopsch that the Germans became thoroughly Romanized, Pirenne nevertheless argued for a complete and rather sudden termination of classical civilization in the seventh century. This conclusion was set forth in its final form in his seminal *Mohammed et Charlemagne*, a volume published posthumously in 1937 (and in English in 1939). In this book, Pirenne devoted over 140 pages to an examination of western Europe during the fifth, sixth and early seventh centuries, when Gothic, Frankish and Vandal kings set up independent fiefdoms on the ruins of the Western Empire. Pirenne's study was not exhaustive, but it was thorough; and what he found was that not only did Roman civilization fail to "decline" in those years, it actually, if anything, revived, and, following an initial period of unrest and destruction, during which the new rulers established their authority in Italy, Gaul, Spain, and North Africa, Latin and Roman civilization began again to flower.

We could fill volumes describing in detail the "neo-Roman" civilization which took shape under the Germanic kings, but I shall confine myself here to reiterate some of the more salient features noted by Pirenne and others.

That from the very beginning the German tribesmen had no intention of destroying Rome and her Empire is revealed in innumerable ways; though perhaps the most graphic illustration comes from the lips of one of the said tribesmen, in the famous declaration of Alaric's brother-in-law Ataulf, as recorded by Orosius:

> To begin with I ardently desired to efface the very name of the Romans and to transform the Roman Empire into a Gothic Empire. *Romania*, as it is vulgarly called, would have become *Gothia*; Ataulf would have replaced Caesar Augustus. But long experience taught me that the unruly barbarism of the Goths was incompatible with the

laws. Now, without laws there is no State (republica). I therefore decided rather to aspire to the glory of restoring the fame of Rome in all its integrity, and of increasing it by means of the Gothic strength. I hope to go down to posterity as the restorer of Rome, since it is not possible that I should be its supplanter.[6]

Pirenne noted that in this statement, Ataulf was making overtures to Honorius, who, however, still refused to treat with him. Being rebuffed by the Western Emperor did not disillusion the "barbarian" chief, who now installed Attalus in the Imperial purple, "in order to reconstruct the Empire with him."[7] This was a project that remained close to the heart of the noble Goth, and before he died, he admonished his brother Wallia to remain loyal to Rome. One year later, in 416, Honorius begged Wallia's help in turning back an enormous host of Vandals, Alans, Seuves and Burgundians, which was then ravaging Gaul and Spain. The assistance was duly given, and, as a reward, the Visigoths were awarded Aquitanian Secunda, and the Emperor duly recognized Wallia as an ally of Rome.

As Pirenne emphasized, this was the pattern all along: The barbarians did not simply march into the Empire and appropriate territories: they were invited in as *foederati*, as allies; and very often this is exactly how they behaved – even during the most disturbed century, the fifth. Thirty years after Wallia defeated the Vandals and Alans, the Visigoths again, this time along with the Franks and Burgundians, proved themselves loyal allies of Rome by helping Atius overcome the Huns: thus saving Western Europe from Attila's tyranny. In Pirenne's words, "The military art of the Romans and the valour of the Germans collaborated. Theodoric I, king of the Visigoths, in fulfilling Ataulf's ambition to become the restorer of the Empire, was slain."[8] Crucially, he notes that in these years, "if the Barbarians had wished to destroy the Empire they had only to agree among themselves, and they must have succeeded. But they did not wish to destroy it."[9]

---

[6] Orosius, *Adversus Paganos*, vii, 43. (ed. K. Zangemeister, 1882, p. 560)
[7] Henri Pirenne, *Mohammed and Charlemagne* (London, 1939) p. 27
[8] Ibid., p. 31
[9] Ibid.,

HOLY WARRIORS

When, about three decades later, the Western Empire was actually abolished, it was not, as some have imagined, an earth-shattering event. In fact, the abolition went almost unnoticed and was merely, in the words of Trevor-Roper, "a political event."[10] This was an internal *coup d'état*: not the destruction of an empire. Odoacer, who now became king of Italy, was a barbarian, it is true, but he was not the ruler of a separate tribe or people, he was a commander of the Imperial forces. And it was as commander of those forces that he dismissed Romulus Augustulus and sent the Imperial insignia back to Constantinople. Zeno, the Emperor of the East, "went so far as to recognize Odoacer as a patrician of the Empire." The simple fact is, "nothing was changed; Odoacer was an Imperial functionary."[11] To those who, in spite of all the evidence, continue to insist that the abolition of the Western Empire was an epoch-making event, we note that just over a decade later, the Eastern Emperor contrived to have Odoacer removed from office. He sent Theodoric, king of the Ostrogoths, into Italy, after granting him the title of patrician of Rome. Finally, in 493, when Odoacer was captured and assassinated, Theodoric, being "duly authorized" by Zeno, took over the government of Italy. He remained king of his own people, the Ostrogoths, but not of the Italians. These he governed as a functionary of the Emperor.

Still, by the end of the fifth century, the whole of the territory of the Western Empire was *de facto* ruled by barbarian kings: Ostrogoths in Italy; Vandals in Africa; Seuves in Galicia; Visigoths in Spain and Gaul south of the Loire; Burgundians in the valley of the Rhone, and Franks in the rest of Gaul. If they had really wished to extirpate Roman society, culture and tradition, they were now in a position to do so. But, as we shall see, they did not. On the contrary, over the next century and a half they did everything in their power to preserve Roman civilization, fostering its language, art, law, custom, architecture and learning. Indeed, the cultural impact of the newcomers upon the lands of the Western Empire was, with the exception of some outlying regions such as Britain, the Rhineland and Bavaria, where the Roman or Romanized population was largely replaced, was minimal. In the other regions, in Italy, Gaul, Spain and North Africa, the Barbarians formed a tiny ruling minority, which depended on the vastly superior indigenous population for almost

---

[10] Trevor-Roper, op cit., p. 71
[11] Pirenne, op cit., p. 32

25

everything. And by the middle of the sixth century intermarriage between the numerically superior Romans and the Barbarians became common, with the result that in a very short time the Germans began to lose all that made them distinct from the great mass of the Romans. Pirenne stressed the extreme superficiality of their cultural impact upon western Europe. Their languages left no trace at all in the Latin-based languages of Italy or Spain, and a paltry 300 words in French.[12] The fact that any trace was left in French is explained by the common border Gaul shared with the German homelands – a border many hundreds of miles long. Even without a Germanic invasion, the peoples of Gaul would have picked up some German words.

The Germans were as swift to embrace Roman law as they were the Latin language. Pirenne notes that by the start of the sixth century, no trace of Germanic law survived anywhere in western Europe, except among the Anglo-Saxons in Britain and those Germans who remained east of the Rhine.[13]

As well as sharing in the language and culture, the Germans seem to have participated in the general moral laxity which is said to have characterized Roman society in late antiquity.[14]

The virtually complete Romanization is perhaps illustrated most graphically in the case of Theodoric, king of the Ostrogoths and ruler of Italy between 493 and 526. At the age of seven, his father gave him as hostage to the Emperor,[15] and he was educated in Constantinople until he was eighteen years of age. "Zeno made him *magister militum* and patrician, and in 474 even went so far as to adopt him. He married an imperial princess. In 484 the Emperor made him consul. Then, after a campaign in Asia Minor, a statue was raised to him in Constantinople. His sister was lady-in-waiting to the Empress."[16]

In 536 Evermud, his son-in-law, surrendered without even token resistance to Belisarius, preferring to live as a patrician in Constantinople rather than defend the cause of his fellow Barbarians.[17] His daughter Amalasuntha was

---

[12] Pirenne, op cit., p. 40

[13] H. Brunner, *Deutsche Rechtsgeschichte*, Vol. 1 (2nd ed., Leipzig, 1906) p. 504

[14] Pirenne, op cit., p. 42

[15] L. Hartmann, *Das Italienische Königreich*, Vol. 1, p. 64 (in *Geschichte Italiens in Mittelalter*, Vol. 1)

[16] Pirenne, op cit., pp. 43-4

[17] Hartmann, op cit, Vol. 1, p. 261

completely Romanized.[18] Theodahat, his son-in-law, boasted that he was a follower of Plato.[19]

Other "Barbarian" rulers were comparable. Thus we find among the Burgundi the noble figure of Gondebaud (480-516), who "in 472, after the death of Ricimer, succeeded to him as patrician of the Emperor Olybrius, and on the death of the latter had Glycerius made Emperor. ... According to Schmidt, he was highly cultivated, eloquent, and learned, was interested in theological questions, and was constantly in touch with Saint Avitus.

"It was the same among the Vandal kings. And among the Visigoths, the same development may be remarked. Sidonius praises the culture of Theodoric II. Among his courtiers he mentions the minister Leo, historian, jurist and poet, and Lampridius, professor of rhetoric and poet. It was Theodoric II who in 455 made Avitus Emperor. These kings were entirely divorced from the old traditions of their peoples...

"And among the Franks there was the royal poet Chilperic.

"As time went on the process of Romanization became accentuated. Gautier remarks that after Genseric the Vandal kings re-entered the orbit of the Empire. Among the Visigoths, Romanization made constant progress. By the end of the 6th century Arianism had everywhere disappeared."[20]

The Germanic States of the West

Pirenne stressed that the Germanic kings were national kings only to their own peoples. Their Roman subjects, who were nominally at least still subjects of the Emperor in Constantinople, were ruled by Roman law and by their own institutions. "For the Romans they [the Germanic kings] were Roman generals to whom the Emperor had abandoned the government of the civil population. It was as Roman generals that they approached the Romans, and they were proud to bear the title on such occasions: we have only to recall the cavalcade of Clovis when he was created honorary consul. Under Theodoric an even simpler

---

[18] Ibid. p. 233
[19] Procopius, ed. Dewing (The Loeb Classical Library), vol. III, pp. 22-24
[20] Pirenne, op cit., p. 44

state of affairs prevailed. He was really a Roman viceroy. He promulgated not laws but edicts only.

"The Goths constituted the army merely. All the civil magistrates were Roman, and as far as possible the entire Roman administration was preserved. The Senate still existed. But all the power was concentrated in the king and his court ... Theodoric assumed merely the title of rex, as though he wished his Barbarian origin to be forgotten. Like the Empress, he lived in Ravenna. The division of the provinces was retained, with their *duces*, *rectores*, *praesides*, and the municipal constitution with its *curiales* and *defensores*, and the fiscal organization. Theodoric struck coins, but in the name of the Emperor. He adopted the name of Flavius, a sign that he had adopted the Roman nationality. Inscriptions call him *semper Augustus, propagator Romani nominis*. The king's guard was organized on the Byzantine model, and so was all the ceremonial of the court. The organization of the judiciary was entirely Roman, even for the Goths; and the Edict of Theodoric was thoroughly Roman. There were no special laws for the Goths. As a matter of fact, Theodoric opposed the private wars of the Goths, and their Germanic barbarism. The king did not protect the national law of his people."[21]

And so it goes on. Pirenne notes that under Theodoric the Goths constituted the garrisons of the cities, who were in receipt of a salary, and they were forbidden to undertake civil employment. "They could not exert the slightest influence upon the Government, apart from those who, with the Romans, constituted the king's entourage." They were, notwithstanding the fact that their king was the ruler of the land, "in reality foreigners, though well-paid foreigners." They were a military caste, whose profession furnished them with a comfortable livelihood.

Even among the Vandals of North Africa, the only Germanic people – apart from the Anglo-Saxons of England – who entered the empire as real invaders, the Roman system of government prevailed. Genseric was not a Roman official like Theodoric, but his entire governmental system was Roman, or became Roman. "He struck coins with the image of Honorius. The inscriptions were Roman. Genseric's establishment at Carthage was like Theodoric's in Ravenna: there was a *palatium*. ..."[22] It seems that the Vandal

---

[21] Ibid. pp. 46-7
[22] Ibid. p. 48

kings even continued to send presentations of oil to Rome and Constantinople.[23] Cultural life was unchanged. "Under Genseric the *termi* of Tunis was constructed. Literature was still practiced. Victor Tonnennensis still believed in the immortality of the Empire."[24]

Spain and Gaul present a similar picture. "Among the Visigoths, before the conquest of Clovis, the kings lived in Roman fashion in their capital of Toulouse, and later, in Toledo. The Visigoths established in accordance with the rules of 'hospitality' were not regarded as juridically superior to the Romans. The king addressed his subjects as a whole as *populus noster*."[25] Everything about the Visigothic kingship was Roman. "The king appointed all his agents. There were both Germanic and Roman dignitaries at his court, but the latter were by far the more numerous. The prime minister of Euric and Alaric II, Leo of Narbonne, combined the functions of *quaestor sacri palatii* and *magister officiorum* of the Imperial court. The king had no bodyguard of warriors, but *domestici* of the Roman type. The dukes of the provinces and the *comites* of the cities were mainly Romans.

"In the cities the *curia* was retained, with a *defensor* ratified by the king. ... For a time the Visigoths appear to have had, in the *millenarius*, a separate magistrate, like the Ostrogoths. But under Euric they were already amenable to the jurisdiction of the *comes*, who presided in the Roman fashion with the assistance of *assessores*, who were legists. There was not the faintest trace of Germanism in the organization of the tribunal."[26]

Pirenne goes on to note that the Code of Euric, drawn up in 475 with the purpose of regulating relations between the Goths and the Romans, was "completely Romanized," whilst the Breviary of Alaric (507), which affected the Romans, was "an example of almost purely Roman law." "The Roman taxes were still collected, and the monetary system was also Roman."[27] Yet this was not all, for, "As time went on, the Romanization became more marked." Whilst, "At first the royal insignia were Germanic ... these were later replaced by

---

[23] Albertini, "Ostrakon byzantin de Négrine (Numidie)," in *Cinquantenaire de la Faculte des Letteres d'Alger*, (1932) pp. 53-62
[24] Pirenne, op cit., pp. 48-9
[25] Ibid. p. 49
[26] Ibid. p. 50
[27] Ibid. p. 51

Roman insignia. ... The old military character of the Barbarians was disappearing."[28] Not only were the Germans under the influence of the Romans with whom they lived, they were constantly under fresh influences deriving from Constantinople. All the signs, Pirenne notes, were that the Visogoth monarchy "was evolving in the direction of the Byzantine system."[29]

So it was too among the Burgundians. After obtaining possession of Lyons, they were on the best of terms with the Empire. Their kings were completely Romanized. "Their courts were full of poets and rhetoricians. King Sigismond boasted that he was a soldier of the Empire, and declared that his country was part of the Empire.[30] These kings had a *quaestor Palatii* and *domesticii*. Sigismond was a tool of Byzantium, who received the title of patrician from the Emperor Anastasius. The Burgundi fought against the Visigoths as soldiers of the Emperor.

"Thus, they regarded themselves as belonging to the Empire. They reckoned their dates from the accession of the consul – that is to say, of the Emperor; the king was *magister militum* in the Emperor's name.

"In other respects the royal power was absolute and unique. It was not divided; when the king had several sons he made them viceroys. The court was peopled mainly by Romans. There was not a trace of warrior bands; there were *pagi* or *civitates*, with a *comes* over them. He had beside him, in order to administer justice, a *judex deputatus*, who was likewise appointed by the king, and who dispensed justice in accordance with the Roman usages."[31]

Even the Frankish Merovingians, whose territories stretched far into the German heartlands east of the Rhine, were thoroughly Roman in their laws and administration. "The Frankish State, until its submission to the Carolingians, was essentially Neustrian and Roman, from the basin of the Seine to the Pyrenees and the sea. However, the Franks who had established themselves there were very few in numbers."[32] Among the Merovingians, nearly all if not all the king's agents were recruited among the Gallo-Romans. Even the best of

---

[28] Ibid.
[29] Ibid. p. 52
[30] Hartmann, op cit, Vol. 1 pp. 218-9
[31] Ibid. p. 53
[32] Ibid. p. 55

the generals of that period, Mummolus, appears to have been a Gallo-Roman.[33] "Even in the governmental offices by which he was surrounded the king had Gallo-Roman *referendarii*."[34]

All of these kings and monarchies were immensely wealthy, and it was a wealth they employed not only in military enterprise but also in patronage of the arts and literature, as we shall see. In Pirenne's words, "No prince of the West, before the 13th century, can have been so rich in money as these kings. The description of their treasuries calls up the image of a river of gold."[35] "To regard them, as they have been regarded, merely as great landed proprietors is a manifest error, of which the only explanation is that they have been compared with [and equated with] the kings who came after them. But the fact is that owing to their wealth in money they were far more akin to the Byzantine kings than to Charlemagne."[36] As well as an enormous revenue derived from manufacture and trade in their own domains, they drew enormous subsidies from Byzantium. We know that the Emperor Maurice sent 50,000 gold *solidi* to Childebert as payment for his alliance against the Lombards.[37] We note also the enormous dowry given to Riguntis in 584,[38] and the 6,000 gold *solidi* of alms given by Childebert to the Abbe of Saint-Germain for the poor. Pirenne notes that these, along with the munificence of Dagobert I, who covered the apse of Saint-Denis with silver, "give us some idea of the wealth of the Frankish kings."[39]

The Ostrogoth and Visigoth kings were even richer.

Another, and crucially important feature of these states, is that they were secular. "The entire administration, in all its phases, was secular." We know that, "Although the kings were generally on good terms with the bishops, not one of the latter filled a governmental office: and here was one of the great differences between this period and the Middle Ages. On the other hand, many of the bishops had been royal *referendarii*. Here we have a striking contrast with

---

[33] Ferdinand Lot, Christian Pfister and Francois L. Ganshof, *Histoire du Moyen Age*, Vol. 1, (Paris, 1929) p. 271
[34] Pirenne, op cit, pp. 56-7
[35] Ibid. p. 59
[36] Ibid. p. 59
[37] Gregory of Tours, *Historia Francorum*, vi, 42
[38] Ibid. vi, 45
[39] Pirenne, op cit., p. 60

the policy of Charlemagne, which was based on the *missi*, half of whom were necessarily bishops, or that of Otto, who entrusted the reins of government to the Imperial bishops. The fact is that on the morrow of the invasion the laity … was still educated."

"The profane Merovingian State was therefore very definitely unlike the religious Carolingian State. And the same may be said of all the other States: Ostrogothic, Visigothic, Vandal, Burgundian. In this respect, then – and this is the essential point – the ancient order of things continued. The king himself was a pure layman, and his power did not depend upon any religious ceremony."[40]

At a later stage, with the commencement of the real Middle Ages, this situation changed radically, and the state become "religionized", with kings depending heavily upon the Church both for legitimacy and for the day to day running of the state bureaucracy. Why this occurred is a point of crucial importance, and we shall return to it at a later stage.

All during the sixth century, and for a time in the seventh, the Emperor in Constantinople was recognized as master of the world. "… the Barbarian kings regarded him [the Eastern Emperor] as their master, striking his effigy on their coins, and they solicited and obtained titles and favours from him. Justinian adopted Theodebert, as Maurice afterwards adopted Childebert."[41] Even after Justinian's death and the loss of Italy and many other western territories, "the Empire was still the only world-power, and Constantinople was the greatest of all civilized cities."[42] In fact, throughout the fifth and sixth centuries, the lands of the West were undergoing a process of Byzantinization. This process had begun even before the formal abolition of the Western Empire in 476, but gathered pace in the final years of the fifth and during the sixth centuries. "Its [Byzantium's] fashions and its art were spread throughout the West by means of navigation. It obtained a foothold in Rome, where there was a host of Greek monks, and everywhere in Southern Italy. Its influence was perceptible in Spain, and of course throughout Africa. In Gaul the *cellarium fisci* was reminiscent of the Byzantine commerciaries."[43]

---

[40] Ibid. p. 61
[41] Ibid. p. 63
[42] Ibid. p. 73
[43] Ibid. pp. 73-4

HOLY WARRIORS

Agriculture was changed little or nothing by the invasions. The appearance of the countryside and the cities remained virtually unaltered. Paulinus of Pella, who was ruined by the Gothic invasion, relates that he was saved by a Goth, who bought a small estate which he owned in the neighborhood of Marseilles. "One could hardly wish for a better illustration of the way pillage was followed by social equilibrium. Here was a deserted estate, yet the invaders did not seize it. As soon as the Germans were established in the country in accordance with the rules of *hospitalitas*, society became once more stabilized."[44] And in fact the great Gallo-Roman and Hispano-Roman estates survived. "There were still enormous *latifundia*. ... The great landowners retained their *villae*, their fortresses." Even in Africa, the Vandals merely replaced the old proprietors: they lived in the Roman villas. Everywhere these estates remained prosperous. Gregory of Tours mentions one Chrodinus who established villas, planted vineyards, erected farm buildings, and organized estates.[45] In Pirenne's words, "Prestations were always paid in money, which shows that goods were circulating, that they were sold in the open market. There is no sign yet of the closed economy of the mediaeval *curtes*."[46] He notes that in Provence during the Merovingian epoch the system of tenure was entirely Roman: "Great quantities of cereals were moved from place to place." In 510 Theodoric sent quantities of corn to Provence on account of the ravages of war in that region.[47] There was a vigorous trade in cereals. Despite of his own enormous resources, Gregory the Great made purchases of grain. In 537-538 a *peregrinus acceptor* made important purchases in Istria. He seems to have been a corn-merchant.[48]

It was the same throughout the former territories of the Western Empire: "Africa, under the Vandals, must have retained the prosperity which was derived from the cultivation of cereals and the olive, since it was still prosperous when the Byzantines returned to it. It does not appear that the aspect of Gaul was in any way less civilized. It seems that the culture of the vine was continued

---

[44] Ibid. p. 75
[45] Gregory of Tours, vi, 20
[46] Pirenne, op cit., p. 77
[47] R. Buchner, *Die Provence in Merowingischer Zeit* (Stuttgart, 1933) p. 30, n.1
[48] Cassiodorus, *Variae*, xii, 22. M.G.H. SS. Antiq., Vol. XII, p. 378

wherever it existed in the time of the Romans. If we read Gregory of Tours we do not by any means obtain the impression of a country in a state of decadence; unless it had been prosperous the landowners could hardly have been so wealthy.

"The retention of the Roman *libra* affords indirect proof of the stability of the economic situation."[49]

We learn that on the large estates there existed workshops which produced various goods, including cloth, tools and pottery of various types. These workshops had already existed during the later years of the Empire.

"The population had retained the form which had been impressed upon it by the fiscal organization, although this had been greatly diminished by the almost complete curtailment of the military and administrative expenditure. In this respect the Germanic conquest may perhaps have been beneficial to the people. On the whole, the great domain had remained the essential social and economic element. Thanks to the domain, the economic basis of the feudal system already existed. But the subordination of the greater part of the population to the great landowners was manifested as yet only in private law. The *senior* had not yet interposed himself between the king and his subjects. Moreover, although the constitution of society was predominantly agrarian, it was not exclusively so. Commerce and the cities still played a considerable part in the general economic, social, and intellectual life of the age."[50]

Commerce and Navigation

International commerce was vibrant during this period; and the Mediterranean still acted, as it had in the Age of the Empire, as a conduit for goods and ideas. Merchandise of all kinds, but especially luxury items, flooded into western Europe from the East. The great bulk of this trade continued, as it had been under the Empire, to be carried on by Syrians. Great trading companies and families, with depots in Alexandria, Rome, Spain, Gaul and Britain, as well as on the Danube, were a vital element in the economic life of the time. "The

---

[49] Pirenne, op cit. p. 78
[50] Ibid., p. 79

invasions," says Pirenne, "did not in any way alter the situation. Genseric, by his piracies [in the first half of the fifth century], may have hindered navigation a little, but at all events it was as active as ever when he had disappeared.

"Salvian (d. circa 484), doubtless generalizing from what he had seen at Marseilles, spoke of the *negociatorum et Syricorum omnium turbas quae majorem ferme civitatum universarum partem occupant.*

"This Syrian expansion is confirmed by the archaeologists, and the texts are even more significant.

"In the sixth century there were large numbers of Orientals in Southern Gaul. The life of Saint Caesar, Bishop of Arles (d. 524), states that he composed hymns in Greek and Latin for the people."[51] There were also many Orientals in northern Gaul, and we have Gregory of Tours testimony to the existence of Greek merchants in Orleans. These advanced, singing, to meet the king.[52] Large numbers of Syrians, it seems, settled in Gaul, where they are mentioned in many inscriptions of the fifth and sixth centuries.[53] One of these is in the chapel of Saint Eloi in Eure, near the mouth of the Seine.[54] Pirenne notes that the latter "was doubtless trading with Britain."[55]

As we shall see, the links between the Byzantine East and Britain under the Anglo-Saxons, were spectacularly confirmed by the discoveries made at the Sutton Hoo burials, discoveries made after Pirenne's death.

In Gaul, Gregory of Tours mentions a *negotiator* of Bordeaux, who possessed a great house in which was a chapel containing relics.[56] Another such merchant was Eusebius of Paris, who purchased the Episcopal dignity and then, finding fault with his predecessor's *scola*, constituted one of his own, which comprised only Syrians.[57] Pirenne notes that the population of Narbonne in 589 consisted of Goths, Romans, Jews, Greeks and Syrians.[58]

---

[51] Ibid., p. 80
[52] Gregory of Tours, viii, 1
[53] Edmond Leblant, *Inscriptions chrétiennes de la Gaule antérieures au VIIIe siecle*, Vol. 1, (Paris, 1856) pp. 207 and 328
[54] Ibid. p. 205, no. 125
[55] Pirenne, op cit., p. 81
[56] Gregory of Tours, vii, 31
[57] Ibid., x, 26
[58] Pirenne, op cit., p. 81

Evidence indicates that there were substantial communities of Syrian traders throughout Western Europe during the fifth and sixth centuries. Procopius mentions, for example, the existence in Naples, during the time of Justinian, of a great Syrian merchant, Antiochus, who was the leader of the Roman party in that city.[59]

As well as Syrians, Greeks and Egyptians, there were many, very many, Jews. These were particularly numerous in Spain, but there were also large communities of them in Italy, Gaul, and even in Germany along the Rhine. Pirenne notes for example that when Naples was besieged by Belisarius, the Jews formed a great part of the merchant population of the city.[60] The existence of sizeable Jewish communities in Ravenna, Palermo, Terracina, and Cagliari, is also mentioned by various writers.[61] The "immense majority" of the Jews, both in Italy and elsewhere, were engaged in commerce.

On the whole, there is a superabundance of evidence to show that during the fifth and sixth centuries, trade within the territories of the Western Empire was of great importance, and that some of this trade was carried on by native merchants, some of whom "were assuredly very wealthy." Pirenne notes that "it is a very long time before we hear of such wealthy merchants again."[62] Some of these merchants, like the Syrians, Greeks and Jews, were involved in the sea-borne trade with the Eastern Mediterranean; a trade that was apparently lively and even growing. "I think we can say that navigation was at least as active as under the Empire."[63]

What did this trade bring into western Europe? It brought a great variety of things, but most especially luxury items. It also brought many of the essentials of civilized life – including, crucially, large quantities of papyrus from Egypt. Thus Pirenne notes that the Royal Diplomas of the Merovingian kings, preserved in the Archives Nationales of Paris, are written on papyrus.[64] The disappearance of papyrus in Western Europe, and its replacement by the extremely expensive parchment, is one of the crucial markers that stand at the

---

[59] Procopius, v, 8, 21
[60] Pirenne, op cit., pp. 82-3
[61] Ibid., p. 83
[62] Ibid., p. 103
[63] Ibid., p. 95
[64] Ibid., p. 92

dividing line between the classical civilization of late antiquity and that of the medieval age. This occurred, as we shall see, in the middle of the seventh century.

Contrary to popular opinion, which sees a decline in urban life after the dissolution of the Western Empire, the cities in fact prospered under the Germanic kings. "The cities [of this time] were both ecclesiastical and commercial in character. Even in the cities of the North, such as Meaux, there were street with arcades which were sometimes prolonged into the suburb. These arcaded houses must have given the cities an Italian appearance, even in the north. They doubtless served to shelter shops, which were generally grouped together; according to Gregory of Tours, this was especially the case in Paris.

"In these cities, besides the merchants, lived the artisans, concerning whom we have very little information. Saint Caesarius speaks of their presence at Arles, in the 6th century. The glass industry seems to have been important; the Merovingian tombs contain many objects made of glass."[65]

Pirenne cites convincing evidence to suggest that the cities of the West during this period remained as large as they had been during the Empire: "The cities had, of course, suffered from the invasions. Bridges had broken down and had been replaced by bridges of boats. But all the cities still existed; moreover, the bishops had restored them. And there is no doubt that just as they were the centres of civil and religious administration, they were also the permanent commercial centres of the country. Here again the ancient economy was continued. We find nothing resembling the great fairs of the Middle Ages – such as those of Champagne."[66] Again, "On reading Gregory of Tours ... we obtain the impression of a period of urban commerce. The *conventus* of the merchants were held in the cities. We hear nothing of the countryside. It is certainly an error, as Waitz has already pointed out, to regard the innumerable localities whose names were impressed by the *monetarii* on the Merovingian coins as the sites of markets. What we do find existing in the Merovingian period, as in antiquity, are *portus* – that is to say, *étapes* and wharves or landing-places, but not markets. The king levied market-tolls (*tonlieux*) in the cities and in the

---

[65] Pirenne, op cit., p. 103
[66] Ibid., p. 104

portus. These were the ancient Roman market-tolls, payable in the same places."[67]

Wealth and the Monetary System

One of the defining characteristics of the Medieval Age was its relative poverty. The money-based system that had prevailed under the Roman Empire disappeared, along with international trade; and this was replaced by local, barter-based economies. There was very little money in circulation, and whatever there was, tended to be silver, rather than gold, as under the Empire. What, then, was the state of the monetary system under the Germanic kings? Did it display any of the characteristics of the feudal age? It did not. As a matter of fact, the monetary system in western Europe seems to have been affected little or not at all by the Germanic invasions. The Germanic kings continued to use the Roman gold *solidus*, and continued to strike coins bearing the effigies of the Emperors.[68] "Nothing attests more clearly the persistence of the economic unity of the Empire. It was impossible to deprive it of the benefit of monetary unity. ... [in the fifth and sixth centuries] The Syrian navigators, on disembarking in the ports of the Tyrrhenian Sea, found there the currency to which they had been accustomed in the ports of the Aegean Sea. What is more, the new Barbarian kingdoms adopted, in their coinage, the changes introduced in the Byzantine currency."[69] All during these centuries, and right up until the middle of the seventh century, the central currency was the gold *solidus*.

Gold alone was the official currency during the fifth and sixth centuries, a point that Pirenne stresses again and again. "The monetary system of the Barbarians was that of Rome."[70] This was in stark contrast to that of the Middle Ages which, beginning in the Carolingian period, was based on silver, and silver alone. "Silver monometallism" is the term used by Pirenne to describe it.

---

[67] Ibid., p. 105
[68] Gunnar Mickwitz, *Geld und Wirtschaft im Romischen Reich des IV. Jahrhunderts nach Christi* (Helsingfors, 1932) p. 190
[69] Ibid., p. 107
[70] Ibid., p. 108

HOLY WARRIORS

The Anglo-Saxons constituted the only exception to the rule: Among them silver the principal metal employed.[71] We note however that in Britain, and only there, the Barbarian Invasions effectively terminated Roman civilization – or, at the very least, produced a far more definitive break with the past than occurred in Gaul, Italy and Spain. Latin was replaced by a Germanic language, and Christianity was – apart from in the far west – extinguished. Yet even in Britain a few gold coins were struck in the southern part of the country; that is to say, as Pirenne remarks, "in those parts which maintained commercial relations with Gaul."[72] There is also reason to believe that these coins were the work of Merovingian minters.[73]

The Merovingian kings themselves struck pseudo-Imperial coins, the series of which closes with the reign of Heraclius (610-641), the first Emperor to come into hostile contact with the Arabs.[74] The significance of this cannot be overstressed, and we shall return to the topic when we come to examine the re-establishment of the Western Empire under the Ottonian kings of the mid-tenth century – supposedly a full three centuries after the Germanic rulers of the West had symbolically terminated their allegiance to Constantinople by ceasing to place the Emperor's image on their coins. This western Roman currency can, as a rule, be distinguished at a glance from the Imperial currency. Yet while differing from the coinage struck in the East, they bear a close resemblance to one another; and it is rarely possible to say whether they were struck by the Visigoths, the Burgundians, or the Franks. Only rarely before the early seventh century did the name of a Germanic king appear on a coin, and the first instance of this occurred (to the horror of Procopius) when Theodebert I was making war in Italy against Justinian, in 539-540. These coins are in fact so much finer than any other Frankish issues that experts believe Theodebert had them struck in Italy. It was only in the reign of Chlotar II (584 – 630) that the name of the king replaced that of the Emperor in the mints of Gaul. The formula *Victoria Augustorum* was replaced by *Victoria Chlotarii*.[75]

---

[71] Ibid.

[72] Ibid.

[73] Arthur Engel and Raymond Serrure, *Traité de numismatique du Moyen Age*, Vol. 1 (Paris, 1891) p. 177

[74] Maurice Prou, *Catalogue des monnaies mérovingiennes d'Autun*, (Paris, 1888) pp. xxvii and xxviii

[75] Ibid. p. xxxix

THE MEDIEVAL PROBLEM

Throughout the fifth and sixth centuries large amounts of gold coins were minted, in numerous locations, throughout Gaul, Spain and Italy. "These constant mintages," says Pirenne, "and what we know from other sources concerning the kings' wealth in gold, and the wealth of the Church and of private individuals, proves that there was a very considerable stock of gold in the West; and yet there were no gold mines, and we cannot suppose that much gold can have been derived from auriferous sands and gravels. How then can we speak of 'natural economy' in the presence of these large amounts of liquid treasure?[76]

An idea of the amount of gold in circulation can be had not only from the archaeological finds, but from documentary evidence. Thus we hear that Bishop Baldwin of Tours distributed 20,000 gold solidi to the poor, whilst gold is mentioned as used profusely in the decoration of garments. There was, as might be expected, a great deal of gold in the possession of private individuals, as is proved by the continual confiscations of gold by the king.[77]

The Gothic and Frankish kings put their treasure to good use. It provided opulent dowries for their daughters, gifts to friends, and lavish alms to the poor. They also lent money at interest, as one Frankish king is on record as doing with the Bishop of Verdun. Pensions were paid to needy ecclesiastics, and lavish churches were raised and decorated. Mention here should be made of the apse of Saint Denis, which was covered in silver. There were in fact great quantities of currency in circulation, and people sought to invest it to their advantage. This was in fact a proto-capitalist economy. Pirenne quotes a case illustrating what he describes as "the trade in money." A Jewish man named Armentarius, together with a co-religionist and two Christians, came to Tours to demand the securities they had advanced to the *vicarius* Injuriosus and Count Eonomius, who had promised to repay the amounts with interest (*cum usuris*). These "tax-farmers" had also lent money to the *tribunus* Medard, who was also requested to make payment. The three powerful debtors invited their creditors to a banquet, in course of which they were set upon and assassinated. Pirenne emphasizes the striking feature that these businessmen lent their money at interest: cum usuries. "This is a proof, and a proof of great importance, of the fact that under the

---

[76] Pirenne, op cit., p. 111
[77] Ibid., p. 111

40

Merovingians interest was regarded as lawful. Everybody lent money at interest, even the king, who authorized a loan, at interest, to the city of Verdun."[78]

Here again we see a situation quite different to that which pertained in the Middle Ages, when the Church forbade the practice of usury. It is true, of course, that even during the period in question, the sixth century, the Church forbade the taking of interest; but it is equally evident that as yet it lacked the authority to enforce the ban. Prelates might berate kings and private citizens who took interest, but they could do little more than berate. The Church's influence was of course important; and it is true that most Christians did heed the warnings of the priests. Even at this time most bankers and money-lenders were Jews. But not everyone involved in this kind of activity was; and this tells us a great deal about the time.

It was a time of wealth; it was a time of opulence. Cities flourished, as they had under the Caesars, and life continued remarkably unchanged from the latter epoch. It was a money and not a barter economy; and the fundamental unit was the gold *solidus*. With this wealth luxury items were imported into the west in great quantities: fabrics, jewelry, spices, wines, and very many other of the things which made life pleasant for the urban elite.

Where then did all this wealth originate? Some at least came from Byzantium, and we know that on occasion the Emperor sent subsidies of up to 50,000 solidi to individual rulers in the West. Some also must have been booty taken in wars. Yet we must agree with Pirenne that, such was the opulence of the western kingdoms, that "commerce alone could have brought this continual stream of gold into the West."[79] And here we must stress another point: The wealth of the Germanic kingdoms, by the end of the sixth century, showed no signs whatever of exhaustion. On the contrary, if anything, these states were becoming ever more wealthy and powerful; a wealth and power which, as we shall see, brought with it a flowering of literature and the arts. This was not an age of decadence, in any way whatsoever; but an age which showed every sign of being the start of a new flowering of civilization.

This was an epoch that could scarcely have been more different from the Middle Ages. Nothing marks this as an age of barter: "All the features of the old economic life were there: the preponderance of Oriental navigation, the

---

[78] Ibid., p. 115
[79] Ibid., p. 112

importation of Oriental products, the organization of the ports, of the *tonlieu* and the impost, the circulation and the minting of money, the lending of money at interest, the absence of small markets, and the persistence of a constant commercial activity in the cities, where there were merchants by profession. There was, no doubt, in the commercial domain as in other departments of life, a certain retrogression due to the 'barbarization' of manners, but there was no definite break with what had been the economic life of the Empire. The commercial activities of the Mediterranean continued with singular persistence. And the same may be said of agriculture, which, no doubt, was still the basis of the economic life, but beside which commerce continued to play an essential part, both in daily life – by the sale of spices, clothing, etc – and in the life of the State – by virtue of the resources which the *tonlieu* procured for it – and in social life, owing to the presence of merchants and the existence of credit."[80]

---

[80] Ibid. pp. 116-7

CHAPTER 2

GERMANIC KINGS AND BYZANTINE EMPERORS

Cultural and Intellectual Life in the fifth and sixth Centuries

 rom what we have learned in the previous chapter it is clear that, far from destroying Roman civilization, the barbarians of Germany did everything in their power to preserve it. They saw themselves as agents of the Empire and rapidly became Romanized in every way. Not only that, they now began to spread that civilization into regions never penetrated by the legions. Thus when the Merovingians conquered the Saxons and Thuringians, they set about establishing churches and various other civilized institutions in the east of Germany. By the year 600, then, the borders of Latin civilization stood at the Elbe.

For all that, it may be argued (and is) that the Germanic rulers essentially failed to preserve Roman civilization in its true essence. It is held that they presided over a declining classical culture, one that had lost all the vigor and originality of Rome in her prime. Literature and even philosophy, it is said, may have survived, but it was decadent and repetitive, a pale relic of the high tradition of the second and third centuries. There was little innovation, we are told, in either art, science, literature, or technology; and all of these gradually declined. The Germans themselves, of course, are not blamed for this. In the decline of culture another culprit is identified: the Christian church; and

43

according to an opinion prevalent since the eighteenth century at least, it was Christianity, as much as the nomads of Germany and Asia, which terminated Classical Civilization. Christianity has been pictured as slowly strangling, with its dogmas and superstitions, the rationalistic and scientific spirit of Greece and Rome. After centuries of Christian supernaturalism, it is held, the rationalism and science of the ancients was eclipsed. The Church deliberately suppressed learning and literacy, gaining a monopoly on the latter. With the ability to read and write confined to clerics, the Church was more able easily to control what people thought.

Although few would now subscribe to the above view in the crude way stated here, there is no doubt that it is still tacitly accepted among large segments of the educated public. It is, in fact, among the educated classes in Europe and the Americas, virtually the default point of view. But it is one that is almost wholly false. As we shall see in the present chapter, the Church of the fourth, fifth and sixth centuries did no more damage to classical civilization than did the Barbarians. On the contrary, the Church, as we shall see, was a bastion of learning – learning of the scientific kind as much as the theological. Furthermore, the Christian faith, from its inception and right through to the sixth and seventh centuries, promoted a humanism and humanitarianism which gradually transformed the lives of people for the better.

By the start of the fifth century Christianity was the official religion of the Empire, both in the East and the West. Yet the civilization of Greece and Rome lived on. Indeed, it showed little signs of decay. True, among poets and other men of letters there was little originality, and the forms of the past were slavishly copied. Nonetheless, literature and cultural life was very much alive – and remained so under the Germanic kings. Pirenne notes, in this regard, that in the Ostrogothic kingdom, "everything continued as under the Empire. It is enough to recall the names of Theodoric's two ministers: Cassiodorus and Boëtius. And there were others. The poet Rusticus Elpidius, the author of a *Carmen de Christi Jesu Beneficii*, was Theodoric's physician and favourite. We may mention also Ennodius, born, probably, at Arles, in 473, who was so profane a writer, although he became bishop of Pavia in 511, as to celebrate the amours of Pasiphae. He was a rhetorician who became, so to speak, a professor of sacred eloquence. We learn through him that the schools of rhetoric in Rome were as busy as ever. He wrote his panegyric of Theodoric between 504 and

508, in the same inflated and pretentious style as that which marks his biography of Anthony, the monk of Lerins. He also wrote of grammar, of rhetoric which 'commands the universe,' and of the bases of the Christian's education."[81]

The reign of Theodoric actually saw the flourishing of some of the greatest minds of antiquity. The most important of these were Boethius and Cassiodorus.

As a thinker, Boethius ranks alongside figures such as Cicero and Seneca. We are told that "Few men have contributed so much to the intellectual sustenance of posterity as Boethius did."[82] He seems to have been born in Rome in 480 (the same year as Saint Benedict), into the distinguished family of the Anicii. Both his parents counted Roman Emperors among their ancestors. His profound knowledge of Greek has led to the supposition that, as a young man, he studied in Athens and perhaps Alexandria. Since his father is recorded as proctor of a school in Alexandria around 470, the younger Boethius may have received some grounding in the classics from him or another close relative.

In 506 the young polymath came to the attention of Theodoric, who wrote him a graceful and complimentary letter. By 520, at the age of about forty, he had risen to the position of *magister officiorum*, the head of all the government and court services. Afterwards, his two sons were appointed consuls, reflecting their father's prestige. In 523, however, Theodoric ordered Boethius arrested on charges of treason, possibly for a suspected plot with the Byzantine Emperor Justin I. Boethius maintained his innocence and attributed the accusations to the slander of his rivals. Theodoric however was feeling threatened by events, and several other leading members of the landed elite were arrested at about the same time. Also, because of his previous ties to Theodahat, Boethius apparently found himself on the wrong side in the succession dispute following the untimely death of Eutharic, Theodoric's presumed heir. Whatever the cause, the philosopher found himself stripped of his title and wealth and imprisoned at Pavia, where he was executed the following year. His remains were entombed in the church of San Pietro in Ciel d'Oro in Pavia.

---

[81] Pirenne, op cit., pp. 119-120
[82] James W. Thompson and Edgar N. Johnson, *Introduction to Medieval Europe, 300-1500* (New York, 1937) pp. 221-2

2: GERMANIC KINGS AND BYZANTINE EMPERORS

Boethius was to be celebrated throughout the Middle Ages, and in Dante's *Paradise* of *The Divine Comedy*, the spirit of Boethius is pointed out by St. Thomas Aquinas, who remarks:

The soul who pointed out the world's dark ways,
To all who listen, its deceits unfolding.
Beneath in Cieldauro lies the frame
Whence it was driven; from woe and exile to
This fair abode of peace and bliss it came.

His best known work is the *Consolation of Philosophy*, which he wrote most likely while in exile under house arrest or in prison while awaiting his execution. The latter was cast as a dialogue between Boethius himself, at first bitter and despairing over his imprisonment, and the spirit of philosophy, depicted as a woman of wisdom and compassion. Alternately composed in prose and verse, the *Consolation* teaches acceptance of hardship in a spirit of philosophical detachment from misfortune. Parts of the work are reminiscent of the Socratic method of Plato's dialogues, as the spirit of philosophy questions Boethius and challenges his emotional reactions to adversity. The work was translated into Old English by King Alfred, and into later English by Chaucer and Queen Elizabeth; many manuscripts survive and it was extensively edited, translated and printed throughout Europe from the 14th century onwards. Many commentaries on it were compiled and it has been one of the most influential books in European culture.

Boethius' stated intention was to translate all the works of Aristotle and Plato from the original Greek into Latin, and then to synthesize the two masters, thus producing a unified philosophy. His completed translations of Aristotle's works on logic were the only significant portions of Aristotle available in Europe until the twelfth century. However, some of his translations (such as his treatment of the *topoi* in *The Topics*) were mixed with his own commentary, which reflected both Aristotelian and Platonic concepts. He also wrote a commentary on the *Isagoge* by Porphyry, which highlighted the existence of the problem of universals: whether these concepts are subsistent entities which would exist whether anyone thought of them, or whether they exist only as ideas. The ontological nature of universal ideas was one of the most vocal controversies in medieval philosophy.

Besides these advanced philosophical works, Boethius is also reported to have translated important Greek texts for the topics of the quadrivium. His loose translation of Nicomachus' treatise on arithmetic (*De institutione arithmetica libri duo*) and his textbook on music (*De institutione musica libri quinque,* unfinished) became the corner-stone of medieval education. His translations of Euclid on geometry and Ptolemy on astronomy, if they were completed, no longer survive.

In his *De Musica*, Boethius introduced the threefold classification of music, namely: (1) *Musica mundana* — music of the spheres/world. (2) *Musica humana* — harmony of human body and spiritual harmony. (3) *Musica instrumentalis* — instrumental music (incl. human voice). He also wrote theological treatises, which generally involve support for the orthodox position against Arian ideas and other contemporary religious debates. His authorship was periodically disputed because of the secular nature of his other work, until the 19th century discovery of a biography by his contemporary Cassiodorus which mentioned his writing on the subject.[83]

Boethius has been called by Lorenzo Valla the last of the Romans and the first of the scholastic philosophers. Nonetheless, there is nothing medieval in his thinking: He is entirely a man of Classical Antiquity, and it is evident that the great transformation which brought Graeco-Roman culture to an end had, in his age, not yet occurred. He was a Christian, and yet, "while accepting the principle of revealed faith, he was not averse to using his own reason to buttress it."[84] Indeed, his thinking is so pervaded by the rationalism of Greece that his Christianity, notwithstanding the fact that the Church considers him a saint, has long been questioned.[85] Such hypotheses however are unnecessary. Christian civilization of the fifth and sixth centuries was not the Christian civilization of the Middle Ages, and the influence of the ancients, of the "pagan" thinkers of Classical Antiquity, had not yet been anathematized or denigrated. It was still

---

[83] *Encyclopedia Britannica,* Vol. 2 Micropaedia, "Boethius".
[84] Thompson and Johnson, op cit., p. 222
[85] Carl Stephenson, *Medieval History: Europe from the Second to the Sixteenth Century* (Harper and Row, New York, 1962) pp. 78-9. There exists a large literature on this topic.

perfectly acceptable for a writer to be a Christian and a follower of Plato. In the words of one author, "… while eager and courageous spirits were contending for the Faith … throughout the Empire, men (and some of them Christian men) were writing and speaking as though no thing as Christianity had come into the world. And the age that witnessed the conversion of Constantine and inherited the benefits of that act was an age that in the East listened to the interminable hexameters of Nonnus' *Dionysiaca*, which contain no conscious reference to Christianity; that laughed over the epigrams of Cyrus; that delighted in many frankly pagan love-stories and saw nothing surprising in the attribution of one of them (the *Aethiopica*) to the Christian bishop Heliodorus; that in the West applauded the panegyrists when they compared emperor and patron to the hierarchy of gods and heroes."[86]

The other great mind of the time was Cassiodorus. Cassiodorus was born at Scylletium, near Catanzaro in southern Italy, of a family that was apparently Syrian in origin. He began his career as councilor to his father, the governor of Sicily, and made a name for himself while still very young as learned in the law. During his working life, as *quaestor* between 507 and 511, as a consul in 514, then as *magister officiorum* under Theodoric and his successor, Athalaric, Cassiodorus kept copious records concerning public affairs. At the Gothic court, his literary manner, which appears overly stylized and rhetorical to a modern reader, was accounted so remarkable that, whenever he was in Ravenna, significant public documents were often entrusted to him for drafting. Ultimately he was appointed praetorian prefect for Italy, effectively the prime ministership of the Ostrogothic civil government and a high honor to finish any career. His promotion seems to have coincided with Boethius' execution, though, understandably enough, he makes no mention of this in his writings.[87]

Athalaric died in early 534, and the remainder of Cassiodorus' public career was engulfed by the Byzantine reconquest and dynastic intrigue among the Ostrogoths. His last letters were drafted in the name of Witigis. Around 537-38, he left Italy for Constantinople where he remained almost two decades, concentrating on religious questions. He noticeably met Junilius, the *quaestor* of

---

[86] H. F. Stewart, "Thoughts and Ideas of the Period," in *The Cambridge Medieval History: The Chrsitian Empire)* Vol. 1 (2nd ed., 1936) p. 596
[87] www.en.wikipedia.org/wiki/Cassiodorus

HOLY WARRIORS

Justinian and his experiences in the East may have contributed to an increasing interest in religion and spirituality.

It may be said of Cassiodorus that he spent his career trying to bridge the cultural divides that were causing fragmentation in the sixth century between East and West, Greek culture and Latin, Roman and Goth, and Christian people with their Arian ruler.

His great project, for which he is mainly remembered, was his attempt to create an institution for the preservation, study and duplication of copies of Christian and Classical literature.[88] He realized his plans "through the establishment at Squillace of a monastery, which he called Vivarium, from the fish ponds (*vivaria*) on its grounds."[89] Here he spent the remainder of his long life with his monks, guiding them in their work. During this time he collected "from Italy and North Africa Greek and Latin manuscripts of such wide variety and scope that his monks had a considerable library to work with."[90] Like his predecessor Boethius, he treasured the intellectual inheritance of Greece and Rome and thus "set a standard and example for the Benedictine monks to follow."[91] And follow they did, as we shall see: Just as he had hoped, the monasteries became the repositories of all knowledge, not just centers of Christian meditation; and the monks of the Benedictine order in particular preserved for us the great bulk of ancient literature that we now possess.

Other important intellects of the period were the following: Arator, who entered the service of the State under the reign of Athalaric, becoming *comes domesticorum* and *comes rerum privatarum*. He entered the Church, apparently during the siege of Rome by Vitiges, and in 544 he publicly recited his poem *De actibus apostolorum* in the Church of San Pietro-in-Vinculi.

Venantius Fortunatus, born between 530 and 540, studied grammar, rhetoric and jurisprudence at Ravenna. In 560 he moved to Gaul, where he came to the attention of Sigebert of Austrasia and other important personages. At Poitiers he made the acquaintance of Saint Radegunda, who had just founded the monastery of the Holy Cross. He became a priest there, and he died Bishop of

---

[88] Thompson and Johnson, op cit., p. 206
[89] Ibid.
[90] Ibid.
[91] Ibid., p. 207

49

Poitiers. His poems were mainly panegyrics, the most notable of which he dedicated to Chilperic and Fredegond. He lauds the Roman eloquence of Caribert, and praises Duke Lupus, a Roman who took pleasure in attracting to the court of his master those of his compatriots who, like Andarchius, were distinguished for their learning.

Roman men of letters were also prominent at the court of the Vandals. Dracontius addressed a poem entitled *Satisfactio* to King Gunthamund (484-496). He was a pupil of the grammarian Felicianus, and there is evidence in his work that the individual Vandals attended the classes of the grammarians in company with the Romans. His family had retained possession of their estates under the Vandals, but was himself later persecuted by Gunthamund, who had him thrown into prison on account of a poem in which he seems to have celebrated the Emperor to the king's disadvantage.

Under Thrasamund (496-523) and Hilderic (523-530) flourished the poets of the Anthology: Florentinus, Flavius Felix, Luxorius, Mavortius, Coronatus and Calbulus, who, although Christians, wrote in the style of pagan antiquity. Their poems celebrate the magnificent *termi* of Thrasamund and the monuments erected at Aliana. In these poems Christianity and Christian sentiments are found side by side with frankly pagan sexual innuendo.

This is hardly what we would expect of an intolerant theocracy.

Technology and Learning

In material terms, in terms of art, architecture, technology and techniques, Roman civilization survived almost unaltered into the fifth and sixth centuries. Indeed, there was progress in all these areas. It was during this time that the importation of crucial technologies and know-how from the Far East, which eventually brought such things as printing, paper, gunpowder, and the compass, to the West, began. Thus we note that silk-production, whose secrets had been smuggled out of China in the middle of the sixth century, began in Europe in the time of Justinian, and had, within a decade or so, spread as far West as Spain. And the mysterious technology of "Greek fire", by which the Byzantines later repulsed the Arab armies, shows that scientific enquiry within the Empire was by no means moribund. It is possible too that the stirrup, whose origins remain mysterious, was adopted in Europe in the sixth century. It has been argued that it was brought to Europe by the nomadic Avars, from whom its use spread to the Byzantines and Franks.

Civilizations that can lay any claim to the name tend to leave an abundance of evidence in the ground. This can be in the form of artifacts and utensils of various kinds, as well as buildings and larger structures. Both of these survive in abundance from the period of the Germanic kings. Indeed, from the amount of archaeology available, it is evident that there was no decrease either in population or in urban life. Everywhere, with the exception of Britain, which was essentially lost to Roman civilization, archaeologists have uncovered the remains of individual settlements and great cities. The technical expertise of the potters, the jewelers, the sculptors and the illustrators of this period is the equal of that of the Imperial epoch. There is not a trace of decline. There is even evidence of advance and improvement. The techniques of metal-working in this period, even in far-off parts of Christendom, such as Ireland, shows an astonishing sophistication, and the microscopic detail of broaches and sacred vessels (as well as in illuminated manuscripts) challenges our notion that these could have been executed without the aid of the magnifying glass.

The most visible evidence of the technical and artistic achievement of any civilization tends to be in its architecture; in the great monuments of stone or brick that it leaves behind. The pride of rulers and the piety of the multitude together ensure that, should a society possess the wealth and the know-how, great temples and great royal residences will be raised. At the very least, such societies will bequeath to posterity massive civic structures, such as defensive walls or irrigation works. Should a civilization fail to leave any of these, then we must seriously question whether it deserves the name at all.

Now, from the mid-seventh to the mid-tenth centuries there is indeed in Europe – and in the Middle East also, as we shall see – a woeful lack of architecture and even of archaeology. The meaning of this three-century hiatus is a question of crucial importance and is one that will be addressed in the Appendix. Yet of the two centuries with which we are here concerned, the fifth and sixth, there is no shortage of monumental structures at all. There was, on the contrary, a great deal of building going on. It is true that the major public works, which were so characteristic of the earlier Empire, were generally (though not always) discontinued. There were no amphitheatres erected during the period of the Franks and Goths. And this is what we should expect, in a Christian society which abjured such entertainments. Yet construction there most certainly was. The Gothic, Frankish and Vandal kings were above all great builders of churches; and some of these, astonishing in their luxury and beauty, survive to this day. Italy is full of the churches and basilicas raised by Theodoric and his successors, whilst the contemporary Merovingians left almost as much in Gaul. As time went on, this building activity only increased, and by the late sixth century monuments comparable to anything raised by the Caesars were being fashioned.

The most outstanding structure of the sixth century was of course the church of San Vitale in Ravenna, built on the orders of Justinian. As a work of architecture and art it bears comparison with the Hagia Sophia in Constantinople. Yet we must not imagine that San Vitale was built by Byzantine craftsmen imported by Justinian. Everything about the building shows it to be typical of the architecture of Italy. The workmanship is astonishing, as the modern visitor will readily observe, but it is not materially different to the earlier churches and basilicas of Ravenna and elsewhere, dating from the time of Theodoric. There is no doubt that this Italian work had a "Byzantine" quality, with its rich mosaics and marble carvings. But such luxurious ornament was found throughout the West. At Clermont in Gaul, in the mid-sixth century, the bishop had a church with marble revetments, forty-two windows, and seventy columns.[92] Fortunatus describes the church of Saint Germain, built in 537, with its marble columns and stained glass windows, and the *Vita Droctovei* speaks of its mosaics and paintings, and the gilt plaques of the roof.[93]

It is true that, for a period during the fifth century, in the midst of the Germanic Invasions, there was some neglect; and Sidonius complains at this time that very little was being done towards the maintenance of the ancient churches. Yet, "when all was quiet again everyone made up for lost time. In all directions churches were built and restored. ... Nicetius of Trèves, Vilicus of Metz, and Carentius of Cologne restored and embellished churches."[94] We are told that, around 550, Leontinus of Bordeaux built nine churches.[95] The Bishop

---

[92] Gregory of Tours, ii, 16.
[93] *Vita Droctovei*, Vol. III, p. 541. From Pirenne, op cit., p. 134
[94] Pirenne, op cit., pp. 134-5
[95] Ibid., p. 134

of Mayence built the church of Saint George and a baptistery at Xanten, whilst in the same period Agricola caused one to be built at Châlons, and Dalmatius raised another at Rodez.[96] Numbers of workmen (artifices) were summoned from Italy, and Bishop Nicetius sent for Italian artifices to come to Treves. Yet there were also local architects.[97]

As in Ostrogothic Italy and Frankish Gaul, so it was in Visigothic Spain. After a falling away of building activity throughout most of the fifth century, this was renewed in the sixth with vigor. Churches and other structures, both private and public, sprang up all over the country. The great majority of the rich Visigothic heritage has of course now disappeared, but enough has survived to convince us that this was a flourishing and opulent epoch. We may mention, for example, what is perhaps Spain's oldest surviving church; the seventh century San Juan, from Baños de Cerrato in the province of Valencia. In Visigoth times, this was an important grain-producing region and legend has it that King Recceswinth commissioned the building of a church there when, on returning from a successful campaign against the Basques, he drank from the waters and recovered his health. The original inscription of the king, cut in the stones above the entrance, can still be discerned. Several bronze belt buckles and liturgical objects – as well as a necropolis with 58 tombs – have been discovered in the vicinity.

The impressive Gothic Cathedral at Valencia itself also has a crypt from the Visigoth era.

Again, the elegant Ermita de Santa María de Lara, at Quintanilla de Las Viñas, near Burgos, is a masterpiece of the Visigothic architectural style. Among its outstanding features is an unusual triple frieze of bas reliefs on its outer walls. Other surviving examples of Visigothic architecture are to be found in the La Rioja and Orense regions. The so-called horseshoe arch, which was to become so predominant in Moorish architecture, occurs first in these Visigothic structures, and was evidently an innovation of their architects. Toledo, the capital of Spain during the Visigothic period, still displays in its architecture the influence of the Visigoths.

---

[96] Gregory of Tours, v, 46.
[97] Mentioned by Fortunatus, *Carmina*, ii, 8. MGH. SS. Antiq., Vol. IV, p. 37

Before finishing, it is worth emphasizing that this Visigothic and Merovingian architecture looks typically late Roman, or Romano-Byzantine. Yet it also bears striking resemblance to Romanesque architecture of the tenth, eleventh and twelfth centuries. It is particularly reminiscent of the early Romanesque of the Ottonian age, which began appearing in the second half of the tenth century. As a matter of fact, the latter work looks like a rather crude version of the later Merovingian work, of the sixth and early seventh centuries, which itself might be described as "proto-Romanesque". This is all the more striking when we realize that Europe as a whole is virtually devoid of architecture during the three intervening centuries – ie between the early seventh and early tenth centuries.[98] Thus we have a situation where an architectural tradition seems to reappear, virtually unchanged, after a gap of three centuries, during which nothing at all was built.

This strange three century hiatus is something we shall encounter again and again, both in the archaeology and in the historiography of this "Dark Age".

Religion and the Church

By the beginning of the fifth century the whole cultural and social outlook of the Empire and its inhabitants was coming increasingly under the influence of Christianity. The Barbarian Invasions had little or no affect upon this process. Yet in view of the fact that Christianity has been blamed for the demise of classical culture almost as much as the barbarians themselves, it is incumbent upon us to consider the role of the Church at this time. It is true, of course, that in the Middle Ages, the Christian Church became both intolerant and – to some degree at least – obscurantist. This however was very definitely not the case during the fifth and sixth centuries. Whatever it was that produced the Church of the Crusades and the Inquisition had not yet made itself felt.

---

[98] Aachen Cathedral, often supposed to have been built by Charlemagne around 800, cannot be dated to this epoch; and quite literally scores of the building's features date it firmly to the eleventh century. Nevertheless, it is true that there are striking parallels to be observed between the Cathedral and Merovingian structures of the sixth and early seventh centuries.

HOLY WARRIORS

Pirenne emphasized the secular character of society during the fifth and sixth centuries. The Empire was becoming Christian, but the Church was not yet dominant. "However great the respect which people might profess for the Church, and however great its influence, it did not constitute an integral part of the State. The political power of the kings, like that of the Emperors, was purely secular. No religious ceremony was celebrated on the accession of the kings ... There is no formula of devotion *gratia Dei* in their diplomas. None of their court functionaries were ecclesiastics. All their ministers and officials were laymen. They [the kings] were heads of the church, appointing bishops and convoking Councils, and sometimes even taking part in them."[99] He goes on to emphasize that "In this respect there is a complete contrast between their governments and those subsequent to the 8th century." In other words, they were not medieval; they lacked the theocratic element that is one of the defining characteristics of medieval Europe. According to Pirenne, "This is explained by the fact that society itself was not yet dependent upon the Church in respect of its social life; it was still capable of providing the State with lay personnel."[100] In short, the Germanic kings of the fifth and sixth centuries had a large population of literate and educated laymen who could perform all the clerical and administrative functions that later only members of the clergy could perform.

There still existed, then, during the fifth and sixth, and the early part of the seventh, centuries, a large class of educated laymen; and these were steeped in the culture of classical antiquity. They all, or virtually all, described themselves as Christians; but their Christianity was not of the exclusive (and sometimes fanatical) variety that pertained in the Middle Ages. The Christian Church and its members "still conformed to a literary tradition whose prestige it respected. It retained the poetry of Virgil and his school, and the prose of the orators."[101] According to Pirenne, "Adhesion to the new faith [Christianity] was universal, but it was only upon a minority of ascetics and intellectuals that its hold was really complete. Many were drawn to the Church by interest: men of rank, like Sidonius Apollinarius, in order to retain their social influence, while the poor and needy sought shelter in it."[102]

---

[99] Pirenne, op cit., p. 136
[100] Ibid.
[101] Ibid., p. 118
[102] Ibid.

55

2: GERMANIC KINGS AND BYZANTINE EMPERORS

Yet the overriding influence of Classical culture was such that it was found even among the most enthusiastic Christian believers: the faith was viewed through the prism of classical philosophy, as we see very clearly in the writings of prominent early Christians, such as Origen. Even Saint Augustine, in many ways the example *par excellence* of the Bible-believing Christian, could not accept baptism until he was persuaded by Ambrose that the first part of Genesis could be viewed allegorically. This was a Christianity very different to that which pertained in the Middle Ages. It was not in any way opposed to the "pagan" philosophers, and indeed many Christian authors used those very philosophers in their defense of Christianity. This is as true of Boethius and Cassiodorus, in the sixth century, as it is of Origen in the third. There was no creeping fundamentalism, no gradual expulsion of classical rationalism; a force which, it appears, was very much alive in the sixth and even early seventh century.

Along with Graeco-Roman culture there prevailed a tolerance quite alien to the medieval spirit. The idea of forcing religious conformity through violence had yet to make its appearance. True, there were isolated instances of fanaticism and even of violence on the part of Christians during the late fourth and early fifth centuries. The two worst of these, that of the persecution of bishop Priscillian and the murder of Hypatia, will be considered presently. In addition, there were the vehement disputes over heresy and condemnations of these by various Christian writers. But these rarely involved anything approaching violence. And tolerance was the order of the day. We recall that Theodoric's nephew Theodahat could, in the early sixth century, proudly describe himself as a follower of Plato,[103] whilst the poets of the Anthology, who flourished under Thrasamund and Hilderic, blended obscenity with Christianity. And it needs to be emphasized that these men actually regarded themselves as Christians. Whatever view we may hold of such writings, there can be little doubt that it could hardly have been produced in an age of religious intolerance.

This was assuredly not the Christianity of the Middle Ages. Nonetheless, it could be argued, as some have tried to, the Church's easy-going attitude in these centuries was due as much to its lack of power, as to any underlying tolerance. The ruling elites in most of the western lands, remember, were not

---

[103] Procopius, Vol. III

actually Catholics but Arians. So, even if the Church had wished to oppress heretics and non-believers, it would not have been able to do so. Yet in two areas, Gaul and the Eastern Empire, orthodox Christianity held the keys to power. How did the Church behave in those regions?

We shall deal with Byzantium shortly. In Gaul, the Merovingian dynasty was Catholic almost from the beginning; and the record shows that in their territories there was as little evidence of religious intolerance as anywhere else. Still, it has to be admitted that several of the later Merovingian rulers issued oppressive decrees against the Jews, including at least one of forcible conversion. This was said to have occurred in 614, at the instigation of Heraclius, who was at that time involved in a desperate war with Persia. During the conflict the Jews of Palestine had allied themselves with the enemy and had committed a terrible massacre of Christians.[104] According to Gregory of Tours, some of the Jews allowed themselves to be converted,[105] whilst others fled to Marseilles, where they were not molested. It is recognized that this persecution was short-lived, and afterwards most converts reverted to Judaism. No violence was done against them. And in contrast to this half-hearted persecution by the secular authorities, Pope Gregory the Great was a stout defender of the Jews. In 591 he reprimanded the laity of Arles and Marseilles who were forcing baptism on them,[106] and rebuked the Bishop of Terracina, who had expelled the Jews from their synagogues. He would not even allow the Bishop of Naples to prevent the Jews from working on feast days and holy days.[107] The only restriction he imposed upon them was in respect of owning Christian slaves, and he requested Brunehaut to promulgate a law forbidding them to own such slaves.[108]

Some minor laws against the Jews were introduced in Gaul during the seventh century; and it is said that when the Visigoths of Spain became Catholic in the early seventh century they began enacting various repressive and discriminatory laws against the Jews. However, there is very good evidence to

[104] Gregory of Tours, vi, 17
[105] Greg. v, 11
[106] P. Jaffé and W. Wattenbach, *Regesta Pontificum Romanorum*, (Lipsiae, 1885) No. 1115
[107] Ibid. No, 1879
[108] Ibid. Nos. 1743-1744.

show that all the documents relating these laws (the Councils of Toledo) are medieval forgeries; and indeed, as we shall see, there is evidence to suggest that all documents that have survived in Europe purporting to come from the seventh, eight, and ninth centuries are fabrications.

Still, it has to be admitted that there was a long history of animosity between Christians and Jews, and we cannot doubt the truth of Gregory of Tours' statement that in his time the Jews were generally disliked by their Gentile neighbors.[109] In earlier times, many of the persecutions launched by the Roman authorities against the Christians were undertaken at the instigation of Jewish religious leaders; and the Jews were a very large and very influential group of people. Nonetheless, the triumph of Christianity did not bring – not until the First Crusade – any violent persecution of the Jews.

This is a topic of fundamental importance, and it is one we shall return to throughout the present work.

Social Conditions in the West

Whatever accusations may be brought against the Christian Church with regard to the Jews, there is no question that, from the very beginning, the Church was a defender of the poor and oppressed. Indeed, almost without exception, it was the poor, the powerless, and the marginalized, who were the first to embrace it. It was said to be a religion of slaves and women. It was also to become the religion of the sick, the dying, the despairing, and of all those for whom the old religion of Greece and Rome, with its all too human and immoral deities, could offer little. To those whose lives were difficult or worse, it gave hope of a better future, and to the bereaved it gave hope of a reunion to come. It was these attributes that in time won over so many and eventually delivered the whole Empire to the faith.

In accordance with its doctrines, real and important material improvements were made to the quality of life. Even before being legalized, the Christians were at work distributing assistance to the poor, the sick and the destitute. With the toleration inaugurated by Constantine, this only increased;

---

[109] Gregory of Tours, v, 11

and the first hospitals for the poor were now established. There were also important legal and legislative improvements. Out of respect for Christ, Constantine banned the practice of crucifixion, and this savage form of punishment was not to be seen again in Europe until, hundreds of years later, it was re-introduced by the Arabs into Spain and southern Italy.[110] Constantine also decreed a ban on gladiator contests. This however was not rigidly enforced, and it was not until 404 that the gruesome ritual came to a definitive end. We are told that a monk named Telemachus, who had travelled to Rome specifically for this purpose, jumped into an arena in the city and tried to separate two combatants. The enraged crowd of spectators however climbed over the perimeter walls and beat the heroic ascetic to death.[111] In response to this ugly incident, the Emperor Honorius permanently banned all such events. This time the law was enforced, and the era of the gladiator was over.

Early Christianity was famously, or notoriously (depending upon one's point of view) pacifist, and the doctrine of non-violence was evidently taken very seriously as late as the beginning of the fourth century, when we have two illuminating cases: that of Maximilianus, an African youth who refused his father's wish that he should join the military, declaring that his conscience would not permit him to embrace the profession of a soldier; and that of Marcellus, a centurion. The latter, on the day of a public festival, threw away his belt, his arms, and the ensigns of his office, and exclaimed in a loud voice that he would obey none but Jesus Christ, the eternal King.[112]

Not surprisingly, the centurion was arrested and executed for the crime of desertion.

When Christianity became the official religion of the Empire such an extreme position could no longer be upheld; not by the Church leadership, at any rate. Nevertheless, Christians were never fully at ease with the idea of killing, even in a defensive war, and there is evidence that the pacifism of the early Church survived well into the tenth and even eleventh centuries. It survived, in fact, till the very dawn of the age of the Crusades. And there is evidence too that it was the unwillingness of large segments of the (now Christian) population of the Empire to enroll as soldiers which led the

[110] *Encyclopaedia Britannica*, Vol. 3 Micropaedia, "Crucifixion".
[111] Theoderet, *Historia Ecclesiastica*, v, 22
[112] Theodore Ruinart, *Acta Sincera*, (1689) p. 302

administration increasingly to the rather dangerous expedient of recruiting Barbarians from Germany and Scythia to fill the ranks.

For all that, there is no question that by the fifth century Christianity was having a powerfully humanizing influence upon life in the Empire; and one of the most conspicuous areas in which the new faith worked on the side of humanity was in the institution of slavery.

Contrary to the beliefs of some modern prominent anti-Christian writers, the new faith brought an immediate and dramatic improvement in the living conditions of slaves. It was also, eventually, instrumental in the abolition of the entire institution. The improvement was an inevitable consequence of the Christian notion that the mistreatment of any human being, whether slave or free, was gravely sinful. In the words of one writer, "The effect of the Church upon the Empire may be summed up in the word 'freedom'."[113] And "Close upon the Church's victory follows legislation more favorable to the slave than any that had gone before."[114] Whilst it is true that "Constantine did not attempt sudden or wholesale emancipation, which would have been unwise and impossible," he nevertheless immediately "sought to lessen his [the slave's] hardships by measures which with all their inequalities are unique in the statute-book of Rome. ... he forbade cruelty towards slaves in terms which are themselves an indictment of existing practice."[115] The Gospel passages of relevance here are too numerous to mention, but we should note in particular the story of the Final Judgment as told in Mark 25: 31-46, where the King (God) tells His servants: "So long as you did it to these, the least of my brethren, you did it to me." It should be remarked also, at this point, that the whole concept of human rights, attributed by many contemporary westerners to the thinkers of the Enlightenment, is rooted in this Gospel concept – a fact admitted by the Enlightenment philosophers themselves. Human rights are a moral as well as a judicial concept. If God will hold each of us accountable for our behavior towards the lowliest members of society, this places the latter on a par, in moral terms, with the highest members of society.

Thus from the start, the lives of slaves improved. This was especially the case with female and younger male slaves, whose function, in the past, was very

---

[113] H. F. Stewart, loc it. p. 592
[114] Ibid.
[115] Ibid., p. 593

often to provide sexual pleasure for their owners. This type of transgression was especially frowned upon by Christians. And so, whilst the owning of slaves was not, to begin with, illegal, mistreatment – from the very start – was. This view led, inexorably, to the abandonment and abolition of the entire slave system. We find therefore, from the earliest times, many Christian leaders, such as Gregory of Nyssa and John Chrysostom, condemning slavery itself and calling for better treatment for slaves. In fact, tradition describes Pope Clement I (92 - 99), Pope Pius I (roughly 158 - 167) and Pope Callixtus I (217 - 222) as former slaves.

As a friend of the outcast and the poor, Jesus himself had given the lead in this issue, and from the beginning the Church made no account of the social condition of the faithful. Bond and free received the same sacraments. Clerics of servile origin were numerous (St. Jerome, *Ep.* lxxxii). As the *Catholic Encyclopedia* states, "So complete -- one might almost say, so leveling -- was this Christian equality that St. Paul (1 Timothy 6:2), and, later, St. Ignatius (*Polyc.*, iv), are obliged to admonish the slave and the handmaid not to condemn their masters, 'believers like them and sharing in the same benefits.' In giving them a place in religious society, the Church restored to slaves the family and marriage. In Roman, law, neither legitimate marriage, nor regular paternity, nor even impediment to the most unnatural unions had existed for the slave (Digest, XXXVIII, viii, i, (sect) 2; X, 10, (sect) 5)."[116]

The above writer continues:

"Primitive Christianity did not attack slavery directly; but it acted as though slavery did not exist. By inspiring the best of its children with this heroic charity, examples of which have been given above, it remotely prepared the way for the abolition of slavery. To reproach the Church of the first ages with not having condemned slavery in principle, and with having tolerated it in fact, is to blame it for not having let loose a frightful revolution, in which, perhaps, all civilization would have perished with Roman society. But to say, with Ciccotti (*Il tramonto della schiavitù* (French trans., 1910) pp. 18, 20), that primitive Christianity had not even 'an embryonic vision' of a society in which there should be no slavery, to say that the Fathers of the Church did not feel 'the horror of slavery,' is to display either strange ignorance or singular unfairness. In St. Gregory of Nyssa (In *Ecclesiastem*, hom. iv) the most energetic and

---

[116] www.newadvent.org/cathen/14036a.htm

absolute reprobation of slavery may be found; and again in numerous passages of St. John Chrysostom's discourse we have the picture of a society without slaves - a society composed only of free workers, an ideal portrait of which he traces with the most eloquent insistence (see the texts cited in Allard, *Les esclaves chrétiens*, p. 416-23).

"Under the Christian emperors this tendency [to ameliorate the conditions of slaves], in spite of relapses at certain points, became daily more marked, and ended, in the sixth century, in Justinian's very liberal legislation (see Wallon, *Histoire de l'esclavage dans l'antiquité* III, ii and x). Although the civil law on slavery still lagged behind the demands of Christianity ('The laws of Caesar are one thing, the laws of Christ another,' St. Jerome writes in *Ep.* lxxvii), nevertheless very great progress had been made. It continued in the Eastern Empire (laws of Basil the Macedonian, of Leo the Wise, of Constantine Porphyrogenitus), but in the West it was abruptly checked by the barbarian invasions."[117]

After the Germanic invasions, there is no question that, for a while, the number of slaves increased, and the conditions of their servitude deteriorated. The German rulers subjected them to legislation and to customs much harsher than those which obtained under the Roman law of the period (see Allard, "Les origines du servage" in *Revue des questions historiques*, April, 1911). Gibbon noted how slavery, "which had been almost suppressed by the peaceful sovereignty of Rome, was again revived and multiplied by the perpetual hostilities of the independent Barbarians."[118] Yet once again the Church intervened. It did so in three ways: redeeming slaves; legislating for their benefit in its councils; and setting an example of humane treatment. Documents of the fifth to the seventh century are full of instances of captives carried off from conquered cities by the barbarians and doomed to slavery, whom bishops, priests, monks, and pious laymen redeemed. Redeemed captives were sometimes sent back in thousands to their own country (ibid., p. 393-7, and Lesne, *Hist de la propriété ecclésiastique en France* (1910), pp. 357-69).

We know from Gregory of Tours and other writers of the time that he Churches of Gaul, Spain, Britain, and Italy were busy, in numerous councils,

---

[117] Ibid.
[118] *Decline and Fall*, Chapter 38

with the affairs of slaves; protection of the maltreated slave who has taken refuge in a church (Councils of Orléans, 511, 538, 549; Council of Epone, 517); those manumitted in ecclesiis, but also those freed by any other process (Council of Arles, 452; of Agde, 506; of Orléans, 549; of Mâcon, 585; of Toledo, 589, 633; of Paris, 615); validity of marriage contracted with full knowledge of the circumstances between free persons and slaves (Councils of Verberie, 752, of Compiègne, 759); rest for slaves on Sundays and feast days (Council of Auxerrre, 578 or 585; of Rouen, 650; of Wessex, 691; of Berghamsted, 697); suppression of traffic in slaves by forbidding their sale outside the kingdom (Council of Châlon-sur-Saône, between 644 and 650); prohibition against reducing a free man to slavery (Council of Clichy, 625). Less liberal in this respect than Justinian (*Novella*, cxxiii, 17), who made tacit consent a sufficient condition, the Western discipline does not permit a slave to be raised to the priesthood without the formal consent of his master; nevertheless the councils held at Orléans in 511, 538, 549, while imposing canonical penalties upon the bishop who exceeded his authority in this matter, declare such an ordination to be valid. A council held at Rome in 595 under the presidency of St. Gregory the Great permits the slave to become a monk without any consent, express or tacit, of his master.

We hear that, "At this period the Church found itself becoming a great proprietor. Barbarian converts endowed it largely with real property. As these estates were furnished with serfs attached to the cultivation of the soil, the Church became by force of circumstances a proprietor of human beings, for whom, in these troublous times, the relation was a great blessing. The laws of the barbarians, amended through Christian influence, gave ecclesiastical serfs a privileged position: their rents were fixed; ordinarily, they were bound to give the proprietor half of their labour or half of its products, the remainder being left to them (*Lex Alemannorum*, xxii; *Lex Bajuvariorum*, I, xiv, 6). A council of the sixth century (Eauze, 551) enjoins upon bishops that they must exact of their serfs a lighter service than that performed by the serfs of lay proprietors, and must remit to them one-fourth of their rents.

"Another advantage of ecclesiastical serfs was the permanency of their position. A Roman law of the middle of the fourth century (*Cod. Just.*, XI, xlvii, 2) had forbidden rural slaves to be removed from the lands to which they belonged; this was the origin of serfdom, a much better condition than slavery properly so called. But the barbarians virtually suppressed this beneficent law (Gregory of Tours, *Hist. Franc.*, VI, 45); it was even formally abrogated among the Goths of Italy by the edict of Theodoric (sect. 142). Nevertheless, as an exceptional privilege, it remained in force for the serfs of the Church, who, like the Church itself remained under Roman law (*Lex Burgondionum*, LVIII, i; Louis I, *Add. ad legem Langobard.*, III, i). They shared besides, the inalienability of all ecclesiastical property which had been established by councils (Rome, 50; Orléans, 511, 538; Epone, 517; Clichy, 625; Toledo, 589); they were sheltered from the exactions of the royal officers by the immunity granted to almost all church lands (Kroell, *L'immunité franque*, 19110); thus their position was generally envied (Flodoard, *Hist eccl. Remensis*, I, xiv), and when the royal liberality assigned to a church a portion of land out of the state property, the serfs who cultivated were loud in their expression of joy (*Vita S. Eligii*, I, xv).

"It has been asserted that the ecclesiastical serfs were less fortunately situated because the inalienability of church property prevented their being enfranchised. But this is inexact. St. Gregory the Great enfranchised serfs of the Roman Church (Ep. vi, 12), and there is frequent discussion in the councils in regard to ecclesiastical freedmen. The Council of Agde (506) gives the bishop the right to enfranchise those serfs "who shall have deserved it" and to leave them a small patrimony. A Council of Orléans (541) declares that even if the bishop has dissipated the property of his church, the serfs whom he has freed in reasonable number (*numero competenti*) are to remain free. A Merovingian formula shows a bishop enfranchising one-tenth of his serfs (Formulae Biturgenses, viii). The Spanish councils imposed greater restrictions, recognizing the right of a bishop to enfranchise the serfs of his church on condition of his indemnifying it out of his own private property (Council of Seville, 590; of Toledo, 633; of Mérida, 666). But they made it obligatory to enfranchise the serf in whom a serious vocation was discerned (Council of Saragossa, 593). An English council (Celchyte, 816) orders that at the death of a bishop all the other bishops and all the abbots shall enfranchise three slaves each for the repose of his soul. This last clause shows again the mistake of saying that the monks had not the right of manumission. The canon of the Council of Epone (517) which forbids abbots to enfranchise their serfs was enacted in order that the monks might not be left to work without assistance and has been taken too literally. It is inspired not only by agricultural prudence, but also by the consideration that the serfs belong to the community of monks, and not to the abbot individually. Moreover, the rule of St. Ferréol (sixth century) permits the abbot to free serfs with the consent of the monks, or without their consent, if, in the latter case, he replaces at his own expense those he has enfranchised. The statement that ecclesiastical freedmen were not as free as the freedmen of lay proprietors will not bear examination in the light of facts, which shows the situation of the two classes to have been identical, except that the freedman of the Church earned a higher *wergheld* than a lay freedman, and therefore his life was better protected. *The Polyptych of Irminon*, a detailed description of the abbey lands of Saint-Germain-des-Prés shows that in the ninth century the serfs of that domain were not numerous and led in every way the life of free peasants."[119]

The end result of all this was that by the tenth or even ninth century the Church had effectively ended slavery in Europe. And this is a fact well-known. In the words of Rodney Stark, "... slavery ended in medieval Europe only because the church extended its sacraments to all slaves and then managed to impose a ban on the enslavement of Christians (and Jews). Within the context of medieval Europe, that prohibition was effectively a rule of universal abolition."[120]

Conditions in the East

We must never forget that, even after the formal abolition of the Western empire in the latter years of the fifth century, all of the lands of the West, with the exception of Britain and North Africa, still remained, theoretically at least, part of the Empire. And for a while in the middle of the sixth century this membership of the Empire became more than theoretical, as Justinian restored Imperial rule throughout Italy, North Africa, and parts of Spain. All during these years, right through the late fifth and sixth centuries, the influence of Byzantium was all-pervasive. The lands of the West remained culturally within the orbit of

---

[119] www.newadvent.org/cathen/14036a.htm
[120] Rodney Stark, *The Victory of Reason* (Random House, New York, 2005) p. 28

the Empire, and everything that happened in Constantinople had repercussions in Spain, Gaul, and even Britain.

Bearing this in mind, we need to look at conditions in Byzantium. As the head of Christendom, the decisions taken there shaped events elsewhere.

Statements by historians about Byzantine history and civilization tend to be diverse and more often than not mutually contradictory. It is often asserted, for example, that Byzantium, which was never overrun by barbarians, experienced no Dark Age and no Medieval period, and that the arts and sciences of Antiquity flourished in Constantinople up to the day it fell to the Turks in 1453, when scholars and philosophers, fleeing the carnage, helped bring about the rebirth of Classical learning in the West. On the other hand, it is asserted – with equal frequency – that Byzantium, with its deep-rooted Christian culture, became the very epitome of all that we call "medieval", and that it was from Byzantium that Christian obscurantism and intolerance transmitted itself to the West, creating there also a darkened and medieval mindset.

It is remarkable that the above viewpoints, though contradictory, are often encountered in works by one and the same author. Which then, we might ask, is right? They cannot surely both be. Did Byzantium preserve Classical civilization intact and avoid a darkened medieval period, or was Byzantium instead herself the source of all "medievalism", both in the East and the West?

In the course of the present work we shall find that neither of the above options amounts to anything more than a hodge-podge of misconceptions and half-truths. Neither in fact is correct. Byzantium, we shall see, though never conquered by Goths or Huns, did have a Dark Age; a Dark Age that corresponded precisely with that of the West (seventh to tenth centuries), and one that was followed by a Medieval Age which, just as in the West, was marked by an enormous decline in literacy and learning, and by the rise of a theocratic and intolerant Church. Yet none of these developments, as we shall see, had anything to do with Christianity, either of the Eastern or the Western variety.

The whole of the former Western Empire, we have seen, remained culturally within the orbit of the Empire throughout the fifth and sixth centuries, and for some time in the latter period large areas came once again within the Empire's political orbit. Indeed, for a while in the sixth century it appeared that the old unified Roman Empire, encompassing the entire Mediterranean littoral, was about to be reborn. This occurred in the time of Justinian.

Justinian's reign may be regarded as constituting a distinct epoch in the history of the Byzantine Empire. Of Illyrian origin, he was a man of great energy and was popularly known as "the Emperor who never sleeps" on account of his work habits. He was said to have been a natural leader, amenable and easy to approach. Since he lacked any power base in the traditional aristocracy of Constantinople, he surrounded himself with men and women of ability, whom he selected not on the basis of aristocratic origin, but of merit. Around 525 he married Theodora, who was by profession a courtesan and about twenty years his junior. In earlier times such a marriage would have been unthinkable. That it was possible at all was due to Justinian's uncle and predecessor, the Emperor Justin I, who passed a law allowing intermarriage between social classes. It goes without saying that the union nevertheless caused a scandal, though Theodora would prove to be highly intelligent and astute, a good judge of character and an able partner of the Emperor. Other talented individuals recruited by Justinian to his administration included Tribonian, his legal adviser; his finance ministers John the Cappadocian and Peter Barsymes, who managed to collect taxes more efficiently than any before, thereby funding Justinian's wars; and finally, his prodigiously talented general Belisarius.

As we have seen, the Emperor's overriding ambition was the *renovatio imperii*, or "restoration of the empire", a project which began in 533-534 with a campaign against the Vandals in North Africa, under the military direction of Belisarius (Justinian himself never left Constantinople). The conquest of North Africa was followed swiftly by a campaign against the Ostrogoths in Italy, where success was not so easily won. Nonetheless, within a few years Italy was once again part of Imperial territory, and a portion of Spain, too, were shortly to come under the administration of Constantinople. Whatever the eventual fate of this project, there can be no doubting that it marked a high point in Byzantine power and culture. For a while, a completely revived Empire, including virtually all the former Imperial territories, seemed a real possibility. And Justinian's achievements were by no means only military: He was also a prolific builder: He filled the Empire with aqueducts, fortifications, palaces and gloriously decorated temples. Most notably, he had the Hagia Sophia, originally a basilica style church that had been burnt down during the Nika riots, splendidly rebuilt according to a completely different ground plan. This new cathedral, with its magnificent dome filled with mosaics, remained the centre of eastern Christianity for centuries. Another prominent church in the capital, the Church of the Holy Apostles, which had been in a very poor state near the end of the fifth century, was likewise rebuilt. Works of embellishment were not confined to churches alone: excavations at the site of the Great Palace of Constantinople have yielded several high-quality mosaics dating from Justinian's reign, and a column topped by a bronze statue of Justinian on horseback and dressed in a military costume was erected in the Augustaeum in Constantinople in 543. It is possible that rivalry with other, more established patrons from the Constantinopolitan aristocracy may have encouraged Justinian's building activities in the capital.

Justinian also strengthened the borders of the empire through the construction of fortifications, and assured Constantinople of its water supply through construction of underground cisterns. During his reign a bridge over the river Sangarius was built, securing a major trade route. Furthermore, he restored cities damaged by earthquake or war and built a new city near his place of birth called Justiniana Prima.

In the words of one writer, "Under Justinian the majesty of Rome shone again, from Spain to the frontiers of Persia, from the Sahara to the Danube. It seemed – superficially at least – as magnificent as ever, secure against all invaders behind its protective Maginot Line."[121] Militarily supreme, the Empire also witnessed a flourishing of intellectual and artistic life. Literacy was commonplace, and writers of the period enjoyed a wide readership. The major events of the time were chronicled by historians such as Procopius (who later turned against the Emperor), Agathias, Menander Protector, John Malalas, the Paschal Chronicle, the chronicles of Marcellinus Comes and Victor of Tunnuna.

Justinian's reign also witnessed the uniform rewriting of Roman law, the *Corpus Juris Civilis*, which was to have a profound influence on European legal systems for centuries, and which still forms the basis of civil law in many modern states. In its totality the legislature is now known as the *Corpus juris civilis*, consisting of the *Codex Justinianus*, the *Digesta* or *Pandectae*, the *Institutiones*, and the *Novellae*. The first draft of the *Codex Justinianus*, a

---

[121] Trevor-Roper, op cit., p. 40

codification of imperial constitutions from the second century onward, was issued on April 7, 529. (The final version appeared in 534.) It was followed by the *Digesta* (or *Pandectae*), a compilation of older legal texts, in 533, and by the *Institutiones*, a textbook explaining the principles of law. The *Novellae*, a collection of new laws issued during Justinian's reign, supplements the *Corpus*. As opposed to the rest of the corpus, the *Novellae* appeared in Greek, the common language of the Eastern Empire; Latin, the traditional language of the Roman Empire, was only poorly understood by most citizens of the East.

The *Corpus* forms the basis of Latin jurisprudence (including ecclesiastical Canon Law) and, for historians, provides a valuable insight into the concerns and activities of the later Roman Empire. As a collection it gathers together the many sources in which the *leges* (laws) and the other rules were expressed or published: proper laws, senatorial consults (*senatusconsulta*), imperial decrees, case law, and jurists' opinions and interpretations (*responsa prudentum*).

The only western province where the Justinianic code was introduced was Italy (in 554), from where it was to pass to Western Europe in the twelfth century and become the basis of much European law. It passed also to Eastern Europe where it appeared in Slavic editions, and became the cornerstone of Russian law.

Some of the most important topics touched by Justinian's code, from our point of view, concerned issues of social justice such as slavery and the treatment of religious minorities. Famously, slavery is, for the first time in history, condemned as immoral. The rationale was explained in the *Institutiones*, (Title III, Book 1, paragraph 2) where we read the following: "Slavery is an institution of the law of nations, against nature, subjecting one man to the dominion of another." Again, in Title II, Book 1, paragraph 2, it states "... the law of nations is common to the whole human race; for nations have settled certain things for themselves as occasion and the necessities of human life required. For instance, wars arose and then followed captivity and slavery, which are contrary to the law of nature; for by the law of nature all men from the beginning were born free."

The spirit of these words needs to be borne in mind when we come to consider Byzantine civilization as a whole.

Tolerance and Intolerance

The moderation of the early Christians, notwithstanding the vandalism carried out during the time of Theodosius, is amply illustrated by the fact that in the age of Justinian, a full two centuries after Constantine, there still existed large populations of pagans throughout the Roman world. These were, it is true, then subjected – by Justinian – to renewed penalties and disapproval; so much so that he has been charged with "suppressing" paganism. And yet, it is admitted, even by Christianity's strongest opponents, that neither Justinian, nor any other Christian ruler of the age, resorted to violence against the persons of non-believers.

The other charge laid at the feet of Christians of this age, and at Justinian in particular, is the accusation that they crushed the scientific and philosophical spirit of Greece and Rome; and indeed that it was these rulers, and their fanatical devotion to an obscurantist Christianity, that ushered in the "Dark Age."

What are we to make of such claims?

Justinian's religious policy reflected the imperial conviction that the unity of the Empire presupposed unity of faith; and it appeared to him obvious that this faith could be only the Orthodox (Nicaean) version of Christianity. Those of a different belief had to recognize that the process of consolidation, which imperial legislation had effected from the time of Constantius II, would now vigorously continue. The *Codex* contained two statutes which decreed the total proscribing of paganism, even in private life. These provisions were supposedly zealously enforced, though there is much evidence to indicate the contrary. Contemporary sources (John Malalas, Theophanes, John of Ephesus) tell of severe persecutions, even of men in high position; yet on no occasion did these "persecutions" include lethal violence against the person. Furthermore, even after the persecutions paganism survived, admittedly in a rather underground way. Cyril Mango notes, for example, the appearance, in art and literature, of themes from pagan culture even into the seventh century.[122] Clearly, this was not suppression of dissent of the type familiar in Medieval Europe.

---

[122] Cyril Mango, *Byzantium: The Empire of New Rome* (Macmillan, London, 1981) p. 265

HOLY WARRIORS

Perhaps Justinian's most notorious decree was enacted in 529, when the Neoplatonic Academy of Athens was placed under state control; effectively strangling this training-school for Hellenism. The intellectual "backbone" of Graeco-Roman philosophy, we are told, was thus broken. There was active suppression of paganism in other areas of the Empire. In Asia Minor alone, John of Ephesus claimed to have converted 70,000 pagans. The worship of Amun at Augila in the Libyan Desert was abolished; and so were the remnants of the worship of Isis on the island of Philae, at the first cataract of the Nile. The Presbyter Julian and the Bishop Longinus conducted a mission among the Nabataeans, and Justinian attempted to strengthen Christianity in Yemen by dispatching a bishop from Egypt.

So, there is no doubt that Justinian can be accused of religious intolerance. Against this, it needs to be emphasized that he tried hard to find accommodation with heterodox Christians, most especially with the Monophysites of Syria and Egypt. This fact cannot be stressed too strongly, as it has been repeatedly suggested that Constantinople's "religious imperialism" caused a fatal weakening of the Empire's unity and may have been partly responsible for the ease with which a short time later the Muslims conquered the Near East. This position is however flatly contradicted by the evidence. There can be little doubt that Byzantium's religious differences with Syria and Egypt were a cause of much controversy and some tension, yet the policy of Byzantium throughout the sixth and early seventh centuries was one of compromise rather than coercion. Repeated attempts were made to find agreement with the Monophysites that would be acceptable to the Western Church. If the Empire failed to preserve the religious harmony and unity of Christendom, it was not for want of trying. And there is no evidence whatsoever that the Christians of Egypt and Syria were alienated from Constantinople to the extent that they co-operated with the Muslims against the Imperial administration. On the contrary, if we are to believe the contemporary accounts, it was the Imperial Viceroy Cyrus of Alexandria, who, in obedience to the command of the Empress Martina, surrendered the strategically vital Alexandria to the Islamic forces – a move which outraged the native Christians.

The belief that the Christians of Egypt and Syria "must" have co-operated with the Muslims is based ultimately on the otherwise incomprensible fact that these vast and populous territories were conquered apparently by little more than

71

a handful of Arabs on camels. Yet the truth, as we shall see in the Appendix, was quite different: it is almost certain that a mighty host of Persian cavalry, in alliance with the Arabs, delivered these regions to Islam.

Whatever the shortcomings of Justinian's religious policies, he most certainly cannot be accused of failure in the field of science and learning: For the evidence indicates that he was a very active patron of the sciences and the arts.

In Justinian's era, and partly under his patronage, there was a continuing interest in the natural sciences, in medicine and mathematics. According to Margaret Deanesley, "an interest in natural sciences ... flowered again ... Actios of Amida, Paulus of Aegina and Alexander of Tralles investigated too the principles of conics and built ingenious machinery. Alexandria was a centre of Greek culture, and Byzantium now and later had commentators on Aristotle who, in their own time, surpassed the learning of Isidore, Bede or Scotus Erigena in western Europe."[123] The mention here by Deanesley of these western luminaries calls our attention to the fact that this flourishing of literature and learning was not confined to the reign of Justinian, or to the eastern regions of the Empire.

All of this artistic, literary and philosophic activity hardly seems to indicate a mentality hostile to science and intellectual enquiry. And the existence throughout the sixth century, both in the East and the West of numerous scholarly as well as ecclesiastical centers speaks of a thriving intellectual life. Thus the closure of the Platonic Academy in Athens, as well as the famous law school in Beirut, both of which are routinely held against Justinian, should not be taken as the defining actions of his epoch. The philosophers of the Academy, many of whom still rejected Christianity, or at least Christian orthodoxy, were perhaps seen as a threat to Justinian's vision of a united spiritual and temporal authority. No one can condone this act, but it must not be regarded as signaling the suppression of classical learning or the scientific spirit. According to Cyril Mango, the suppression of pagan culture at this time was much less thorough than is popularly imagined, and he notes, for example, that the Academy continued functioning (though in a somewhat diminished way) for several decades after the date of its supposed closure (529),

---

[123] Margaret Deanesley, *A History of Early Medieval Europe, 476 to 911* (Methuen, London, 1965) p. 207

and that at Alexandria philosophy was still being taught by the pagan Olympiodorus until after Justinian's death.[124] And the scientific, artistic and literary activity which characterized the whole of the epoch hardly speaks of an oppressive and obscurantist theocracy.

Having said that, Classical civilization, properly speaking, with its urban culture, its widespread literacy and tradition of liberal education, did come to an end in Byzantium, just as surely as it came to an end in Gaul and Spain. Byzantium too would experience its Dark Age, when cities declined, literacy almost vanished, and poverty prevailed. This Dark Age began in the East, as it began in the West, in the middle of the seventh century. Yet it had nothing to do with Christianity. What caused it will be the subject of the next chapter.

Heretics and Jews in the East

As noted above, Justinian is famous, or infamous, for his intolerant attitude towards heretics and non-Christians. Thus in his Code he provides for the expulsion or even execution of some groups, such as Manicheans. As far as we know, the latter sanction was carried out only once, when "several" Manicheans were put to death, in the Emperor's presence, in Constantinople. Even one death is too many, but these events have to be viewed in the context of the times. The Manicheans were a sect of Persian origin, and the entire history of the Roman Empire, from its very beginning, was punctuated by wars with the Persians. In the words of Cyril Mango, "Among the sects that inspired the greatest fear was that of the Manichees, on the mistaken assumption that they were, in addition to their dangerous doctrines, agents of the [Persian] enemy."[125] Should we should doubt Mango's analysis, we need only note the fact that over two centuries before Justinian, the pagan Emperor Diocletian had likewise accused the Manicheans of being Persian agents and had persecuted them severely:

> We have heard that the Manichees very recently like new and unexpected monstrosities have taken their rise among the race of the Persians which is at enmity with us, and have progressed thence into

---

[124] Mango, op cit., p. 135
[125] Ibid., p. 94

our empire, and that they commit many crimes there; for our information is that they disturb the quiet populations, and even work the greatest harm to whole cities: our fear is that in the course of time as usually happens they will attempt through the accursed morals and savage laws of the Persians to infect men of less wicked nature, ie the modest and peaceful race of the Romans and our whole dominion with, as it were, the poison of a malignant serpent. And because all the manifestations of their religion which your Prudence revealed in your account set out the carefully devised and thought out contrivances of obvious malefactors, we therefore set out due and fitting pains and penalties for them. For we order the authors and leaders of the sect, to be subjected to a very severe penalty, namely, to be burnt, along with their abominable scriptures: but their followers, who are persistently obstinate we order to be punished with death, and we ordain that their property be confiscated to our treasury. If any persons of the official classes, or of any rank, no matter what, or of superior status, have betaken themselves of this unheard of, base, and utterly infamous sect, or to the doctrine of the Persians, see that their property is attached to our treasury and that they are themselves committed to the mines (quarries) of Phaeno or Proconnesus.[126]

Justinian's persecution of the Manicheans, while deplorable, was thus primarily a political rather than a religious act, and cannot be seen as proof of the Emperor's willingness to use violence against others on purely religious grounds. And the intertwining of politics with religion, as well as long-established Roman Imperial policy, must always be borne in mind when we look at the supposedly religious conflicts of this age. In particular, the traditional hostility towards Persia, which had begun in the first century BC, was to color the actions and policies of the Emperors, both Christian and pagan, right up to Justinian's time and beyond. The power of Persia was to be an ever-present threat, and over the centuries many Roman armies were destroyed and the reputations of generals ruined in these perennial and apparently perpetual wars.

---

[126] *Lex Dei sive Mosaicarum et Romanorum Legum Collatio*, xv, iii, ed. Kübler, in *Iurisprudentiae Anteiustinianae Reliquiae*, Ed. 6, II.2 pp. 381-3 (Teubner): A. Adam, *Texte zum Manichäismus* (Kleine Texte 175), pp. 82-3.

HOLY WARRIORS

The war with Persia flared again during the time of Justinian and his predecessor Justin. Justinian's opponent was Chosroes I, one of the most able rulers of the Sassanid Dynasty; and the conflict between the two emperors dragged on for twenty-two years (540 – 562).

One tactic employed repeatedly by the Persians was to encourage the rebellion of religious or ethnic minorities on the eastern fringes of the Roman Empire. These were promised, upon the event of a Persian victory, their own independent states, allied with Persia. It was this promise which had precipitated the terrible slaughters carried out by Jewish rebels in Cyprus, Egypt and Cyrene during the time of Trajan. On this occasion (115 AD), according to Dion Cassius, the Jewish insurgents massacred 240,000 Greeks in Cyprus; 220,000 in Cyrene, and "a very great multitude" in Egypt.[127] Fifteen years later, during the reign of Hadrian, the Jews, once more in expectation of Persian/Parthian assistance, rose against the Empire. This insurrection was quelled only after a frightful massacre and the virtual extinction of the Jewish race in the land of Israel.[128]

The disappearance of the Jews in Israel did not prevent the Parthians, and later the Sassanids, continuing their policy of fomenting rebellion along Rome's eastern borders. Thus Armenia, which occupied a large portion of the boundary between the two empires, and whose inhabitants held unorthodox religious views, was frequently disturbed by the intrigues of the Sassanid kings. And the situation had not changed in the time of Justinian. Shortly after his accession to the throne (527), a serious rebellion broke out among the Samaritans, a semi-Jewish sect of northern Palestine. Very many Christians were killed at this time, and it took two years of fierce fighting to bring the war to a close. And this conflict, it must be stressed, was only one in a long series of Samaritan rebellions, which culminated in a "terrible" revolt in the year 555.[129] Theophanes states that after the rebellion of 527 the fugitive Samaritans endeavored to enlist the aid of Chosroes I against the Romans by offering him their country as well as an army of 30,000 Jews and Samaritans. Shortly after this, Chosroes I did indeed go to war against Byzantium. Whether the appeal of

---

[127] Dion Cassius, lxviii, 1145
[128] Ibid., lxix, 1162
[129] eg. Malalas, *Chronicle*, xviii, 445; and Theophanes, *Chronographia*, i, 274.

75

the rebel Samaritans had any effect we cannot say; but the authorities in Constantinople certainly believed the danger was real enough: For it was then (532) that Justinian published the first of his famous anti-Jewish decrees. According to Cyril Mango, "The change from a policy of grudging toleration to one of forced conversion and persecution seems to have been brought about by political events. The Jews proved to be disloyal to the Empire."[130] Mango notes how Christians were massacred in Yemen around 529 by the Jewish convert Du-Nuwas, an event which seems to have had a decisive effect upon Justinian's thinking. Furthermore, "the Jews took the side of the enemy when Asia Minor and Palestine were invaded by the Persians.[131]

The *Jewish Encyclopedia* can in no way be described as an organ of Christian apology, and its judgment must be seen as important. According to it: "The consequences of persistent rebellion [by Jews and Samaritans against the Empire] were soon felt." In 532, just five years after his coronation, "… the emperor issued a decree to the effect that in cases of dispute the Jews could act as witnesses against one another, but not against Christians; heretics, including Samaritans, could not act as witnesses even against one another (*Corp. Juris*, i. 5, 21). 'The synagogues of the Samaritans shall be destroyed, and if they dare to build others, they shall be punished. They may have no testamentary or other legal heirs except Orthodox Christians' (*ib.* i. 5, 17; comp. i. 5, 18-19). They were forbidden to leave legacies or presents. In 551, Bishop Sergius of Cæsarea succeeded in softening the emperor's severity toward them and securing the repeal of these disgraceful laws (*Novella* 129). In other respects the status of the Jews and Samaritans was the same. Novella 45 of the year 537 begins as follows: 'Relating to the law that Jews, Samaritans, or heretics are not to be exempt from the office of magistrate on pretext of their belief, but that, on the contrary, they shall bear the burdens of the magistracy without enjoying its privileges.' In 545 it was ordained that no heretic should, under any circumstances, acquire real estate from a church or religious institution. 'If an Orthodox Christian has sold or willed to a Jew or pagan or Arian a piece of land on which there is a church, the church of that locality shall seize such property.' 'Heretics may not build a "spelunca" for their heresies, nor may the Jews erect any new synagogues' (*Novella* 131, ch. 14). The following decrees were issued

---

[130] Mango, op cit. p. 92
[131] Ibid.

in favor of the Orthodox Church in newly conquered Africa: 'Jews may not keep Christian slaves, nor may they make proselytes by circumcision.' 'Their synagogues shall be rebuilt in the style of churches.' 'Jews, pagans, Arians, and other heretics may not have *speluncas* nor observe any of the ceremonies of the Orthodox Church' (*Novella* 37, of the year 535)."[132]

The fraught relationship between Jews and the Empire became even more strained after the death of Justinian. Shortly after ascending the throne, Heraclius was involved in a new and devastating conflict with Persia. This time the Jews, and not the Samaritans, took the lead, and in 614 a combined Jewish-Persian army invested Jerusalem. After a twenty-day siege, the city was taken and the Christian population massacred.[133] The Jews, under Benjamin of Tiberias, then formed a semi-autonomous state until 617, when, fearing a resurgent Rome, the latter changed sides and helped oust the Persians. We are told that, in return for this favor, Heraclius had promised him and his followers amnesty for their earlier treachery but that, influenced by some fanatical monks, the Emperor reneged on his promise and ordered a general massacre of the Jews.[134]

Before moving on, it needs to be stated that the authenticity of almost everything related to the life of Heraclius – after his first two or three years – is very much open to question; and this is a topic we shall be examine at a later stage. Whatever happened, there is no doubt that, by the beginning of the seventh century the relationship between the Empire and her Jewish subjects continued to be strained, and this would have far-reaching and eventually tragic repercussions. Nonetheless, whatever ill-feeling there was between Jews and Christians, it is important to remember that it had a geopolitical rather than a religious origin. The perpetual rivalry between Persia and Rome caused the smaller nations on the borders to be in a state of continuous agitation and ferment. Rebellion was ever in the air; and with it revenge and repression.

It has become commonplace to see in these events the beginning of medieval obscurantism and religious fanaticism. Bat Ye'or, for example, a fierce critic of Islam and its treatment of religious minorities, nevertheless sees early Islam as an improvement on the Byzantine system: "It is undeniable," she says,

---

[132] Retrieved from: www.jewishencyclopedia.com-JUSTINIAN.
[133] www.en.wikipedia.org/wiki/Revolt_against_Heraclius.
[134] Eutychius, ii. 241

"that the Arab-Islamic colonization [of the Near East], especially at the beginning, was a considerable improvement over the theocratic Byzantine rule."[135]

Yet such conclusions seem to have more to do with deep-rooted prejudices than with historical fact. Apart from the handful of Manicheans killed in Constantinople, there is no evidence that anyone was put to death solely for their religious beliefs in the entire Byzantine epoch. Even the Manicheans could have saved their lives by renouncing their faith; and, as we have seen, their execution had at least as much to do with politics as religion: As a Persian sect they were suspect.

Significantly, till the day it fell to the Turks in 1453, no Jew that we know of ever suffered the death penalty in Byzantium for his faith. Procopius was a fierce and vindictive enemy of Justinian, never tiring (at least in the *Secret History*) of accusing him of tyranny. Nevertheless, the same writer could apparently find nothing worse in the Emperor's behavior towards the Jews than forcing them to celebrate Passover at the same time as or later than the Christian Easter:

> Justinian, not content with subverting the laws of the Roman Empire every day, exerted himself in like manner to do away with those of the Jews; for, if Easter came sooner in their calendar than in that of the Christians, he did not allow them to celebrate Passover on their own proper day or to make their offerings to God, or to perform any of their usual solemnities. The magistrates even inflicted heavy fines on several of them, upon information that they had eaten the paschal lamb during that time, as if it were an infraction of the laws of the state.[136]

And the testimony of the Jewish historians themselves is surely the best commendation we can offer for Justinian. In the words of the *Jewish Encyclopedia*: "Justinian, whose reign so greatly affected the Jews, is hardly mentioned in the Jewish sources. A passage in a responsum of the Geonim

[135] Bat Ye'or, *The Dhimmi: Jews and Christians under Islam* (London, 1985) p. 132
[136] Procopius, *Secret History of the Court of Justinian*, xxviii

relating to the interdiction of the reading of the Torah refers, according to Grätz, to Justinian's decree, but it may be more correctly referred to Yezdegerd's interdiction (Halberstam, in Kobak's *Jeschurun*, vi. 126). The Samaritans, for whom Justinian's reign became fateful, do not mention him at all in their chronicles. The Jewish chronicles copy from Christian sources the statement that he was a great and just ruler, and they know nothing whatever of his tyrannous treatment of the Jews. David Gans quotes from the *Yuhasin* the statement that during one whole year in the time of Justinian the sun did not shine (*Zemah Dawid*, anno 566)."

Monasteries and Monasticism

An extremely important cultural innovation of the East which eventually spread to the West and had there a profound influence, was that of monasticism. Monasticism began in Egypt, where the austerities of Saint Anthony, who took up residence first in the tombs near Thebes and then in a remote part of the Eastern Desert, were imitated by a host of other devout believers. By the mid-fourth century, many religious-minded young men, heeding the call of Saint Basil the Great, began to live in monastic communities devoted to the same austere life of prayer as the hermits, yet without the complete isolation of the latter. Living in a community of faith, it was realized, had some distinct advantages over the life of the anchorite.

Initially, monks did not see themselves as educators or men of letters: they were merely followers of Christ who wished to tread the path of spiritual perfection by relinquishing all worldly desires and possessions, as he had instructed. Nonetheless, even by the fourth century we find them involved in study and education. Saint John Chrysostom tells us that already in his day (circa 347 – 407) it was customary for people in Antioch to send their sons to be educated by the monks.

Monasticism probably began in the West during the fourth century, and it made great headway in particular in Ireland, a region of which we shall have more to say presently. The story of monasticism in the West however really begins with Benedict of Nursia, Saint Benedict, a contemporary of Boethius and Cassiodorus. Around 525 he established twelve small communities of monks at Subiaco, thirty-eight miles from Rome, before heading fifty miles south to

2: GERMANIC KINGS AND BYZANTINE EMPERORS

Monte Cassino, where he established the great monastery that would forever be associated with him. It was here that he formulated his famous Rule, the excellence of which was reflected in its almost universal adoption throughout Western Europe in the centuries that followed. Under the Rule of Benedict, the monks lived a life of prayer, work and study, and subsisted at a level comparable to that of a contemporary Italian peasant.

Although the monk's purpose in retiring from the world was to cultivate a more disciplined spiritual life, in the end the Benedictine Houses would play a much wider and historically-significant role. The monks may not have intended to make their communities into centers of learning, technology and economic progress; yet, as time went on, this is exactly what they became. Indeed, one can scarcely find a single endeavor in the advancement of civilization during Late Antiquity and the Early Middle Ages in which the monks did not play a central role. It is well-known, of course, that they preserved the literary inheritance of the ancient world (much more completely, in fact, than was previously realized), yet they did much more. According to one scholar, they gave "the whole of Europe ... a network of model factories, centers for breeding livestock, centers of scholarship, spiritual fervor, the art of living ... readiness for social action – in a word ... advanced civilization that emerged from the chaotic waves of surrounding barbarity. Without any doubt, Saint Benedict was the Father of Europe. The Benedictines, his children, were the Fathers of European civilization."[137]

We could fill volumes enumerating the achievements of the Benedictines. That they single-handedly preserved much of ancient literature is well-known. Not so widely known is the enormous quantity of that literature that they saved. We are accustomed to think that, following the collapse of the Western Empire, most of the literary heritage of Greece and Rome was lost in the west and was only recovered after contact with the Arabs in Spain and Italy during the eleventh century and after the fall of Constantinople during the fifteenth. Yet this notion is quite simply untrue. The great majority of the literature of Greece and Rome that has survived into modern times was preserved by the monks of the sixth and seventh centuries and was never in fact forgotten. Thus for example Alcuin, the polyglot theologian of Charlemagne's court, mentioned that

---

[137] Réginald Grégoire, Léo Moulin, and Raymond Oursel, *The Monastic Realm* (New York, Rizzoli, 1985) p. 277

his library in York contained works by Aristotle, Cicero, Lucan, Pliny, Statius, Trogus Pompeius, and Virgil. In his correspondences he quotes still other classical authors, including Ovid, Horace, and Terence. Abbo of Fleury (latter tenth century), who served as abbot of the monastery of Fleury, demonstrates familiarity with Horace, Sallust, Terence, and Virgil. Desiderius, described as the greatest of the abbots of Monte Cassino after Benedict himself, and who became Pope Victor III in 1086, oversaw the transcription of Horace and Seneca, as well as Cicero's *De Natura Deorum* and Ovid's *Fasti*.[138] His friend Archbishop Alfano, who had also been a monk of Monte Cassino, possessed a deep knowledge of the ancient writers, frequently quoting from Apuleius, Aristotle, Cicero, Plato, Varro, and Virgil, and imitating Ovid and Horace in his verse.

By the end of what is generally termed the Early Middle Ages (ie by the tenth and eleventh centuries) we find that monasteries all over Europe were in possession of enormous libraries stacked with the works of the classical authors, and that knowledge of Greek and even Hebrew was widespread. This is important, because it illustrates the continuity between this period and the world of Late Antiquity (fifth and sixth centuries), and shows that the so-called Dark Age is little more than a mythical construct – a topic to which we shall return at a later stage. It shows too that Christian Europe did not need to depend upon other societies and cultures (such as the Islamic) to reacquaint it with letters. Thus we find for example that Gerbert of Aurillac, later Pope Sylvester II, taught Aristotle and logic, and brought to his students an appreciation of Horace, Juvenal, Lucan, Persius, Terence, Statius, and Virgil. We hear of lectures delivered on the classical authors in places like Saint Alban's and Paderborn. A school exercise composed by Saint Hildebert survives in which he had pieced together excerpts from Cicero, Horace, Juvenal, Persius, Seneca, Terence, and others. It has been suggested that Hildebert knew Horace almost be heart.[139]

If the monks were classical scholars, they were equally natural philosophers, engineers and agriculturalists. Certain monasteries might be known for their skill in particular branches of knowledge. Thus, for example,

---

[138] Cited from Charles Montalembert, *The Monks of the West: From St. Benedict to St. Bernard.* 5 Vols. (Vol. 5) (London, 1896) p. 146

[139] John Henry Newman, in Charles Frederick Harrold, (ed.) *Essays and Sketches,* Vol. 3 (New York, 1948) pp. 316-7

lectures in medicine were delivered by the monks of Saint Benignus at Dijon, whilst the monastery of Saint Gall had a school of painting and engraving, and lectures in Greek and Hebrew could be heard at certain German monasteries.[140] Monks often supplemented their education by attending one or more of the monastic schools established throughout Europe. Abbo of Fleury, having mastered the disciplines taught in his own house, went to study philosophy and astronomy at Paris and Rheims. We hear similar stories about Archbishop Raban of Mainz, Saint Wolfgang, and Gerbert of Aurillac.[141]

The monks, from the time of Benedict onwards, established schools all over Europe. Indeed, our word "school" is related to the word "Scholastic", a term used to broadly define the system of thought and philosophy developed by the monks of this period. Scholastic thinking was based largely on Aristotle, and represented real continuity with the classical traditions of philosophy and rationality.

As well as teachers and educators, the monks established the first hospitals. These were the first institutions ever to exist proving free medical care to all, irrespective of financial circumstances. In the words of one writer: "Following the fall of the [Western] Roman Empire, monasteries gradually became the providers of organized medical care not available elsewhere in Europe for several centuries. Given their organization and location, these institutions were virtual oases of order, piety, and stability in which healing could flourish. To provide these caregiving practices, monasteries also became sites of medical learning between the fifth and tenth centuries, the classic period of so-called monastic medicine. During the Carolingian revival of the 800s, monasteries also emerged as the principal centers for the study and transmission of ancient medical texts."[142]

As noted by the above writer, their interest in healing led the monks naturally into medical research, and in course of time they accumulated a vast knowledge of physiology, pathology, and medication. Their studies of herbs and natural remedies led them into the investigation of plants, and they laid the foundations of the sciences of botany and biology.

---

[140] Ibid., p. 319

[141] Ibid., pp. 317-9

[142] Günter B. Risse, *Mending Bodies, Saving Souls: A History of Hospitals* (Oxford University Press, 1999) p. 95

Fig. 1. Church of Sant' Apollinare, Ravenna, early 6th century.

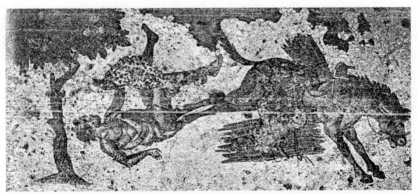

Fig. 2. Mosaic of Great Palace Pavement, Constantinople, probably late 6th century. (after Mango). Classical figurative art continued to flourish until the first half of the 7th century

Fig. 3 Byzantine silver plate with maenad, 613-630. (after Mango). Themes from pagan classical art were common throughout the territory of the Roman Empire until the mid-seventh century

Fig. 4. Page from the Book of Kells, probably early 7th century. The Hiberno-Saxon illuminated manuscripts of this period, which used blue pigment derived from Afghanistan lapis-lazuli, are by common consent among the finest and most technically brilliant works of miniature art ever produced.

HOLY WARRIORS

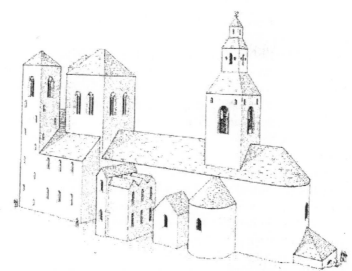

Fig. 5. Reconstruction of 7th century English Winchester Cathedral. (after M. Biddle). By the 6th and 7th centuries such structures, based on Roman architerctural models, were being constructed throughout the formerly barbarian lands of Britain and eastern Germany. Classical civilization was expanding its boundaries

As part of the Rule of Benedict, the monks were committed to a life of work, study and prayer, and the work part often involved manual labor in the fields. This led to a renewed respect for this type of activity amongst the aristocracy who, by the late Roman period, had come to regard manual work with contempt. Their labors in the fields produced a deep interest in agriculture and agricultural techniques. New technologies were developed by the monks, including, almost certainly, the windmill. Everywhere, they introduced new crops, industries, or production methods. Here they would introduce the rearing of cattle and horses, there the brewing of beer or the raising of bees or fruit. In Sweden, the corn trade owed its existence to the monks.

When Benedict established his Rule, much of Europe was still an uncultivated wilderness. This was true primarily of those areas which had never been part of the Roman Empire, such as Germany, but even of parts of Gaul and Spain, as well as Britain and Ireland remained in this condition into the sixth and seventh centuries. These areas the monks brought under cultivation, often deliberately choosing the wildest and most inhospitable tracts of country to set up their houses. Many of the virgin forests and marshes of Germany and Poland were brought into cultivation for the first time by the monks. "We owe," says one writer, "the agricultural restoration of a great part of Europe to the monks." According to another, "Wherever they came, they converted the wilderness into a cultivated country; they pursued the breeding of cattle and agriculture, labored with their own hands, drained morasses, and cleared away forests. By them Germany was rendered a fruitful country." Another historian records that "every Benedictine monastery was an agricultural college for the whole region in which it was located."143 Even nineteenth century French historian Francois Guizot, a man not especially sympathetic to Catholicism, observed: "The Benedictine monks were the agriculturalists of Europe; they cleared it on a large scale, associating agriculture with preaching."144

It would be possible to fill many volumes outlining the contribution made by the monks, particularly those of the Early Middle Ages, to the civilization and prosperity of Europe. Their role cannot be emphasized strongly enough; yet it is one that has been curiously overlooked by many historians. In the 1860s and 1870s, when Comte de Montalembert wrote a six-volume history of the monks of the West, he complained at times of his inability to provide anything more than a cursory overview of great figures and deeds, so enormous was the topic at hand. He was compelled, he said, to refer his readers to the references in his footnotes, in order that they might follow them up for themselves.

The Flowering of Learning in Christian Ireland and Britain

Christianity's positive effect upon learning is very clearly illustrated in the case of Britain and Ireland. Here were various societies, some of which had never been part of the Roman Empire (Ireland and Scotland) and others wherein Roman culture was almost completely effaced by a massive Barbarian invasion (England). Yet throughout the British Isles, Christianity took strong root in the

---

143 Alexander Clarence Flick, *The Rise of the Medieval Church* (New York, 1909) p. 223
144 See John Henry Cardinal Newman, loc cit., pp. 264-5.

fifth and sixth centuries, and produced an astonishing flowering of learning. So striking was this in the case of Ireland that the island gained, in the sixth and seventh centuries, the reputation as the "Land of Saints and Scholars."

Famously, Christianity was said to have been introduced to Ireland by Saint Patrick, a native of western Britain, who had apparently been captured by Irish slave-traders whilst still a boy, and forcibly brought to the land with which his life was to become so intimately connected. After escaping and training for the priesthood, he returned to Ireland as a missionary, where his teaching found fertile ground. Within a very short time, most of the country was converted; the last conquest, so it has often been said, of the Roman Empire.

Patrick is traditionally credited with preserving the tribal and social patterns of the Irish, codifying their laws and changing only those that conflicted with Christian practices. He is also credited with introducing the Roman alphabet, which enabled Irish monks to preserve parts of the extensive Celtic oral literature. The historicity of these claims remains the subject of debate and there is no direct evidence linking Patrick with any of these accomplishments. Nevertheless, they are all clearly connected with the appearance in the country of Christianity; and from Patrick's time at least Irish scholars excelled in the study of Latin learning and Christian theology in the monasteries that flourished shortly thereafter. Nor was their knowledge confined to Latin: as we shall see, there exists ample evidence to show that Greek too, and the Greek writers – not all of them ecclesiastical – were taught in the Irish centers.

In effect, Ireland was now, by the late fifth century, added to Roman civilization. What the legions had failed to do, Christians missionaries accomplished within a decade or two. Churches and cathedrals appeared throughout the land; and monastic settlements became miniature universities. Irish men of learning travelled to Rome and beyond in search of knowledge and books. The influence of Egypt, both in terms of art and religious ideas, began to be felt on the western shores of the Atlantic. Influenced by the Anglo-Saxons, who had seized the mainland of Britain, Irish artists now developed a new style, described as Hiberno-Saxon, which combined the old Celtic motifs of the region with the interlinking animals and serpents which the Anglo-Saxons had brought from Germany (ultimately under the influence of the Goths). The new style was now applied to some of the most astonishing artwork ever created. Illuminated books and metalwork, whose microscopic detail is justly celebrated, make us wonder whether the insular artists were in possession of an understanding of the magnifying lens. And the materials used in these masterpieces, such as lapis-lazuli from Afghanistan (the source of ultramarine blue), convince us that both the Book of Kells and the Lindisfarne Gospels were created before the middle of the seventh century, when the Arabs closed the Mediterranean to trade.[145]

The quality and sheer technical competence of Hiberno-Saxon art is perhaps best illustrated by the comments of art historian J. O. Westwood: "I have examined, with a magnifying glass, the pages of the Gospels of Lindisfarne and the Book of Kells, for hours together without ever detecting a false line or an irregular interlacement; and when it is considered that many of these details consist of spiral lines, and are so minute as to be impossible to have been executed with a pair of compasses, it really seems a problem not only with what eyes, but also with what instruments, they could have been executed. One instance of the minuteness of these details will suffice to give an idea of this peculiarity. I have counted in a small space, measuring scarcely three-quarters of an inch in width, in the Book of Armagh, not fewer than one hundred and fifty-eight interlacements of a slender ribbon-pattern, formed of white lines edged by black ones upon a black ground. No wonder that an artist of Dublin, lately applied to by Mr Chambers to copy one of the pages of the book of Kells, excused himself from the labour on the grounds that it was a tradition that the lines had been traced by angels."[146]

Art historian Kenneth Clark remarked on the fact that the technical excellence of the work evinced in the Book of Kells and the Lindisfarne Gospels was never equaled. They are, he said, "almost the richest and most complicated pieces of abstract decoration ever produced," and are "more sophisticated and refined than anything in Islamic art."[147] This in spite of the fact that among the Muslims (owing to the ban on representational art), calligraphy became the primary outlet of artistic expression.

From the latter years of the fifth century Ireland herself now began to send out missionaries, first to the still-pagan Picts of Caledonia, and shortly-thereafter to the pagan Angles and Saxons, who had by then settled much of Britain. Very quickly, a distinctive type of Christianity, now called "Celtic,"

---

[145] See www.irish-society.org/Hedgemaster%20Archives/book_of_Kells.htm
[146] Westwood, quoted in Thompson and Johnson, op cit., pp. 212-3
[147] Kenneth Clark, *Civilisation* (BBC publication, London, 1969) p. 11

took shape, a Christianity which was, within a few generations, to completely transform the British Isles.

One of the best-known of these Irish missionaries was Columba, who left Ireland for western Scotland following a conflict over a book and its copy. Eventually he settled in Iona, off the coast of Scotland, where he established a monastic settlement that was to become renowned across Europe as a centre of Christian education. Columba had pledged to "convert as many souls for Christ" as he could and his new monastery was designed specifically for this undertaking. His monks were sent throughout Europe.

When King Oswald of Northumbria in England wanted a center of learning to be established for the education of Anglo-Saxon boys, he called upon the great monastery of Iona to provide him with a spiritual guide. The task was taken up by another Irish monk, Aiden, who, traditionally in 635, but probably earlier, arrived at Lindisfarne Island, which soon became the base and cradle of Celtic Christianity in north-east England. From there, the whole of Northumbria was converted and became, within a short time, a major center of Christian civilization.

Two of the first pupils accepted into the Lindisfarne monastery were Anglo-Saxon brothers called Cedd and Chad. The elder of these two, Cedd, was sent to Mercia, in the English midlands, where he quickly transformed the region. He was so successful that when King Sigbert of the East Saxons (Essex) asked for a similar mission, it was Cedd who was sent with one companion. Cedd's first church in Essex was built of wood, but this was soon replaced by a more permanent structure using cut-stones from a nearby Roman fort. This new church, now called Saint Peter's on the Wall, was modeled on the churches of Egypt and Syria, illustrating the profound influence that the Eastern Church then exerted in the far-off regions of the west. The Egyptian influence shows too that this structure must have been completed before circa 640, when Arab piracy closed the Mediterranean.

The monastery attached to Saint Peter's on the Wall was said to have incorporated a hospital, a guest-house and a library. All in the middle of a supposed Dark Age!

One of the most notable of Ireland's scholars, as opposed to saints, of this period, was John Scotus Erigena (or Eriugena). As well as being a theologian, he was a Neoplatonist scholar and a poet. His work illustrates, in a most dramatic way, the absurdity of the notion of a European "Dark Age". For John Scotus was a major philosopher, who travelled to various parts of Europe, who was in communication with the Byzantine Emperor, and who had a thorough knowledge of Greek, as well as Latin. About the age of thirty, we are told, he moved from Ireland to France, where he took over the Palatine Academy at the invitation of King Charles the Bald. He succeeded Alcuin of York as head of the Palace School. It is generally believed that he remained in France for at least thirty years, during which time he undertook, at the request of Byzantine Emperor Michael III the translation into Latin of the works of Pseudo-Dionysius. He also added his own commentary, thus being the first to introduce the ideas of Neoplatonism from the Greek into the Western European intellectual tradition.

Erigena was a "truly original thinker," a Christian universalist who he believed that all people and all beings, including animals, reflect attributes of God, towards whom all are capable of progressing and to which all things ultimately must return. His thought was Neoplatonist to the core, and "while recognizing the validity of authority in thought and accepting the authority of the Scriptures, he insisted upon the equal validity of reason."[148] "Authority," he wrote, "sometimes proceeds from reason, but reason never from authority. For all authority which is not approved by true reason seems weak. But true reason, since it is established in its own strength, needs to be strengthened by the assent of no authority."[149] To Erigena, hell was not a place but a condition and punishment was purifying, not penal. He was a believer in *apocatastasis*, which maintains that all moral creatures – angels, humans and devils – will eventually come to a harmony in God's kingdom.

Erigena based his beliefs on the Greek writings of the early Christian fathers, like Origen, and considered himself an orthodox Christian thinker. And his knowledge of Greek is a crucial chronological marker – as crucial as the ultramarine pigments in the Book of Kells. Having travelled to the East and studied there, Scotus Erigena must have lived and worked before the middle of the seventh century: For after that time, as we shall see, such travel would have been absolutely impossible.

---

[148] Ibid., p. 258
[149] Ibid.

HOLY WARRIORS

The sixth and early seventh centuries therefore saw the expansion, rather than the withering away, of Latin and Classical civilization. The great works of Greek and Roman literature were now known and debated in the formerly barbarian lands of Ireland and Caledonia. Paganised Britain, or England, was again being Romanized, this time mainly through the offices of Christianity. Churches and cathedrals, based on Roman and Near Eastern models, began to appear throughout the British Isles and in the previously savage lands of eastern Germany, on the borders of the Elbe. Around these ecclesiastical centers towns and cities began to form in regions never reached by the armies of Imperial Rome. Far from being in terminal decline, Classical civilization was on the move.

CHAPTER 3

SARACENS, VIKINGS AND HUNGARIANS

Definitive end of Classical Civilization

ccording to historians writing before the appearance of Pirenne's *Mohammed and Charlemagne*, the period of the Germanic kingdoms (notwithstanding the evidence to the contrary) was one of slow and gradual decline. True, for a while, it was conceded, there was a semblance of continuity. The Visigoths, Franks and Vandals made a real attempt to perpetuate the civilization of Rome, which they never intended to destroy, and some Roman institutions survived under them for a couple of centuries. Yet in the end the barbarous nature of these peoples prevailed, and the whole of Europe was plunged inexorably into an epoch of illiteracy, poverty, backwardness and superstition.

Even after the publication of Pirenne's watershed work, the above was the narrative that continued to be presented in histories of the period; and it is a version of events that survives to this day. Consider the following from a popular author of medieval history, published by Macmillan in 1953 and reprinted as recently as 1970: "The gradual decline of civilization in Gaul, which had been in progress since the third century, became more rapid in the Merovingian period. The Franks were essentially warriors rather than traders, and they had no interest in urban life. Moreover their kings did not consider the

93

encouragement of trade and commerce by keeping roads and bridges in repair, policing the trade routes, and protecting merchants and their goods, any part of their royal function. Although the ancient cities on the Mediterranean coast retained some sea-borne commerce, trade almost disappeared in the interior. By the end of the Merovingian era, Gaul was essentially an agricultural region with a localized agrarian economy. There was little money in circulation and few traders moved along the roads."[150] The overwhelming impression given here, and in countless similar and even more recent publications, is of a long and painful decline – a gradual descent into anarchy and illiteracy under the auspices of a barbarous people who had no real understanding or appreciation of civilized life. No mention here of the lively trade and economy of the sixth century, which brought luxury products on an enormous scale from the Eastern Mediterranean to northern Gaul and even into Anglo-Saxon England. No mention of the lively intercourse between the Near East and Ireland, or of the evidence of regular trading links as far as Afghanistan and China. No mention of the revival of architecture throughout Europe during the sixth century, which saw the erection in Gaul, Spain, Italy and North Africa of enormous and luxurious palaces, villas and basilicas in the Roman style, decorated with the finest mosaic work, marble and stained glass. The above writer does however concede that, until the time of Gregory of Tours (late sixth century), there was little sign of civilizational decline – on which he nevertheless places so much emphasis – in Gaul. Yet, "after that generation [of Gregory of Tours] disappeared, learning became extremely rare and literacy rather uncommon."[151] So, the decline which a few paragraphs earlier the writer had declared to be gradual and inexorable, now appears to be sudden and rather unexpected. So, we might ask, was this descent into illiteracy sudden, or was it gradual? And who, or what, might have caused it?

The Muslim conquerors of Spain, who arrived in the Iberian Peninsula shortly after the time of Gregory of Tours, were astonished at the size and opulence of its cities; the cities of the Visigoths. Their annalists recall the appearance at the time of Seville, Cordova, Merida and Toledo; "the four capitals of Spain, founded," they tell us naively, "by Okteban [Octavian] the

---

[150] Painter, op cit., pp. 67-8
[151] Ibid., p. 68

Caesar." Seville, above all, seems to have struck them by its wealth and its illustriousness in various ways. "It was," writes Ibn Adhari,

> ... among all the capitals of Spain the greatest, the most important, the best built and the richest in ancient monuments. Before its conquest by the Goths it had been the residence of the Roman governor. The Gothic kings chose Toledo for their residence; but Seville remained the seat of the Roman adepts of sacred and profane science, and it was there that lived the nobility of the same origin.[152]

Not much sign of decline here! Another Arab writer, Merida, mentions Seville's great bridge as well as "magnificent palaces and churches,"[153] and we should note that archaeological confirmation of this picture is forthcoming. In particular, the discovery near Toledo in 1857 of a collection of richly wrought Visigothic votive crowns encrusted with precious stones brought the descriptions of the Arab conquerors to mind in the most vivid way possible.[154]

At what point, then, the reader might ask, did the real break with the Roman past occur? Henri Pirenne, who perused the subject his entire professional career, came, towards the end of his life, to a dramatic conclusion: The great change occurred with the arrival of the very men who wrote the above description of Gothic Spain "over a hundred years after the death of Justinian," and its cause "was, in one word, Mahomet."[155]

This is by no means a very controversial statement. It has long been known that by the middle of the seventh century, the whole of the Christian world, both in the east and in the west, was under sustained attack; an attack which, for a time, seemed likely to wipe Christian civilization off the map.

---

[152] Cited from Louis Bertrand and Sir Charles Petrie, *The History of Spain* (2nd ed, London, 1945) p. 17

[153] Ibid., pp. 17-8

[154] Richard Fletcher, *Moorish Spain* (London, 1992) p. 18 The Arab and Berber conquerors were struck by the effeminacy of the Visigoths of Spain. Not, one might say, a very attractive characteristic, but hardly one associated with fierce barbarians. After the Battle of Guadalete the body of the Visigoth king Roderick could not be found; yet his horse, with its richly-embroidered saddle was found, as were a pair of gold sandals embroidered with imperial eagles.

[155] Ibid. p. 72

3: SARACENS, VIKINGS AND HUNGARIANS

Some of Christendom's enemies came, like those of the fourth, fifth and sixth centuries, from the barbarian lands of the north and east. But by far the most serious opponent was a new one, one which hailed from the south and east: An enemy imbued with a zeal and even a fanaticism entirely lacking in the opponents from the barbarian regions of the north and east. This enemy was Islam.

The whole of the Near East and North Africa, which are now the core areas of Islam, were at one time almost exclusively Christian. These regions, including Mesopotamia, Syria/Palestine, Egypt, Libya, Tunisia, Algeria and Morocco, were not converted peaceably to the faith of Muhammad, but were conquered and subdued by Muslim armies, and their peoples either forcibly converted, enslaved, or persecuted and discriminated against over a span of many centuries. The end result was that a vast area was lost to Christianity. It is true, of course, that the Muslim invasions of this period, though the most dramatic and most permanent, were, in the words of Trevor-Roper, "not the only invasions of those years." There were also "other invasions, some of them independent of the Moslem conquests, others involved with them. These were the invasions of the nomads. For the period between the fifth and eighth centuries, between the political and social end of the Roman Empire, is one of the great periods of nomadic irruptions. There were land-nomads and sea-nomads, both of whom suddenly, with their superior mobility, enveloped and overpowered the settled populations of the civilized world."[156] There can be no doubt that the nomad irruptions of this period, which began in the latter years of the sixth century with the invasion of the Avars, caused much disruption on their own. And yet it was "the Moslem conquests which absorbed and directed" even these.

We shall argue that, in reality, the irruption of the Avars was followed rapidly by the arrival of the Magyars, in the early seventh century, and that these invasions almost precisely coincided with the appearance of the Vikings and the arrival of the Muslims. A faulty chronology has separated several of these almost simultaneous events by two to three centuries. And yet, even leaving out the contribution of the Magyars and the Vikings to this seventh-century mayhem, it is very clear that, in the words of Trevor-Roper, "The early years of

---

[156] Ibid. p. 75

the eighth century – the years when the invasions of the Avars and the Lombards had been followed by the conquests of the Arabs, were indeed the darkest age of Europe."[157]

As we shall see, a necessary correction of the chronology identifies in a most unmistakable way the Arab conquests as the force which brought classical civilization to an end; and yet even without this correction, the contribution of the Arabs to Europe's "darkness" at this time is undeniable.

Signs of the Break

What made Pirenne so certain that it was Islam, and not the Germanic Invasions, which had terminated classical civilization? There were two factors: Firstly, there was the fact, examined by us in the previous chapters, that the culture of Western Europe remained virtually unchanged in the two centuries which followed the fall of Rome to Alaric. As we have observed in scores of details, under the Germanic kings, "Roman" life continued much as it always had. Secondly, all of the things, or many of them, which made this culture Roman, disappeared quite suddenly in the seventh century. And the things which disappeared were those which spoke of contact between the West and the highly cultured centers of the East. It was evident, from this sudden change, that something had completely disrupted the Mediterranean world. Something had appeared which had terminated the centuries-long trade and cultural contacts of the eastern and western Mediterranean worlds. It was evident that that "thing" was Islam.

In Chapter 2 we examined the question of culture and religion. Pirenne concentrated on economics and trade. Until the seventh century, he noted, "the luxuries of the table were ... supplied by the East."[158] Gregory of Tours, for example, in the sixth century, refers to the wines of Syria which were exported from Gaza.[159] He tells us too that a widow of Lyons used to take two gallons of Syrian wine to her husband's tomb every day.[160] And there are several other

---

[157] Ibid. pp. 85-8
[158] Pirenne, op cit., p. 88
[159] Gregory of Tours, vii, 29
[160] *Liber in Gloria Confessorum*, circa 64, ed. Krusch, p. 785

references to eastern wine in sixth and seventh century documents, which Pirenne refers to. Doubtless also, foodstuffs were imported from the East, he says. Gregory of Tours spoke of a hermit in the neighborhood of Nice who ate nothing but roots brought to him from Alexandria.[161] The really important branch of Oriental commerce in foodstuffs was however the spice trade. Pirenne quotes Pliny the Elder, who gave his estimate of the enormous sum spent, in his time, on spices imported from India, China, and Arabia. And their diffusion throughout the Empire was not disrupted by the Germanic Invasions. "They continued," he says, "to form a constituent of the everyday diet."[162] He found abundant evidence of the everyday use of exotic eastern spices until the middle of the seventh century.

Papyrus of course was a vital import from the East throughout the period of the Empire; and it continued to be during the fifth and sixth centuries. In Pirenne's words: "It was a necessary constituent of social life. The juridical and the administrative life of the Empire, the very functioning of the State, necessitated the practice of the art [of writing], and the same may be said of social relations. The merchants had their clerks, *mercenarii literati*. Masses of papyrus must have been required by those who kept the registers of the fisc, by the notaries of the tribunals, by the private correspondents, and by the monasteries."[163] He continues: "The fragility of papyrus in the northern climate explains why so little is left; but we must be under no illusion as to the quantity which was formerly employed. And the wealth of information which we possess concerning Gaul, thanks to Gregory of Tours, should not make us forget the fact that still more papyrus must have been used in Italy and Spain, and that this must have necessitated an exceptionally active import trade."[164]

The loss of papyrus supplies, as we shall see, had a devastating effect upon European culture. Kings and commoners, churchmen and laymen, were compelled to fall back upon the tremendously expensive parchment. The consequences of this are not difficult to imagine. In Europe during the Middle Ages, as more than one commentator had remarked, precious parchment was used again and again, with ancient texts frequently erased and lost forever to

---

[161] Gregory of Tours, vi, 6.
[162] Pirenne, op cit p. 89
[163] Ibid, pp. 91-2
[164] Ibid, pp. 92-3

scholarship. We cannot doubt that the disappearance from Western Europe by the eleventh century of many of the Greek and Latin masterpieces was due entirely to this cause.[165]

Oil too, according to Pirenne, was imported into Europe in large quantities up until the seventh century; this time mainly from North Africa; whilst silk was another important Oriental product that found its way to the far West as far as the sixth and seventh centuries.

It is astonishing that all of these products, some of them essential to the administration of a civilized polity, disappear from the West almost completely by the middle of the seventh century. For Pirenne, this was a fact of immense significance; one that had not, until his time, been fully understood or even noticed by historians. What had occurred to put an end to the Mediterranean trade? There was only one possible explanation: Islam. And Pirenne here quotes the Arab writer Ibn-Khaldun, who boasts that by his time "the Christians could no longer float a plank upon the sea."

"It is necessary to insist upon this point," says Pirenne, "since some excellent scholars do not admit that the Musulman conquest can have produced so complete a break."[166] Such historians have pointed to the journeys of some individual pilgrims or scholars as proof that Mediterranean traffic continued. But the coming and going of a few pilgrims of scholars do "not in any way prove the existence of commercial relations..."[167] These were isolated exceptions to the rule, and "We must not confuse the circulation of merchandise with the movement of pilgrims, scholars and artists." And at this point he proceeds to demonstrate the absence, from the mid-seventh century onwards, of all the important products which, up to that time, the West had imported in large quantities from the East.

"Papyrus," he says, "was the first to disappear. All the works written in the West on papyrus of which we have knowledge are of the 6th or 7th century. Until 659-677 nothing but papyrus was used in the royal Merovingian chancellery. Then parchment made its appearance."[168] And it is hard to quarrel with Pirenne on this point. The Middle Ages, by definition, were the age of

---

[165] See eg. Briffault, op cit., p. 206
[166] Pirenne, op cit p. 166
[167] Ibid., pp. 167-8
[168] Ibid., 169-170

parchment, on which was executed the famous illuminated manuscripts of the period. What had happened to the papyrus which, until that time, had been employed throughout the West? The normal assumption, that the Barbarian Invasions disrupted Roman trade, simply will not do. The Roman world continued alive and well until the start of the seventh century; under the Germanic kings, who tried so hard to emulate Roman potentates.

Along with papyrus, everything else goes. Eastern spices cease to be mentioned. Those that continue to occur, such as madder, cumin and almonds, are those which can be cultivated in Gaul. There is however "not a single reference" to pepper, cloves, nard, cinnamon, dates or pistachios.[169] Wine from Gaza, celebrated by Gregory of Tours, also disappears, as does oil from Africa. "Similarly, the use of silk seems to have been almost entirely unknown at this period."

All of this was accompanied by an increasing rarity of gold. "Evidently gold had ceased to arrive from the Orient."[170] One of the primary indicators of the transition from the civilization of classical antiquity to that of the Middle Ages was the relapse from a money to a natural economy; one based on barter. There is no question that from the seventh century, the money economy began to disappear, as did all the other features characteristic of what we now call classical civilization.

Reaction to Pirenne's thesis, which was published posthumously, was varied. On the whole, it was agreed that he had hit on something of great importance. By the 1930s, when he completed his researches, it was well understood that the old concept of Germanic invaders destroying Roman civilization and immediately introducing a Dark Age was false. Roman civilization, it was agreed, had continued more or less unchanged into the early seventh century. After that, there was a change. After that, the culture and mind-set we now call medieval or feudal began to appear. Pirenne's explanation – that the change was caused by the arrival of Islam – seemed to be as good as any other. Yet he was criticized; and it is instructive to note that this criticism centered on problems of chronology. One of his fiercest critics, Alfons Dopsch, was not slow to point out a glaring anomaly: That the appearance of feudalism, with its castle-building and manorial organization, only appears at the end of the

[169] Ibid., p. 171
[170] Ibid., p. 173

tenth century – three centuries after the date indicated by Pirenne. As such, said Dopsch, medievalism probably had more to do with the coming of the Vikings than with the coming of the Muslims.[171]

There is some validity in Dopsch's argument, and the various chronological problems of this period is a question we shall return to again and again throughout our study. Nonetheless, Dopsch's central point, that it was not the Muslims who ended classical civilization, is invalid. He was never, for example, able to disprove Pirenne's exposition of the massive disruption in Mediterranean trade that had occurred in the seventh century. To deny that this disruption had a profound and long-lasting impact upon western Europe is impossible. The impoverishment of the West, by the second half of the seventh century, is all too obvious. Yet amid the general disappearance of economic activity in the Mediterranean, there was one type of trade which did survive. Indeed, it not only survived but flourished as never before. But this was a trade so terrible and so repulsive that its very existence goes part of the way to answering the great question begged by the destruction of trading relations in the first place: Why was the arrival of Islam such a cataclysmic event?

The trade I refer to was the slave trade.

The Muslim Conquests

The explosion of the Muslim armies from Arabia early in the seventh century is a fact of history that is well documented and has been much written about. That its impact was devastating is not so well recognized. It was indeed an event as disruptive as anything that has happened in Europe's history; yet this, notwithstanding the efforts of Henri Pirenne to elucidate the issue, is still overlooked.

After sweeping through Syria, Egypt and North Africa, the Muslim armies, almost without a pause, entered Europe. In 711[172] the Berber Tarik led

---

[171] B. H. Slicher Van Bath, *The Agrarian History of Western Europe, AD 500 – 1850* (Edward Arnold, London, 1963) (Trans. from the Dutch, of *De agrarische geschiedenis van West-Europaa (500 – 1850)* p. 31
[172] Most of these dates, I will argue, need to be reduced; the earliest by the least. Thus I consider the Muslim invasion of Egypt to have occurred about

an invasion force across the Straits of Gibraltar, and within little more than seven years most of Visigothic Spain was subdued. In 720 the Arab armies crossed the Pyrenees. They took Narbonne and sacked the greatest monasteries of southern France, after which they continued their northward march as far as Poitiers. They had, says Gibbon in one of his most celebrated passages, within a space of roughly fifteen years, prolonged their victorious line of march more than 1,000 miles from Gibraltar to the banks of the Loire: "The repetition of an equal space would have carried the Saracens to the confines of Poland and the highlands of Scotland; and the Rhine is not more impassable than the Nile or Euphrates, and the Arabian fleet might have sailed without a naval combat into the mouth of the Thames. Perhaps the interpretation of the Koran would now be taught in the schools of Oxford, and her pulpits might demonstrate to a circumcised people the sanctity and truth of the revelation of Mohammed." (Ch. 49) "From such calamities," says Gibbon, "was Christendom delivered by the genius and fortune of one man." That man was, of course, Charles Martel, the "mayor of the palace" and effective ruler of the Frankish kingdom who, at the battle of Poitiers, defeated the Arabs at this, the farthest point of their advance.

Yet the Muslim invasion of Spain and then France was in fact but one theatre of a general attack on Europe from the south. A series of Arab assaults on Sicily, in 652, 667 and 720 failed; Syracuse was conquered for the first time temporarily in 708, but a planned invasion in 740 failed because of a rebellion of the Berbers of the Maghreb that lasted until 771 and civil wars in Africa lasting until 799. Sardinia however became Islamic by several stages beginning in 711, 720 and 760 respectively. The Italian island of Pantelleria had been conquered by the Arabs in 700, and was attacked again a century later, when the Arabs sold the monks they captured into slavery in Spain.[173]

Further to the east, the very centre of Christianity, the second Rome itself, Constantinople, was not immune. An Arab army, led by Muawiyah I, laid siege to Constantinople between 674-678. Unable to breach the Theodosian Walls, the Arabs blockaded the city along the Bosporus, but their fleet was eventually destroyed by the famous "Greek Fire" of Kallinikos (Callinicus) the Syrian.

twenty years before the traditional date of 639, whereas the Islamic invasion of Spain probably occurred around 630, rather than the traditional 711. See the Appendix to the present volume for a fuller discussion.
[173] Pirenne, op cit., p. 159

Although this was a decisive defeat, within just over half a century the Arabs were back. In 718 an 80,000-strong army led by Maslama, the brother of Caliph Suleiman of Umayyad, crossed the Bosporus from Anatolia to besiege the capital of the Eastern Empire by land, while a massive fleet of Arab war galleys commanded by another Suleiman, estimated to initially number 1,800 ships, sailed into the Sea of Marmara to the south of the city. After some desperate fighting, and the use once again by the defenders of "Greek Fire," this onslaught was also repulsed.

Just how devastating was this Muslim onslaught? It has, of recent years, been the fashion to underplay or even ignore the destructive effect of Islam upon Europe. In particular, the supposedly civilized and advanced state of Muslim Spain, in the eighth, ninth and tenth centuries, is contrasted to the reputedly primitive conditions prevailing in Christian Europe north of the Pyrenees. And yet the Islamic attacks unleashed a veritable torrent of violence. This was war without end and without rules. The earliest attacks on Italy and the islands having been repelled, the Muslims simply waited a while, then returned; again and again. By the late eighth century the battle for Corsica raged incessantly. The island was taken by the Muslims, then retaken by the Christians, then taken again by the Muslims.[174] Amidst this general and incessant violence, "even the destruction by a tempest of a Saracen fleet of a hundred ships in 813 only checked for a time the *razzias* of the Spanish Arabs, who continued to pillage Civita Vecchia, Nice, Sardinia, and Corsica ..."[175] The war continued unabated, and after 830 the cities of central and southern Italy were at the mercy of the Muslims. Brindisi and Tarento were ravaged (838), Bari conquered (840), and the Byzantine and Venetian fleets defeated. In 841 the Muslims ravaged Ancona and the Dalmatian coast, and it seemed that Italy was about to be annexed. An attack on Rome itself was launched in 846. This failed to take the city, but in 876 and 877 the Saracens were back, this time ravaging the Campagna, and the Pope was compelled to bribe the invaders with an annual tribute of 25,000 *mancusi* of silver. In 883 the Abbey of Monte Cassino was burned and destroyed, and the Abbey of Farfa besieged. Subiaco was destroyed and the valleys of Anio and Tivoli pillaged. Amidst this general carnage Campagne became a desert: *reducta est terra in solitudinem*. In Pirenne's words, it was

---

[174] Ibid.
[175] Ibid., p. 160

only the intervention of the Byzantine fleet that allowed Italy to escape "from the grip of Islam."[176]

Around 890 a band of Moorish pirates from Andalusia landed at Saint Tropez and dug themselves in on a hilltop nowadays known as La Garde Freinet. From there they raised west to Marseilles, north to Vienne, and even to the abbey of Saint Gall in Switzerland. They were not expelled until 972.[177]

The number of wrecks of tenth-century Muslim ships found off the coast of Provence suggests considerable traffic – in slaves and plunder – with the rest of the Muslim world.[178]

I shall argue that many of the above events happened a good deal earlier than the "traditional" dates, and that those normally placed in the eighth and ninth centuries probably actually occurred closer to the second half of the seventh century. Nonetheless, it is apparent that, whatever absolute dates we choose, the war between Islam and Christendom was virtually endless. Thus as late as the tenth and eleventh centuries the battle for Spain raged unabated throughout the whole land. In the tenth century alone a fortress like Toledo was conquered and lost again several times. By 980 there emerged in Al-Mansur a conqueror in the old style. He burned Leon, Barcelona and Santiago de Compostela, and even advanced over the Pyrenees. His march of conquest only ended with his death in 1002. Yet throughout the century that followed the war for the possession of the country continued to rage.

Christendom's encounter with Islam was to have long-term and profound consequences, consequences which have not, until now, been either properly understood or appreciated. The Mediterranean, previously a highway, now became a frontier, and an extremely dangerous frontier at it. "With Islam," says Pirenne, "a new world was established on those Mediterranean shores which had formerly known the syncretism of the Roman civilization. A complete break was made, which was to continue even to our own day. Henceforth two different and hostile civilizations existed on the shores of *Mare Nostrum*. ... The sea which had hitherto been the centre of Christianity became its frontier. The

---

[176] Ibid., p. 163
[177] John Julius Norwich, *The Middle Sea: A History of the Mediterranean* (Chatto and Windus, London, 2006 p. 94
[178] Ibid., p. 94

Mediterranean unity was shattered."[179] According to Pirenne, "This was the most essential event of European history ... since the Punic Wars. It was the end of the classic tradition. It was the beginning of the Middle Ages, and it happened at the very moment when Europe was on the way to becoming Byzantinized."[180]

Before moving on, we need to stress one important point: Notwithstanding the Arab seizure of the most populous and prosperous provinces of the Byzantine Empire, and the attacks on Constantinople herself, it has been customary to downplay the impact of the Muslim conquests upon the Eastern Empire. Even Pirenne believed that Byzantium somehow coped better with the Arabs than the West. It is generally assumed that Classical Civilization survived in the East, and that the region was less "medievalised" than the West. We are, or have been until recently, informed by historians that the eighth, ninth and tenth centuries in Byzantium were "three centuries of glory," and that during this time "The Byzantine Empire was the richest state in Europe, the strongest military power, and by far the most cultivated."[181] We are further informed that, "During these three centuries while Western Europe was a land of partly tamed barbarians, the Byzantine Empire was a highly civilized state where a most felicitous merger of Christianity and Hellenism produced a fascinating culture."[182]

Over the past few decades archaeology has proved that nothing could be further from the truth. As a matter of fact, the once-proud Eastern Rome was devastated by the Arab assaults. The same poverty and illiteracy that we find in the West we now find also in the East. Cities decline and the science and philosophy of the Greeks and Romans disappear. Indeed, just as in the West, a "dark age" descends. In the words of Cyril Mango; "One can hardly overestimate the catastrophic break that occurred in the seventh century. Anyone who reads the narrative of events will not fail to be struck by the calamities that befell the Empire, starting with the Persian invasion at the very beginning of the century and going on to the Arab expansion some thirty years later – a series of reverses that deprived the Empire of some of its most prosperous provinces,

---

[179] Pirenne, op cit., pp. 152-3
[180] Ibid., p. 164
[181] Painter, op cit., p. 35
[182] Ibid.

namely, Syria, Palestine, Egypt and, later, North Africa – and so reduced it to less than half its former size both in area and in population. But a reading of the narrative sources gives only a faint idea of the profound transformation that accompanied these events. ... It marked for the Byzantine lands the end of a way of life – the urban civilization of Antiquity – and the beginning of a very different and distinctly medieval world."[183] Mango remarked on the virtual abandonment of the Byzantine cities after the mid-seventh century, and the archaeology of these settlements usually reveals "a dramatic rupture in the seventh century, sometimes in the form of virtual abandonment."[184] With the cities and with the papyrus supply from Egypt went the intellectual class, who after the seventh century were reduced to a "small clique."[185] The evidence, as Mango sees it, is unmistakable: the "catastrophe" (as he names it) of the seventh century, "is the central event of Byzantine history."[186]

Constantinople herself, the mighty million-strong capital of the East, was reduced, by the middle of the eighth century, to a veritable ruin. Mango quotes a document of the period which evokes a picture of "abandonment and ruination. Time and again we are told that various monuments – statues, palaces, baths – had once existed but were destroyed. What is more, the remaining monuments, many of which must have dated from the fourth and fifth centuries, were no longer understood for what they were. They had acquired a magical and generally ominous connotation."[187]

That the Arab conquests should have one and the same effect upon the East and the West provides the definitive proof in favor of Pirenne. The East was not invaded by Goths and Huns; Constantinople did not fall. On the contrary, by the latter sixth century, the Eastern Empire was again flexing its considerable muscles and reasserting Imperial rule throughout many of the western lands. And even those regions which were not conquered by Justinian, such as Gaul and Germany, nevertheless recognized the suzerainty of the Emperor and were completely within Byzantine's cultural and political orbit. Yet by the mid-seventh century the Roman lands, both East and West, were

---

[183] Mango, op cit., p. 4
[184] Ibid., p. 8
[185] Ibid., p. 9
[186] Ibid.
[187] Ibid., p. 80

involved in a common destruction; a destruction that involved the abandonment of cities, a general loss of literacy, and the death of Classical civilization.

The Mediterranean in the Seventh and Eighth Centuries

There can be no doubt that the conquest of the Near East and North Africa by any enemy, whether Persian, Arabian, or Egyptian, would have had a disruptive effect on trade and cultural contact. Yet we would not expect the conquest of one empire by another to have terminated all trade in the entire Mediterranean. From the beginning of history, empires had come and gone around the shores of the Middle Sea, yet trade and economic life had continued. With the rise of Islam, it is clear, this did not happen. All trade between the Christian West (and Christian East) and the newly-Islamic East was terminated, definitively. We know this for certain by the data brought forth by Pirenne. Why did it happen? Did the Caliphs forbid merchants to trade with infidels?

The truth is far worse.

One of the fundamentals of the Islamic faith, of which more will be said in the chapter to follow, was the acceptability, even the duty, of Muslims to wage war against the infidel. As we shall see, Islam divided the world into two starkly opposing camps: that of Islam, the *Dar al-Islam*, and that of the unbelievers, which was known as the *Dar al-Harb*. But *Dar al-Harb* literally means "House of War". *Jihad* or Holy War, as we have seen, was a fundamental duty of all Muslim rulers. Truces were allowed, but never a lasting peace.[188] "Since the jihad [was] ... a state of permanent war, it [excluded] ... the possibility of true peace, but it [did] ... allow for provisional truces in accordance with the requirements of the political situation."[189] Thus also Robert Irwin notes how "Muslim religious law could not countenance the formal conclusion of any sort of permanent peace with the infidel."[190] In such circumstances, it is evident that, when the Islamic forces were in a position of strength, almost all contact between them and the outside world was warlike.

---

[188] Koran, 8: 40; 9: 124; 24: 56.
[189] Bat Ye'or, op cit., p. 46
[190] Robert Irwin, "Islam and the Crusades: 1096-1699," in Jonathan Riley-Smith (ed.) *The Oxford History of the Crusades* (Oxford, 1995) pp. 237

3: SARACENS, VIKINGS AND HUNGARIANS

And this was not war as is waged between two kingdoms, empires, or dynasties: This was total war, war that did not distinguish between combatants and non-combatants, and war that did not end. In this spirit, Islamic generals launched attack after attack against the southern shores of Europe during the seventh and eighth centuries; and these "official" actions were supplemented by hundreds, even thousands, of lesser raids, carried out by minor Muslim commanders and even by private individuals: For it was considered legitimate that the Muslim faithful should live off the infidel world. Whatever spoils could be taken, were divinely sanctioned.

Thus the coming of Islam signaled a wave of banditry and piracy in the Mediterranean such as had not been seen since before the second century BC, when such activities were severely curtailed by Roman naval power. Indeed, it seems that this new Islamic piracy surpassed in scope and destructiveness anything that had come before. We could mention here, from the seventh and eighth centuries and later, quite literally hundreds of accounts of attacks in Greece, Italy, southern France, Spain, Sicily, Sardinia, and Corsica, carried out by Muslim freebooters and slave-traders. Neither Eastern nor Western Christendom was safe, and Crete, for a long time, was the centre of the Mediterranean slave-trade; a dubious honor she retained till the island was retaken by the Byzantine Emperor Nicephorus II Phocas around 956.[191] These cut-throats, it seems, did not confine themselves to capturing towns and their inhabitants, but plundered churches and monasteries too, putting their occupants to the sword or selling them into slavery. The entire Mediterranean, east and west, was now off-limits for trade and, "In the Occident ... the coast of the Gulf of Lyons and the Riviera to the mouth of the Tiber, ravaged by war and the [Muslim] pirates, whom the Christians, having no fleet, were powerless to resist, was now merely a solitude and a prey to piracy. The ports and the cities were deserted. The link with the Orient was severed, and there was no communication with the Saracen coasts. There was nothing but death."[192]

The history of Muslim freebooting in the Mediterranean has never, I feel, been properly written. This is a great omission, as its effect upon history and the development of western civilization was profound, even decisive: For it was Muslim piracy, much more than regular warlike activity, that brought classical

---

[191] John Julius Norwich, op cit., p. 94
[192] Pirenne, op cit., p. 184

civilization in the west to an end. This was the force which terminated, once and for all, the cultural and economic contacts between east and west, and which gave birth, as Pirenne rightly saw, to what we now call the Middle Ages. Of the situation at the time, we might agree with the judgment of a Dutch economic historian who wrote: "One could say, in modern parlance, that an iron curtain now divided the Mediterranean, whose littoral had once formed an economic whole."[193]

The pillaging and slave-raiding which began in the seventh century never really came to an end. It continued incessantly, with varying degrees of intensity, until the beginning of the nineteenth century, and was to have a devastating effect not only on trade, but on the culture of every society bordering the Mediterranean, and eventually on the whole of European civilization. Both East and West were devastated. Nor was the pillaging confined to the sea and coastal regions. From the mid-seventh century onwards Arab forces struck at Constantinople both by sea and by land, through the Middle of Asia Minor. In the latter case "not once or twice," as Cyril Mango noted, "but practically every year ... for nearly two centuries."[194] The consequences of this prolonged process, he notes, "are easy to imagine: much of Asia Minor was devastated and depopulated almost beyond repair."[195] And we should not imagine, as some authors do, that the revival of Europe during the eleventh century and the advance through the Mediterranean of fleets of Crusaders brought Muslim piracy – at least temporarily – to an end. This was emphatically not the case. Large, heavily armed fleets might move safely through the Mediterranean, but it was very different for merchant vessels. These, travelling alone, or in small and lightly-defended groups, were never safe. The Mediterranean remained a very dangerous place for all merchant shipping until the early nineteenth century!

In the meantime, however, the Muslim expansion was to have a more immediate and devastating effect: For it was now to launch a veritable tidal wave of violence throughout northern Europe also.

---

[193] B. H. Slicher Van Bath, op cit.
[194] Mango, op cit., p. 25
[195] Ibid., p. 26

3: SARACENS, VIKINGS AND HUNGARIANS

A Tidal Wave of Violence

As we have seen, the great barbarian migrations, which commenced in the fourth century and led to the collapse of the Western Roman Empire in the fifth, did not end with that event. On the contrary, by the beginning of the sixth century, a veritable flood of nomadic peoples entered Europe from the east. The first of these, forming as it were the tail end of the main Germanic movements, were the Langobards, or Lombards, who arrived in Italy in 568 and seized control of most of the country. Hard on the heels of this people there appeared a bewildering succession of nomads, tribes of Slavs, Bulgars, Avars, and eventually Hungarians. The latter people, in particular, penetrated deep into western Europe, and threatened to repeat the depredations of the Huns of the fifth century, with whom they claimed a blood relationship.

A final wave of Germanic barbarians, this time from Scandinavia, appeared on the scene about the same time as the Hungarians. These were the Vikings, piratical seafarers who famously ravaged the whole of northern Europe and even, in the end, seized control of whole countries, such as England.

I remind the reader at this point that the chronology of this period, the darkest period of the so-called Dark Ages, is in serious doubt; and there is much evidence, some of it to be examined in the Appendix, that the appearance of the Vikings and Hungarians almost precisely coincided with the arrival of the Muslim threat from the south. Indeed, the Viking raids were intimately and directly related to the Islamic expansion. Hugh Trevor-Roper puts it thus: "What were these Vikings doing? What sudden force drove these piratical Northmen to range over the seas and rivers of Europe, creating havoc? It used to be supposed that it was merely a sudden, unexplained growth of population in Scandinavia which lay behind this extraordinary outburst. No doubt this was true: so vast an expansion cannot have been sustained by a static population. But the scope and direction of the raids point also to other motives. There were opportunities abroad as well as pressures at home; and these opportunities link together the Viking raids and the Moslem conquests."[196]

Trevor-Roper goes on to describe the vast wealth accumulated by the Muslim Caliphate in its expansion across Asia and Africa, and how, with this

---

[196] Trevor-Roper, op cit., p. 90

wealth, it could purchase what it wanted from Europe. What the Muslims wanted, above all, was "eunuchs and slaves." He continues: "It was one of the functions of the Vikings to supply these goods. Half traders, half pirates, they ranged over all northern Europe, and in their ranging, or through the method of piracy, they collected furs and kidnapped human beings. For preference they dealt in heathen Slavs, since Christian States had less compunction in handling a slave-trade in heathen bodies – they could always quote that useful text, *Leviticus* xxv, 44. So the Vikings fed both Byzantium and the rich new civilization of Islam with the goods which they demanded and for which they could pay. In doing so they penetrated all the coasts and rivers of Europe."[197] In the above quotation Trevor-Roper repeats the erroneous notion, prevalent until the last decades of the twentieth century, that Byzantium somehow escaped the ravages of the Saracens and that in her territory there continued to flourish an intact and prosperous branch of ancient Rome. Constantinople, he imagines, like Damascus, was a wealthy recipient of Russian slaves. Yet by the end of the seventh century, as we saw, the formerly great power of Eastern Rome was little more than an impoverished rump, cut off, just as surely as the West, from the wealth and learning of Asia. If there was a slave trade in Byzantium, it was only as a link in the chain that brought eunuchs and concubines from Russia to Damascus and Baghdad. What little gold Byzantium possessed in the tenth and eleventh centuries was from the taxes levied Muslim merchants of human flesh, who frequented the Viking-supplied markets of the ancient capital. The gold derived from this infamous trade was known as *aurum arabicum*, Arab gold, or, as humane men preferred to call it, *aurum infelix*, unhappy gold. By the tenth century large quantities of this Arab gold and silver had found its way to Scandinavia. Viking longboats were apparently not infrequent visitors to Islamic ports in Iberia, and the occasional Arab traveler returned the compliment by visiting Scandinavia.

Whilst, as Trevor-Roper says, the majority of European slaves delivered to the Arabs were Slavs, not all of them were. Indeed, the Vikings plundered all of western Europe to supply the markets of the Caliphate. Dublin, for example, established by the Vikings in Ireland, was a major slave market, with most of the captives bought and sold coming from Ireland and Britain. Nonetheless,

---

[197] Ibid., pp. 90-1

there is no doubt that the majority of slaves sold to the Muslims were heathen Slavs, and there is no doubt also that some of the Christian rulers of western Europe were complicit in the trade. Venice, for example, acted as a depot for the collection and sale of Slavic captives from Dalmatia. Marseilles too, it seems, also was active. In the words of Trevor-Roper: "For if the Vikings were the pioneers, the princes of Europe, or some of them, were the middlemen in the new slave-trade. They licensed it and they profited by it, though they left the direct traffic in it to the Jews, who could move most easily across the frontiers of the two societies. We have plenty of evidence of this trade and its routes ... Liutprand of Cremona, the ambassador of the West who, in the tenth century, stood agog before the kaleidoscope pageantry of the Byzantine court, tells us that it was the merchants of Verdun who, for the immense profit of the trade, made boys into eunuchs and sold them through Moorish Spain to the rich Moslem world ... The trade has left its mark in the languages of both Christendom and Islam. *Sclavi*, 'Slavs', has formed, in every European language, the word for slaves; and the same word, *Sakaliba*, has provided the Arabic word for eunuchs."[198]

The involvement of some "Christian" rulers in this new slave-trade would have far-reaching consequences, as would the involvement of Jewish traders. For, as we shall see, as the Muslim threat grew, and as all of Spain and parts of France were overwhelmed, suspicions that "the Jews" were secretly allied to the Muslims increased.

Effects on European Consciousness

It is hard for us, at a distance of a thousand years, to imagine the effects these invasions had upon the peoples of Europe. Henri Pirenne rightly, in the opinion of the present author, identified the Muslim onslaught as the event which brought Classical civilization to a definitive end and launched what has come to be known as the Middle Ages. Pirenne focused his attention on economics. The loss of Egypt to Islam closed off what had been the breadbasket of Rome; and

---

[198] Ibid., p. 92

thus of urban civilization.[199] Without a ready supply of surplus food, no large cities can survive. And sure enough, the seventh and eighth centuries saw the decline of urban life throughout Europe, both in the West and in the East, along with the appearance of an increasingly rural society. By the tenth century, Rome herself, as well as Constantinople, had shrunk to little more than what would earlier have been considered small provincial towns – though they still remained the biggest urban centers in Europe. The severing of trade with the eastern Mediterranean also impoverished Europe culturally. The links, both economic and cultural, which had for example brought Egyptian monasticism to the islands and crags of western Ireland and Byzantine silverware to the court of an Anglo-Saxon prince in eastern England, now came to an end. Terminated too was the supply of lapis-lazuli from Afghanistan, which had provided the Christian monks with their ultramarine pigment for decorating the famous illuminated manuscripts. Papyrus supplies from Egypt also dried up, forcing Europeans to turn to the more expensive animal skins for writing material. This can only have had a detrimental effect on literacy as a whole.

Pirenne, and others, have viewed these events as signaling the beginning of the Medieval Age. The present writer is in agreement. But what exactly do we mean by "Medieval"? The word is commonly used in English in a rather derogatory sense, as implying backward and out-of-date, but also narrow and ignorant.

Now there can be no doubt that although (as I hope to illuminate at the end of the present work) there was no Dark Age, no period when civilization completely collapsed, the real Medieval Age did indeed see a decline in learning and the arts. This decline however touched not only the arts and sciences, but also thinking. For the Medieval Age saw a very definite movement away from the rationality of Greece and Rome towards a simplistic and literalist interpretation of all things. This was nowhere more apparent than in religious ideas. The Church Fathers, including even the most literalist of them, such as Augustine, had rightly viewed much of Genesis, especially its earliest parts, as allegorical, and had no problems with this. Whilst it is true that, even in the second, third and fourth centuries, most ordinary Christians did not share the allegorical interpretation of Genesis and the other early books of the Old

---

[199] Pirenne, op cit.

3: SARACENS, VIKINGS AND HUNGARIANS

Testament, it is undeniable that this was how the highest ranks of the Church thought. Yet by the seventh and certainly the eighth century the situation had changed completely. Now we find ourselves in the intellectual world of the Medieval. Every word of the Bible, both Old and New Testaments, is seen as literally true, and this biblical literalism is accompanied by a general hardening of attitudes all round. Thus we know, as just one example, how the killing of Hypatia by a mob of fanatics in Alexandria early in the fifth century was viewed with sorrow by the Christian writer Socrates Scholasticus, who wrote shortly after the event. He spoke of the "bigoted zeal" of her attackers. Yet by the eighth century another Egyptian Christian writer, John of Nikiu, could describe Hypatia as "a pagan" who was "devoted to magic" and who had "beguiled many people through Satanic wiles." And whilst Socrates Scholasticus condemned her killing, John of Nikiu approved it, speaking of "A multitude of believers in God" who, "under the guidance of Peter the magistrate ... proceeded to seek for the pagan woman who had beguiled the people of the city and the prefect through her enchantments."

John of Nikiu was an Egyptian, writing in Egypt about three-quarters of a century or perhaps slightly more after the Muslim conquest. His opinions were his own, and were not necessarily shared by all Egyptian Christians of the eighth century. Nonetheless, it seems fairly clear that he had already absorbed much from Islam – a faith which saw both God and the Devil as essentially other, essentially outside. Thus neither God, who was completely transcendent, nor the Devil, who was equally transcendent, were in any way present in the souls of men; nor did men share in the attributes of God and the Devil. In Islam, neither God nor the Devil wore a human face. Human beings were the helpless playthings of both God and the daemons, an attitude which led to fatalism, but also to the view that the Devil and his agents were everywhere. That Islam could so early have influenced the thinking of Christians should not surprise, as we have abundant proof of its deep impact elsewhere in the eighth century in the famous "Iconoclasm" controversy, where Byzantine Christians, adopting the anti-image prejudice of Islam, set about destroying much of the figurative artwork of Eastern Christendom. Iconoclasm began sometime between 726 and 730 when the Emperor Leo III, "the Isaurian," ordered the removal of an image of Christ prominently placed over the Chalke Gate in Constantinople, as a prelude to the destruction of sacred statues and images throughout the Empire.

HOLY WARRIORS

That this concept was directly derived from Islam is well-known, and denied by no one. Yet all these attitudes, redolent of a return to a primitive, Old Testament view of life, are precisely what we now understand as Medievalism. Belief in magic and the power of Satan, and the idea that his agents lurked everywhere, was to become one of the defining characteristics of the Medieval Age.

As will become clear in the next chapter, it was Islam and not Christianity which demanded the abdication and abandonment of the faculty of reason. In Islam, faith and reason are fundamentally incompatible – an attitude deriving from the capricious behavior of Allah himself in the Koran.

As we saw, Henri Pirenne dated the appearance of the Medieval world to the Islamic conquests and to the severing of trade and economic links between the western and eastern Mediterranean. The loss of these links did damage the west's economy; and it damaged the general level of culture. Europe became backward. Yet it was not so much European science and technology, or even art, which suffered, so much as European humanity. For the war initiated by the Muslim advance across North Africa and Spain was to become a ferocious clash of civilizations; an epoch-making battle which progressively degraded the minds of those who participated, on both sides, and which finally killed, once and for all, the humanitarian impulse of both early Christianity and Classical culture.

A centuries-long period of fear, insecurity and, increasingly, paranoia, was initiated by these events. The war for possession of the Iberian Peninsula, as well as for other regions of southern Europe was to rage, without respite, for many centuries. Muslim armies carried the war north of the Pyrenees into France, whilst French ports on the Mediterranean were regularly raided for slaves by Muslim corsairs. Italy was not spared these depredations, and the south of the country actually, for a while, suffered the fate of Spain, as did the islands of Sicily and Sardinia. And it should not be forgotten that the Muslim threat, once it appeared, never departed. Mediterranean Europe would never again know peace: For even if the immediate threat of overrunning all of Europe receded in the course of two centuries, new wars, equally dangerous to the security of Europe, first involving the Almoravids in the West and the Seljuk Turks (and later the Ottoman Turks) in the East, continued to rage. And the brief interludes between these conflicts failed to leave the Mediterranean lands in peace: Muslim pirates and slave-traders preyed on the coasts of southern Europe without respite for almost a thousand years, bringing to these regions a state of almost perpetual war.

Fig. 6. The world of Islam and Christianity, around 720. By the end of the seventh century Christendom had been reduced to a rump comprising the Frankish Kingdom and Byzantium, and little else.

Back in the eighth century, things must have seemed even more bleak: The advance of the Saracens had been unstopped and unstoppable in a march of conquest that had taken them, within a century, from the borders of Arabia to the centre of France. This new enemy, as we have seen, was unlike any Christians had faced before. Here was a foe determined not only to conquer and subdue the Christians, to take their lands and wealth and enslave them; but to extirpate or at the very least subvert the Christian faith itself. As we shall shortly see, the Muslim conquest of Spain produced, instead of a Golden Age of science and learning, a bloodbath and an interminable war of attrition. The Christians, having lost the whole of North Africa, now found their Muslim foes advancing through Europe itself. The *Reconquista,* the battle to retake the Iberian Peninsula, began almost immediately after the initial invasion: and it was here, in Spain, that the first "crusades" began.[200] Indeed, it was from their Muslim foes that the Christians learned the very idea of "Holy War," a fact admitted even by Bernard Lewis.

At the same time, Viking raiders, tempted by the promise of Islamic gold, brought devastation across northern Europe. The plunder, rape, pillage and kidnapping they unleashed on the British Isles brought to an abrupt end the Golden Age of the Celtic Church. And whilst the Muslims raided southern France, the Vikings raided the north – as well as northern Germany. Thus in Germany they burned Aachen, Trier, and Cologne, whilst in France they plundered Rouen, burned Nantes, and ravaged the valley of the Garonne, from which point they moved south to Spain and sacked Seville. Within a relatively short time, Bordeaux, Tours, Blois, Orleans, Poitiers, and Paris had been sacked one or more times.[201] The Viking assault, like the Islamic, constituted an ongoing and interminable threat; and at the very peak of the carnage Western Europe was assailed by yet another wave of nomads from the steppes. The Magyars, for a time, became a threat as serious almost as the Muslims, and they pushed their raiding parties deep into the western parts of Germany, crossing into Gaul on at least one occasion, where they advanced as far as Reims.[202]

The sense of terror these events created can only have had a profound effect upon the consciousness of Europe. And so too did the growth of the new slave-trade to satisfy Muslim demands. Here we need to bear in mind the fact that some western rulers, perhaps desperate to raise money to fend off Viking and Hungarian attack, became involved in that trade. Such commerce can only have had a profoundly corrupting effect. And we need to consider too the involvement of some Jewish merchants in the trade and the consequent growth of suspicions about the Jews – one of which was that they had assisted the Muslims in the conquest of Spain. These suspicions, as we shall see, were to have far-reaching and fatal consequences. Connected to this, we must bear in

---

[200] The Reconquista is normally dated from the victory of Don Pelayo in Asturias, probably in 718 or 719. It is interesting that the Reconquista thus began almost immediately after the initial Muslim Conquest. This makes sense, and is a vital clue to the confused chronology of the period. As we shall see at the end of the present volume, a mistake of no less than three centuries is indicated.
[201] Painter, op cit., p. 90
[202] Ibid., p. 93

mind also the penetration into Europe of Islamic ideas – ideas about war and about the Jews.

A fierce and irrational hatred of the Jews is of course another of the most execrable characteristics of what is now seen as the Medieval mentality. But it was the system of governance, or rather the fragmentation of central power into the hands of local military strong men, that was to be the characteristic most classically associated with the Medieval Age. This was Feudalism, a system also directly linked to the arrival of Islam.

The Growth of Feudalism

The defining characteristic of medieval culture was feudalism. According to the *Oxford Dictionary* feudalism is: "the dominant social system in medieval Europe, in which the nobility held lands from the Crown in exchange for military service, and vassals were tenants of and protected by the nobles, giving their lords homage, labour, and a share of the produce." As such, it was by definition, a system characterized by a fragmentation of power and authority, where the central government, in the form of the monarchy, was limited by the power of the aristocracy. The latter group, the lords and the barons, maintained a great deal of independence and the monarchy had to deal with them as best it could. These men pursued their own interests, sometimes with remarkable ruthlessness, and the Crown frequently had little or no control over how they governed their own territories.

There can be little doubt that the groundwork for the feudal system was laid in the period of the Gothic and Frankish kingdoms, whose rulers never enjoyed the power or authority of Roman Emperors, and who had to deal frequently with troublesome vassals. Nevertheless, Pirenne has shown that the Merovingians in Gaul and the Visigoths in Spain had been well on the way to re-establishing a centralized system of government, complete with thriving urban centers and bureaucratic institutions. The complete disintegration of central authority came later, along with the dwindling of urban life and the decline of literacy.

It is in fact widely recognized that feudalism, in its proper and fully-developed sense, only appeared in Europe in the second half of the tenth century. The Europe of this time was "a society where violence was endemic and in itself unremarkable."[203] This fact, continues the writer of the above words, "constitutes perhaps the greatest mental adjustment to make" when considering this period. "Violence was everywhere, impinging on many aspects of life. Legal disputes, for instance, were often resolved by means of trial by battle or by recourse to painful and perilous ordeals. ... Vendettas within and between kindreds were frequent. Seldom neatly contained aristocratic combats, they had wide repercussions, for crude but effective economic warfare was regularly waged on opponents' assets, and that meant peasants, livestock, crops, and farm buildings. Brutality was so common it could be ritualistic."[204]

This then was the reality of life in the early feudal world, or much of it at least.

Many and various are the theories advanced to explain the rise of such a system. Since the 1950s historians have generally come to see the "dislocation" of royal power in the ninth and tenth centuries as the prelude to feudalism proper, which itself only appears in the last decades of the tenth century. This change is known to French medievalists as the *mutation féodale*, the feudal transformation. The theory is summarized thus by Marcus Bull: "From around the middle of the tenth century ... the large regional blocs which were the remnants of the Frankish polity themselves became subjected to centrifugal pressures from petty warlords, many of whom had risen to prominence as the princes' deputies in the localities. Repeating the earlier pattern of fragmentation, but now on a much smaller scale, the local lords flourished by combining their economic muscle as landowners and their residual public powers with regard to justice and military organization. Peasants found themselves subjected to increasingly burdensome rents and labour obligations. Courts ceased to be public forums which served the free population of their area and became instruments of private aristocratic might, privileged access to which was gained by entering into the lord's vassalage."[205]

---

[203] Marcus Bull, "Origins," in Jonathan Riley-Smith, (ed.) *The Oxford History of the Crusades*, p. 16
[204] Ibid., p. 17
[205] Ibid., p. 22

3: SARACENS, VIKINGS AND HUNGARIANS

The above describes a society ruled by petty warlords who were themselves little more than criminals or thugs made good. It reads not unlike a description of Sicily prior to the suppression of the Mafia in the 1920s.

But what circumstances could have placed so much power in the hands of local warlords? The obvious answer is the Vikings. Large-scale attacks on a country, as carried out by invading armies, tend to increase the authority of the central power. The invading hosts need to be met by forces of equal size, and this inevitably leads to the control of enormous forces and resources by a single individual or by a small group of individuals. The Viking raids were not like that. These were small-scale attacks involving hundreds rather than thousands of warriors. They preyed upon peasant and village communities. They appeared suddenly and disappeared with equal speed. Such a foe demanded a local response. Groups of warriors in a particular locality, under the leadership of a minor aristocrat with military experience, were the only way to deal with a threat such as that posed by the Vikings. And it is surely to this, or at least chiefly to this, that we must trace the origin of feudalism.

It can thus be seen that feudalism, an oppressive system in which violence was endemic, was a manifestation – in northern Europe at least – of the response to the Viking threat. Similar petty feudal aristocracies, offering "protection" to small communities, sprang up in southern Europe, where the piracy came from Saracen raiders. Since the Viking raids themselves were largely elicited by the Muslim desire for European slaves, it is thus clear that what we consider to be the endemic violence of early medieval Europe was a direct consequence of the Muslim threat.

Before moving on we should note, yet again, a question relating to chronology.

We have seen that whilst feudalism proper is dated only to the second half of the tenth century, the Viking raids which precipitated this development are said to have commenced almost two centuries earlier (ie around 790). This does not make sense, since we can hardly expect the peasants and villagers of northern Europe to have endured two centuries of murder and enslavement before finally organizing some sort of resistance. The mark of that resistance, and the defining sign from an archaeological viewpoint of the rise of the feudal order, was castle-building. These, originally of wood, began to be constructed throughout northern Europe only in the final decades of the tenth century. Why take two hundred years to organize such a basic and obvious mode of defense? All of this suggests that the Viking raids have been seriously misdated, and that they only began in the middle of the tenth century.

And it is interesting to note at this point that Henri Pirenne's thesis, which saw the coming of Islam as the main force behind the rise of medievalism, also ran into the same chronological problem: It was not only castle-building, but also the change-over to the barter economy, that had to wait till the tenth century for its appearance. Thus Van Bath writes; "Pirenne's theories raised immediate opposition from Dopsch. He agreed as to the change-over from money to natural economy, but set it at a later date, namely the end of the Carolingian era [tenth century], the time of the Viking invasions and the raids of the Magyars and Saracens."[206] Dopsch's view, according to Van Bath, "is more consistent with the rise and development of the feudal system and the manorial organization than is that of Pirenne."

If this were the only indication of a major chronological mistake, it would perhaps be not so pressing; yet, as we have seen elsewhere and shall see further, much other evidence points in the same direction, and the advent of Islam itself, with which the Viking epoch is so closely related, gives much indication of having begun also in the tenth century; or, even more probably, both Islamic and Viking ages commenced in the seventh century.

More on this in due course.

[206] Van Bath, op cit., p. 31

CHAPTER 4

CONDITIONS UNDER ISLAM

Propaganda and History

ccording to Henri Pirenne, Islam caused the Dark Age in Europe. This is in stark contrast to the politically-correct narrative – popular especially in the English- and French-speaking worlds – which sees Islam not as the cause of the Dark Age but as the cure. In this viewpoint, it was Islam's science and learning which, arriving in Europe in the early eighth century, began the process of delivering the continent from the darkness into which it had been plunged in the fifth century by the barbarian tribes. According to this, the seventh, eighth, ninth and tenth centuries, constituted an Islamic "Golden Age," and the Muslim armies which assaulted Europe from the east, south and west were altogether superior, in terms of culture and civilization, to their European opponents. Thus for example historian Bernard Lewis contrasts the sophisticated Muslims who entered Spain with that of their Spanish and Frankish opponents, whose economy was "little better than Neolithic."[207]

In agreement with that picture, we are told endlessly, in publication after publication, of the "splendid" civilization that arose in the Caliphate of Cordoba, as Muslim Spain became in the tenth century. The debt owed by medieval

---

[207] Bernard Lewis, *God's Crucible: Islam and the Making of Europe, 570 – 1215* (W. W. Norton and Co., 2008)

4: CONDITIONS UNDER ISLAM

Europe to Islamic scholars such as Averroes (Ibn Rushd), with his commentaries on Aristotle are endlessly trumpeted, as are the slightly later works of Moses Maimonides, especially his Aristotle-inflected *Guide to the Perplexed*. It is emphasized, again and again, that Muslim scholars preserved and translated the works of classical authors like Aristotle, most of which had been lost in Europe in the wake of the Barbarian Invasions, and that these were reintroduced into Europe through the agency of Arabic translations during the eleventh and twelfth centuries. Arab contributions to mathematics and science are emphasized again and again, and the "splendid" art and architecture of the Islamic region is contrasted with the supposedly low (or non-existent) state of these skills in contemporary Europe.

Along with science and the arts, the Islamophiles praise the enlightened tolerance of the Arabian faith. Again and again we are told how the Muslim conquerors of Syria, Egypt, North Africa and Spain permitted both Christians and Jews to practice their own faiths without hindrance; and that, subject to the payment of a special tax, Christians and Jews enjoyed almost the same rights as Muslims. This Muslim tolerance is contrasted with the gross intolerance of Christians, who had earlier severely persecuted non-Christians and even heretical Christians, destroying their places of worship and imposing heavy financial penalties for non-compliance.

In the above view, then, Islam arrived in Europe as a breath of fresh air; an enlightened and civilized force from the Near East, which breathed new life into the arts and sciences of a benighted and barbarous Europe, and laid the foundations for Europe's own Renaissance in the fifteenth century.

What are we to make of such claims?

Without going a step further, we have already shown that at least part of the above narrative – namely that Islam encountered a dark and barbarous, "almost Neolithic" Europe – is a complete and utter myth. It is a myth emphatically countered both by written history and by the findings of archaeology. It is a myth denied even by the Arab chroniclers themselves, who praise the fabulous wealth and learning of the Spanish cities their forces seized. And it is a disgrace that historians such as Bernard Lewis should still be speaking in such terms.

Granted then that Europe in the sixth and early seventh centuries was not a barbarian world far behind the Islamic: What then of the second part of the

124

claim: That the Muslims, if not far in advance of the Europeans, were at least highly civilized and cultured people; and that they were generally tolerant and enlightened, when compared with the Christians?

This question is partly answered by the fact, noted in the preceding chapter, of the torrent of violence launched throughout the Mediterranean by Muslim armies during the seventh and eighth centuries. It may, in this regard, be argued that all armies produce destruction: That war itself, and not just Islamic war, causes destruction. According to the Islamophiles, after this initial stage, peace was established. Once the Christians of North Africa and Spain submitted, they were permitted to live in peace and to worship freely. And that this life, enjoyed by Christians and Jews under the mantle of an Islamic polity, was superior to that of Christians and Jews in other parts of Europe at the time. In short, Islam's boundaries may have been bloody, but her innards were peaceful and enlightened.

Is this correct? Clearly the view of Pirenne on the one hand and the Islamophiles on the other cannot both be correct. Either Islam brought a Dark Age, or it ended one: These are two diametrically opposed and indeed mutually exclusive positions. Between these two there can be no reconciliation, no synthesis. One is right and the other wrong. But which is which? Who is telling the truth?

Islamic Tolerance?

Although Islam or Islamic power was spread by the sword, it is true that followers of other religions, specifically "Religions of the Book" (ie those of a biblical origin, namely Judaism and Christianity), were permitted to continue the practice of their faiths. Other faiths, such as Buddhism and Hinduism, which had no biblical roots, fared much less well. Nonetheless, in all of the lands conquered by the Muslims it was possible, for centuries afterwards, to find sizeable Jewish and Christian minorities, and these groups were accorded what was known as *dhimmi*, or "protected" status. Jews and Christians must pay a poll tax, named a *jizya*, from which Muslims were exempt. Aside from this, Jews and Christians were almost equal to Muslims before the law.

That at least is the story told in publication after publication. Along with it we find, in the thinking of many modern historians and theologians, the idea that Islam was a kindred faith; one of the three "Arbahamic" traditions. Such writers are wont to remind their readers that Islam has biblical roots and that the prophets of the Old Testament are honored in the Koran. We are reminded too that Islam regarded Jesus as a prophet.

There is no question that Islam does display Jewish and Christian roots, or at least influences: Characters and events of the Old Testament are found frequently in the Koran. Yet Judaism, as we shall see, was not regarded by Muslims in a fraternal light: rather the Jews were seen as treacherous apostates who murdered and rejected the prophets of God.

Islam's relationship with Christianity is and always has been just as fraught. It is not true that Muslims honored Christ, for they did not believe that Jesus was the Christ (ie the "Anointed One" or Messiah). They did however honor Jesus, whom they name Isha; but the Jesus of Islamic tradition has nothing in common with the figure encountered in the New Testament. According to Islam, Isha (Jesus) taught pure Islam – including all that Islam espouses, such as polygamy, the death penalty for adultery and apostasy, spreading the faith by violent struggle, etc – and the Jesus of the Gospels is a fabrication invented by Christian propagandists in the late first century, or thereabouts. Furthermore, Isha did not die on the cross – a lookalike took his place – and he did not rise from the dead.

It is evident from this alone that Islam, whatever politically-correct historians and theologians might say, has little in common with Judaism (certainly not sixth century Judaism) and almost nothing in common with Christianity. It is equally clear that, given the profound doctrinal and theological differences, its relationship with the followers of these faiths must always have been strained, to say the least. And, as we shall see, the notion that the "Peoples of the Book," the Jews and Christians, enjoyed some kind of favored status in Islamic societies is little more than a cruel fiction.

In his book *Moorish Spain* Richard Fletcher states that: "Moorish Spain was not a tolerant and enlightened society even in its most cultivated epoch."[208] In the essay "Andalusian Myth, Eurabian Reality", Bat Ye'or and Andrew G.

---

[208] Fletcher, op cit., p. 173

Bostom examine the myth of the supposed "tolerance" enjoyed by Christians and Jews in the Iberian Peninsula: "Segregated in special quarters, they had to wear discriminatory clothing. Subjected to heavy taxes, the Christian peasantry formed a servile class attached to the Arab domains; many abandoned their land and fled to the towns. Harsh reprisals with mutilations and crucifixions would sanction the Mozarab (Christian dhimmis) calls for help from the Christian kings. Moreover, if one dhimmi harmed a Muslim, the whole community would lose its status of protection, leaving it open to pillage, enslavement and arbitrary killing."[209]

This humiliating status provoked many revolts, punished by massacres. Insurrections erupted in Saragossa in 781 and 881, Cordova (805, 818), Merida (805-813, 828 and the following year, and in 868), and again in Toledo (811-819). Many of the insurgents were crucified, as prescribed in the Koran (5:33):

"The revolt in Cordova of 818 was crushed by three days of massacres and pillage, with 300 notables crucified and 20 000 families expelled. Feuding was endemic in the Andalusian cities between the different sectors of the population: Arab and Berber colonizers, Iberian Muslim converts (Muwalladun) and Christian dhimmis (Mozarabs). There were rarely periods of peace in the Amirate of Cordova (756-912), nor later. Al-Andalus represented the land of jihad *par excellence*. Every year, sometimes twice a year, raiding expeditions were sent to ravage the Christian Spanish kingdoms to the north, the Basque regions, or France and the Rhone valley, bringing back booty and slaves. Andalusian corsairs attacked and invaded along the Sicilian and Italian coasts, even as far as the Aegean Islands, looting and burning as they went. Thousands of people were deported to slavery in Andalusia, where the caliph kept a militia of tens of thousand of Christian slaves brought from all parts of Christian Europe (the Saqaliba), and a harem filled with captured Christian women."[210]

In Granada, up to five thousand Jews perished in a pogrom by Muslims in 1066. The Berber Almohads in Spain and North Africa (1130-1232) wreaked enormous destruction on the Jewish and Christian populations. Suspicious of the sincerity of converts to Islam, Muslim "inquisitors" (i.e., antedating their Christian Spanish counterparts by three centuries) removed children from such

[209] Bat Ye'or and Andrew Bostom, "Andalusian Myth, Eurabian Reality," www.jihadwatch.org/dhimmiwatch/archives/001665.php
[210] Ibid.

families, placing them in the care of Muslims. A prominent Andalusian jurist, Ibn Hazm of Cordoba (d. 1064), wrote that Allah has established the infidels' ownership of their property merely to provide booty for Muslims.[211]

None of this sounds like the attitude or behavior of a tolerant or enlightened faith. And yet, it is true that, during the Middle Ages the Muslims at least tolerated the existence of Christians and Christian churches within their territories. As "People of the Book" (ie the Bible), the Christians and Jews were entitled to the status of *dhimmi*, or "protected" peoples. Subject to the paying of a special tax, the *jizya*, Christian and Jewish populations in the conquered territories were permitted to live more or less in peace and to worship as they had before. But even as we extol the generosity of the followers of Islam on this count, it is important to point out that the status of the *dhimmi* communities was not nearly as desirable as some naïve westerners have recently imagined, as we shall shortly see. Indeed, so appalling were conditions for these communities that, in the course of centuries, they shrank to vanishing-point throughout the Near East and North Africa. It is also worth remembering that a victor is more inclined to be, and can afford to be, magnanimous. We need not repeat here the calamities suffered by Christians at the hands of Muslims during the century and a half after Muhammad's death, and how a caliphate was founded on the ruins of Christian kingdoms from Syria and Egypt to Spain and the Pyrenees. We recall the overwhelming sense of gloom felt by Christians as they observed these events unfold, and the growing sense of terror that the faith of Christ was about to be extinguished even in the heart of Europe. And whilst it is true that most of the conquered Christians were permitted to retain their faith and its practice, the massacre and enslavement of the conquered populations, very often on the slightest pretext, was common.

To describe the treatment of the *dhimmi* communities of Jews and Christians as one of benevolent tolerance is thus to do violence to the meaning of words. The *dhimmi*, by definition, had virtually no rights before the law. His existence, as Bat Ye'or explains in her detailed examination of the topic, was merely tolerated – a toleration that could be withdrawn as any time by his Muslim masters. Subject to an enormous array of humiliating constrictions –

---

[211] Ibid.

amongst which was the wearing of distinctive clothing for easy identification – the *dhimmi* Jew or Christian could be assaulted, degraded, or even slaughtered in the street with little hope of legal redress. Should a Jew or Christian take such a complaint to the authorities, his Muslim attacker invariably claimed his victim had insulted the Koran or Muhammad. Two Muslim witnesses were needed to substantiate this claim, but these were always forthcoming; and since the word of the *dhimmi* Christian or Jew counted for nothing against that of a Muslim, the *dhimmi* was invariably put to death. The frequent occurrence of the latter effectively prevented any Christian or Jew attempting to find justice at a Muslim court of law.[212]

But even the grudging acceptance of the existence of *dhimmi* communities has to be viewed in the context of how Islam came to power: the conquering Muslims of the seventh, eighth and ninth centuries could scarcely enslave or forcefully convert the entire populations of the subdued territories. Such a policy would perchance have involved them in dangerous revolts, revolts which may easily have extinguished the numerically small numbers of conquering Arabs. Far better to appease the conquered peoples with a semblance of toleration and recognition, whilst at the same time imposing punishing financial burdens and closing to them the most important and prestigious positions in society. This has been explained most lucidly by Bat Ye'or.

"The conditions of minorities in Christian countries has often been compared with the fate of the *dhimmis* under Islam, although such generalizations concerning vast territories and periods of time are inappropriate. Rather than looking for similarities between the two, one should acknowledge an essential difference. During the first two centuries of their conquest – and certainly at the outset – the Arabs were themselves a minority. In order to impose their laws, their language, and their foreign culture on ancient civilizations, they had to proceed with caution. A general uprising of the subject populations would have compromised the success of their conquest."[213]

The financial question too is one that cannot be ignored. Christians and Jews, we have noted, were compelled to pay a "poll tax" or *jizya,* an annual tribute which, considering the great numbers of conquered Christians, amounted to a fabulous sum for the government of the Caliphate. In such circumstances, it

---

[212] Bat Ye'or, op cit., pp. 56-7
[213] Ibid., 67-8

will be obvious that it was financially advantageous to have Christians and Jews as subjects, and to keep them as Christians and Jews. Muslims were exempt from this kind of taxation. So lucrative was the *jizya* system that Muslim rulers did not, in most cases, actually want Christians to convert. Christian conversions meant loss of revenue. In the words of Louis Bertrand, "In general the Caliphal government did not want to see the Christians turn Musulman. The treasury lost too much if they did, inasmuch as it was they who paid the major part of the taxes."[214] Bat Ye'or comments: "Baladhuri related that when Iraq fell to the Arab conquerors, the soldiers wanted to 'share out' the region of Sawad between themselves. The caliph Umar b. al-Khattab permitted them to divide the booty, but decreed that the land and the camels should be left to the local farmers so as to provide for the Muslims: 'If you divide them among those present, there will be nothing left for those who come after them.' And Ali, the Prophet's son-in-law said of the non-Muslim peasants of Sawad, 'Leave them to be a source of revenue and aid for the Muslims.'"[215] Bertrand rightly concludes; "It is difficult to find, as most of our historians do, an attitude of tolerance and broad-mindedness in this entirely self-interested line of conduct."[216]

Thus the sole reason for Islam's begrudging acceptance of the continued existence of Jews and Christians was that they should form the basis of a servile population upon which the Muslims, the ruling elite, could enjoy what can only be described as a parasitical existence in perpetuity.

This then was Arab policy: heavy taxation coupled with periodic violent persecutions of the subject Christians. Egypt, for example, remained predominantly Christian until the thirteenth century, when a ferocious campaign of massacre and repression initiated by the Fatimid rulers compelled the majority to convert to Islam. The end result of such policies, enacted throughout the Muslim-controlled territories, was a progressive diminishing of Christian numbers – eventually in many places to vanishing point – and a commensurate augmentation of Muslim numbers.

We should note too that whilst the Muslims had a doctrinal reason for honoring the founder of Christianity, Christians had no such reason for revering

---

[214] Bertrand, op cit., p. 33
[215] Bat Ye'or, op cit., p. 68
[216] Bertrand, op cit., p. 33

the founder of Islam. Christian prophecy did not look forward to the coming of a prophet who would wage violent war against their faith, and who would both practice and sanction several of the most obnoxious things condemned by Christ: polygamy, the death sentence for adultery, strict rituals surrounding clean and unclean food, easy divorce, etc. Indeed, if Muhammad were to find a place in the predictions and imaginings of the early Christian writers, it was as the Antichrist – a figure with whom he was, by very many Christian authorities, identified.

And just how tolerant can we really consider a faith that considers it not only legitimate but a duty to spread its message by force of arms; and which, at the same time, prescribes the death penalty for those abandoning it? How tolerant is a faith which reduces to second class citizenship even the followers of those other few religions which it actually permits to exist? And how tolerant is a faith which considers it legitimate to plunder and destroy the temples and shrines of those religions it considers idolatrous or polytheistic; and which regards the adherents of such faiths as fair game, to be killed or enslaved, or forcibly converted, at the whim of the Muslim conquerors?

Taking all of this into account we can only conclude that those who describe Islam as tolerant do not understand it.

Islamic Learning: the Myth

As noted above, it is a widely-held belief, and so it is stated in one authoritative publication after another, that Islam experienced a Golden Age in the seventh, eighth and ninth centuries. During this period, it is held, Muslim scholars contemplated the mysteries of the universe: they mapped the earth and the stars; they evolved new mathematical systems; they wrote advanced treatises on subjects as diverse as medicine and philosophy; and they raised architectural masterpieces, palaces and places of worship that had no peer in the savage world of contemporary Europe.

Presiding over this flowering of science and arts were semi-legendary Caliphs such as Harun al-Rashid (for whom was composed Scheherazade's *Thousand and One Nights*) in a vast and fabulously wealthy Baghdad, then the home to an estimated one million souls. Contemporary Cordoba, the capital of

4: CONDITIONS UNDER ISLAM

Al-Andalus, was said to compare with Baghdad in terms of wealth, and was home – apparently – to half a million.[217] No city of Christian Europe, it is said, had at that time more than 50,000 people.

Indeed, it was to Islam and the Islamic world, we are told, that the benighted peoples of Europe owed the revival of their own civilization: For it was Islamic scholars who, displaying a respect for learning entirely absent amongst Europeans, preserved the masterpieces of the Classical world, and subsequently transmitted them again to Europe as soon as the natives of that continent were willing or able to appreciate and value them. And, so the story goes, Islam remained culturally and materially superior to Europe until the whole edifice was destroyed by the barbarians of Europe (Crusaders) and the barbarians of Central Asia, the Mongols.

That, at least, is the story now told in almost all learned publications. The importance of the topic, from an ideological point of view, can be gauged by the enormous Wikipedia web-page titled "Islamic Science," replete with hundreds of references, which has recently appeared on the Internet. The story told above is essentially that appearing in the Wikipedia page. It is a version of history which is not, one might be surprised to learn, the product of our modern politically-correct age. Indeed, the notion of an advanced and cultured Islam, contrasted with a benighted and primitive Europe during the seventh to eleventh centuries, is one that has a long pedigree. The germs of it are found in Gibbon, but it owes its origin to the notion of a European Dark Age stretching from the fifth century to the tenth. Before Henri Pirenne, this notion went unchallenged, and led, eventually, to a whole genre of literature which virtually accredited Islam with the saving of western civilization. In the early years of the twentieth century, one of the most outspoken exponents of this view was our old friend Robert Briffault, who, we remember, viewed the Germanic peoples as incorrigible savages. Typical of Briffault's utterances is the following: "It was under the influence of the Arabian and Moorish revival of culture, and not in the

---

[217] Yet, as we shall see shortly, barely a trace, hardly a brick or inscription, of this half-million strong metropolis has been found by archaeology – and that after a very intensive search indeed. As a matter of fact, the earliest provable and substantial Islamic settlement of Cordoba is dated to the tenth century; but it was a settlement tiny compared to the half-million-strong Cordoba of legend. Interestingly, the million-strong Baghdad of Harun Al-Rashid is just as elusive. Not a trace has been found.

fifteenth century, that the real Renaissance took place. Spain, not Italy, was the cradle of the rebirth of Europe. After steadily sinking lower and lower into barbarism, it [Europe] had reached the darkest depths of ignorance and degradation when the cities of the Saracenic world, Baghdad, Cairo, Cordova, Toledo, were growing centres of civilization and intellectual activity."[218] Again, "It is highly probable that but for the Arabs modern European civilization would not have arisen at all; it is absolutely certain that but for them, it would not have assumed the character which has enabled it to transcend all previous phases of evolution."[219]

In support of these statements, Briffault refers to a series of Arab inventions, discoveries and innovations. He refers to the astronomers Al-Zarkyal and Al-Farani, who postulated that the orbits of the planets was elliptical rather than circular, as Ptolemy believed.[220] He notes how Ibn Sina (Avicenna) is said to have employed an air thermometer, and Ibn Yunis to have used a pendulum for the measurement of time.[221] He points to the work of Al-Byruny, who travelled forty years to collect mineralogical specimens, and to that of Ibn Baitar, who collected botanical specimens from the whole Muslim world, and who compared the floras of India and Persia with those of Greece and Spain.[222] He lauds the Arab achievement of having introduced the zero into mathematics (though he admits this came originally from India), and points to the Arab invention of algebra, which was to revolutionize mathematics.[223] As if all this were not enough, he asserts that the Arabs invented the empirical method itself, which stands at the foundation of all modern science, and points to the achievements of Arab chemists, or alchemists, whose "organized passion for research ... led them to the invention of distillation, sublimation, filtration, to the discovery of alcohol, or nitric acid and sulphuric acids (the only acid known to the ancients was vinegar), of the alkalis, of the salts of mercury, of antimony and bismuth, and laid the basis of all subsequent chemistry and physical research."[224]

---

[218] Briffault, op cit., pp. 188-189
[219] Ibid. p. 190
[220] Ibid. pp. 190-191
[221] Ibid. p. 191
[222] Ibid. p. 198
[223] Ibid. p. 194
[224] Ibid. p. 197

4: CONDITIONS UNDER ISLAM

It should be noted that, notwithstanding the work of Henri Pirenne, the above viewpoint is still widely encountered, both in the English-speaking and French-speaking worlds. Thus the Wikipedia "Islamic Science" page quotes Rosanna Gorini, who notes: "According to the majority of the historians, Al-Haytham was the pioneer of the modern scientific method. With his book he changed the meaning of the term optics and established experiments as the norm of proof in the field. His investigations are based not on abstract theories, but on experimental evidences and his experiments were systematic and repeatable."[225] The same page, which is massive, enumerates the supposedly astonishing achievements of the Arab or Muslim scientists. The work of Averroes (in philosophy), Avicenna (in medicine), Geber (in chemistry), Al-Kindi (Earth sciences), Abu Rayhan al-Biruni or Byruny (in astronomy and medicine), Ibn Zuhr (in surgery), and Ibn al-Haythan, or Alhacen (in optics) are all mentioned. The latter in particular is seen by some enthusiasts as being the inventor of the modern scientific method.

What are we to make of these claims?

Islamic Learning: the Reality

That there is a germ of truth in some of the above claims is beyond doubt. To begin with, there is no question that the early Islamic world was fabulously wealthy. How could it be otherwise, when it conquered and, within a very short time, controlled virtually all of the ancient centers of culture and population of the Near East? By circa 650 Islamic armies had subdued everything from Egypt and Libya in the west, to Persia and Afghanistan in the east. The wealth, and learning, of those regions, including the enormous population centers, with their libraries and universities, were all now at the disposal of Muslim rulers. As well as the actual plunder accrued in a successful war of conquest, the Muslims, as we have seen, imposed heavy taxes upon the natives who refused to convert to Islam, whilst the treasures of ancient and venerable churches were more often

---

[225] Rosanna Gorini, "Al-Haytham the Man of Experience. First Steps in the Science of Vision," *International Society for the History of Islamic Medicines*. (2003) Institute of Neurosciences, Laboratory and Psychobiology and Psychopharmacology, Rome, Italy.

than not simply looted. This was usually disguised as an act of religious piety, since church treasures were frequently in the form of statues or gold-covered images – idols, which it was the sacred duty of Muslims to destroy. In Egypt, even the tombs of pharaohnic times were plundered.[226] In addition, the Muslims discovered new sources of gold and silver. In Khorasan, to the east of Persia, and in Transoxiana beyond it, between Kashmir and the Aral Sea, "vast mines of silver" were discovered, whilst the Arab conquest of Nubia, to the south of Egypt, opened the gold mines of that region to their use.[227] And these new sources of wealth were of such richness that they could scarcely have done else than produce an epoch of prosperity.

For a while, some Muslim rulers did patronize universities and other seats of learning. Scientific and philosophic treatises were indeed composed, and there is no doubt that Arab, or at least Arabic-speaking scholars were in possession of many Classical texts not generally available in Europe. These men, it is evident, made important contributions, in various areas of scientific and scholarly endeavor. In addition, the Arabs, or rather the Arab rulers of the Near East (for the great majority of the population remained non-Arab in language and non-Muslim in religion for several centuries after the conquest), learnt the secrets of paper-making, printing, the compass, and various other crucial technologies from the Chinese between the eighth and eleventh centuries, which technologies they utilized and eventually (inadvertently) spread to Europe. But what of the argument that Islam encouraged the arts and sciences? Here, the Islamophiles are on much shakier ground. The Arabs who emerged from Arabia with Caliph Umar were mostly illiterate nomads, whose knowledge of what we call science was non-existent. Like all barbarians, they were of course deeply impressed, to begin with at least, by the advanced and civilized cultures which they overran. Egypt, Babylonia, and Persia were ancient civilizations with unique attributes. Each had long-established universities, libraries and traditions of learning. When the Arabs conquered these regions there is evidence that they permitted these institutions, for a time at least, to continue. Furthermore, these nations, and Persia in particular, were conduits through which flowed new ideas and techniques from the great civilizations of the Far East, from India and China. Much, indeed most, of the new technologies

---

[226] Trevor-Roper, op cit., p. 90
[227] Ibid.

and methods that medieval Europeans learned from the Arabs, were not Arab or even Near Eastern at all, but Chinese and Indian. Europeans used the Arabic names for these things (such as "zero", from the Arabic *zirr*), because it was from Arab sources that they learned them. But they were neither Arab nor Middle Eastern.

This is in fact the case with the great majority of the "Arab" learning outlined by such enthusiasts as Briffault. The claim, for example, that the Arabs discovered the distillation of alcohol, which Briffault makes, is quite simply false. Alcohol had been distilled in Babylonia prior to the Arab conquest.[228] Under the Arabs, distillation techniques were improved; but they did not invent distillation. Again, the claim that the Persian Al-Khwarizmi invented algebra is untrue; and it is now widely admitted that the Greek mathematician Diophantes, building on the knowledge of the Babylonians, was the first to outline the principles (in his *Arithmetica*) of what we now call algebra.[229] Al-Khwarizmi did make a number of important innovations, such as the quadratic equation and the introduction of the decenary numerical system from India, but in many other respects his work was not as advanced as that of Diophantes. Furthermore, he clearly owed much to the fifth century Indian mathematician and astronomer Aryabhata, whose 121-verse *Aryabhatiya* expostulated on astronomy, arithmetic, geometry, algebra, trigonometry, methods of determining the movements of the planets and descriptions of their movements, as well as methods of calculating the movements of the sun and moon and predicting their eclipses. And we note too that Aryabhata was manifestly the source of the astronomical ideas attributed to Al-Zarkyal and Al-Farani, which Briffault places such store in.

There is another important consideration to remember: Whilst "Arab" scientists and philosophers of this time used Arab names and wrote in Arabic, the great majority of them were not Arabs or Muslims at all, but Christians and Jews who worked under Arab regimes. The Saracen armies which conquered the Near East in the seventh century imposed their faith and their language in the corridors of power; and the subdued peoples were forced to learn it. At no time,

---

[228] Charles Simmonds (1919). *Alcohol: With Chapters on Methyl Alcohol, Fusel Oil, and Spirituous Beverages.* (Macmillan, 1919). p. 6ff.
[229] See eg. Carl B. Boyer, *A History of Mathematics, Second Edition* (Wiley, 1991) p. 228

not even at the beginning, did genuine Arabs and Muslims show much interest in science and scholarship. Aristotle's work was preserved in Arabic not initially by Muslims at all, but by Christians such as the fifth century priest Probus of Antioch, who introduced Aristotle to the Arabic-speaking world. In fact, during the eighth and ninth centuries, "the whole corpus of Greek scientific and philosophical learning was translated into Arabic, mainly by Nestorian Christians."[230] We know that "Schools, often headed by Christians, were ... established in connection with mosques."[231] The leading figure in the Baghdad school was the Christian Huneyn ibn Ishaq (809-873), who translated many works by Aristotle, Galen, Plato and Hippocrates into Syriac. His son then translated them into Arabic. The Syrian Christian Yahya ibn 'Adi (893-974) also translated works of philosophy into Arabic, and wrote one of his own, *The Reformation of Morals*. Throughout the Muslim world it was Christians and Jews (especially the latter), who did almost all the scientific research and enquiry at this time. And there is much evidence to suggest that the efforts of these scholars were often viewed by their Muslim masters with the deepest suspicion. Certainly there was not the encouragement to learning, much less to new research, that is so frequently boasted.

Even the limited number of "Arab" scholars who were not Jews and Christians were rarely Arabs. We are told that Al-Kindi was "one of the few pure Arabs to achieve intellectual distinction."[232] More often than not they were actually Persians. This was the case, as we saw, with the mathematician Al-Khwarizmi, and also with the great philosopher Avicenna, among many others. The Persian origin of so much "Arab" learning reminds us again that a great deal of what has been attributed to the Arabs was in reality Persian, and that, prior to the Islamicization of Persia in the seventh century, the country had, under the Sassanids, been a cultural and intellectual crossroads, bringing together the latest mathematics from India, the latest technology from China, and the latest philosophy from Byzantium; and making important contributions to all of these herself. This leads to the suspicion that "Al-Khwarizmi" and "Avicenna" (Ibn-Sina), were scholars of the Sassanid period, whose works were

---

[230] Thompson and Johnson, op cit., p. 175
[231] Ibid., p. 176
[232] Ibid., p. 178

translated into Arabic and their names "Arabized" during the Abbasid period – probably in the early eighth century.

Having said that, there is no question that for a short time – much shorter than in generally realized – the Arabs did permit and even encourage new research. That most of this research was not carried out by real Arabs is almost beside the point. At this stage, Islam did at least permit learning and research. But then again what kind of learning was it, and what was its purpose? Even Briffault admits that the early Arabs, those supposedly imbued with an almost unquenchable thirst for knowledge, had little or no interest in the histories and cultures of the great civilizations they conquered.[233] The truth of this is demonstrated in the fact that by the eighth century Arab writers had no idea who constructed the Great Pyramid or indeed any of the monuments of Egypt. Yet this knowledge had been widely available in the writings of such Classical authors as Herodotus and Diodorus, whose works were preserved in the great libraries of Egypt and Babylonia. Take for example the comments of Ibn Jubayr, who worked as a secretary to the Moorish governor of Granada, and who visited Cairo in 1182. He commented on "the ancient pyramids, of miraculous construction and wonderful to look upon, [which looked] like huge pavilions rearing to the skies; two in particular shock the firmament ..." He wondered whether they might be the tombs of early prophets mention in the Koran, or whether they were granaries of the biblical patriarch Joseph, but in the end came to the conclusion, "To be short, none but the Great and Glorious God can know their story."[234] The complete ignorance of the Arabs in this regard strongly suggests that they did indeed (as Christian polemicists for centuries argued) destroy much Classical literature – at least that literature not of any practical or utilitarian import. In Persia too, the newly-converted Muslims quickly lost track of their own inheritance. By the time of poet and mathematician Omar Khayyam (11th-12th century), the natives of the country had forgotten almost everything about their illustrious history. Thus the ancient city of Persepolis, capital of the Achaemenid kings Darius I and Xerxes, was believed by the poet to have been

---

[233] Briffault, "Of the poets and historians of Greece, beyond satisfying their curiosity by a few samples, they [the Arabs] took little account." op. cit., p.192
[234] Andrew Beattie, *Cairo: A Cultural History* (Oxford Univeristy Press, 2005) p. 50

built by the genie king Jamshid; and the same daemon was credited by him with raising the pyramids of Egypt. Islamic chroniclers in Egypt itself had their own mythical figures and genie-kings to whom they attributed the erection of the pyramids. Such was their regard from the literature of the classical age and for the critical method!

Within a short time worse was to follow. Muslim rulers began to systematically plunder the ancient monuments of Egypt, and an official department existed whose purpose was the location and despoilation of pharaohnic tombs. The larger monuments were plundered for their cut-stone, and Saladin, the Muslim hero lionized in so much politically-correct literature and art, began the process by the exploitation of the smaller Giza monuments. From these, he constructed the citadel at Cairo (between 1193 and 1198). His son and successor, Al-Aziz Uthman, went further, and made a determined effort to demolish the Great Pyramid itself.[235] He succeeded in stripping the outer casing of smooth limestone blocks from the structure (covered with historically invaluable inscriptions), but eventually cancelled the project owing to its cost.

And that attitude to learning was displayed in the treatment meted out to two of the biggest luminaries of Muslim Spain, Averroes and Maimonides. Despite being an Islamic judge, Averroes was banished, his books burnt, and he was forced to emigrate to Morocco (in 1195) where he died in 1198. Maimonides in his turn had to flee in order to escape Almohad persecution. He was to state that "the Arabs have persecuted us [Jews] severely, and passed baneful and discriminatory legislation against us ... Never did a nation molest, degrade, debase, and hate us as much as they." Jews could teach rabbinic law to Christians, but Muslims he said, will interpret what they are taught "according to their erroneous principles and they will oppress us. [F]or this reason ... they hate all [non-Muslims] who live among them." But the Christians "admit that the text of the Torah, such as we have it, is intact."

Louis Bertrand issued this cautionary note to those who extol Islamic learning: "When we are told about Musulman tolerance and about the cult of literature, science, and art at the court of the Caliphs, when the praises of the universities of Cordova, Seville, and Toledo are sung to us, it would be very naïve to judge them by our standards, and to see in these universities something

---

[235] Ibid.

like the Sorbonne, even that of the Middle Ages."[236] Illustrating his point, Bertrand looks at the work of the Arab historians. "The Arab 'histories,' as they are generously called, can only be regarded from our point of view as dry annalists or, in general, compilers without any critical faculty. As Gobineau has already remarked, in connection with the Persian writers, they do not possess the sense of what we understand by truth, or, more exactly, the sense of Yes and No. They have a hazy idea of the boundaries of history and poetry, properly so-called.

"Thus their histories are strewn with long fragments of poetry, to which they attribute the value of historical evidence; they accept the most fabulous legends and traditions without interpreting them; they fall into all kinds of Oriental exaggeration; and, when they quote figures, they let themselves go to astronomical valuations. As for marshalling of narrative and methodical exposition, nothing could be further from their habits of mind. Everything is put on the same plane – trivial incidents and important events which led to changes of regime or the fall of empires."

Bertrand complains too of the chopping of narrative into annual sections, a feature that "produces extraordinary complexity and intricacy, something like the inextricable labyrinth of lines in an arabesque." In the end; "These histories – if one dare give them that name – only too often leave us with the impression of an absurd and unintelligible chaos."[237]

Schools certainly existed in the Spanish Caliphate; yet they were not schools as we imagine them: "These schools ... were strictly sectarian, and the teaching was purely religious. Those which Hakam [II] subsidized were intended to 'teach the Koran' to poor children of the capital. That did not even mean that the children were taught to read and write in Arabic. Teaching the Koran means teaching recitation of the suras of the Holy Book by heart."[238] As for the "universities", Bertrand notes: "Learning, as we understand it, had only the most restricted place in them. It was regarded with suspicion by the religious intolerance of the faquis, which was often translated into very drastic prohibitions and persecutions. During periods of extreme rigour, all that was permitted to students of mathematics was to acquire the knowledge necessary to

---

[236] Bertrand, op cit., p. 22
[237] Ibid.
[238] Ibid., p. 75

orientate the mosques in the direction of Mecca and determine the seasons, the phases of the moon, and the exact hour of prayer. Everything else was regarded as dangerous."[239]

Some areas of research were more acceptable to the religious sensibilities of the imams: "Medicine and botany, by reason of their practical utility, escaped the severity of religious censorship. There were famous Spanish doctors and surgeons ... who were mostly of Christian or Jewish origin." Yet the medicine practiced "makes us smile to-day." And, "All this so-called science had nothing in common with ours. It was the liquidation of the old Greco-Latin empiricism plus an Alexandrine and Oriental endowment. It was a farrago which the modern age had to abandon." Bertrand concludes that, "The bulk of this teaching – terrible in its verbalism and almost entirely theological – reduced itself to some ideas of medicine, mathematics, and astronomy, but especially of astrology, alchemy, and demonology. The occult part of the Judeo-Arab learning was what most attracted the Christians, not only of Spain, but also of the whole of medieval Europe."[240]

The rejection of reason is said by some apologists for Islam to have been the fault of philosopher/theologian Al-Ghazali (1058-1111). Yet, as Catholic priest and physicist Stanley Jaki has explained, the rejection of reason is implicit in the Koran. There is no question that Al-Ghazali, one of the pillars of Islamic jurisprudence, "denounced natural laws, the very objective of science, as a blasphemous constraint upon the free will of Allah."[241] Yet from the very beginning, "Muslim mystics decried the notion of scientific law (as formulated by Aristotle) as blasphemous and irrational, depriving as it does the Creator of his freedom."[242] Robert Spencer quotes social scientist Rodney Stark who notes that Islam does not have "a conception of God appropriate to underwrite the rise of science. ... Allah is not presented as a lawful creator but is conceived of as an extremely active God who intrudes in the world as he deems it appropriate. This prompted the formation of a major theological bloc within Islam that condemns

[239] Ibid., p. 76
[240] Ibid., p. 157
[241] Stanley Jaki, op cit., p. 242
[242] Stanley Jaki, *The Savior of Science* (Regnery Gateway, Washington DC, 1988) p. 43

all efforts to formulate natural laws as blasphemy in that they deny Allah's freedom to act."[243]

Allah's freedom to act is seen all too clearly in the outlandish events of Muhammad's life, where sacred moral laws are broken by the Prophet and his followers, only to be vindicated – afterwards – by new "revelations" from Allah.

Allah's total freedom to act resulted in fatalism and the death of reason; a universe dominated by forces that are utterly incomprehensible. If my house is destroyed by lightning, it is the will of Allah; it has nothing to do with my failure to install a good lightning-rod. This was the very essence of what we now call "Medievalism". Islamic cosmology was explained thus by Maimonides:

Human intellect does not perceive any reason why a body should be in a certain place instead of being in another. In the same manner they say that reason admits the possibility that an existing being should be larger or smaller than it really is, or that it should be different in form and position from what it really is; eg, a man might have the height of a mountain, might have several heads, and fly in the air; or an insect might be as small as an insect, or an insect as huge as an elephant.

This method of admitting possibilities is applied to the whole Universe. Whenever they affirm that a thing belongs to this class of admitted possibilities, they say that it can have this form and that it is also possible that it be found differently, and that the one form is not more possible than the other; but they do not ask whether the reality confirms their assumption ...

[They say] fire causes heat, water causes cold, in accordance with a certain habit; but it is logically not impossible that a deviation from this habit should occur, namely, that fire should cause cold, move downward, and still be fire; that the water should cause heat, move upward, and still be water. On this foundation their whole [intellectual] fabric is constructed.[244]

---

[243] Robert Spencer, *Religion of Peace? Why Christianity is and Islam isn't,* (Regnery, Washington DC, 2005) p. 154, citing Rodney Stark, op cit., pp.20-1
[244] Moses Maimonides, *The Guide for the Perplexed* (M. Friedländer, trans.) (Barnes and Noble, New York, 2004)

HOLY WARRIORS

The rejection by Islam and the Islamic world of science and reason is illustrated by a number of significant events, such as the burning by El Mansur (Caliph of Cordoba, late tenth/earth eleventh century) with his own hand, of the "materialist and philosophical works of the library associated with Hakam II,"[245] as well as by the major and obvious facts, such as that by the thirteenth century Europe had overtaken the Islamic world in virtually every field of science and technology – though Islam had, just a few centuries earlier, inherited all the great centres of Greek and Babylonian learning, when Europe had to start from scratch. And here we need only note, by way of example, that during the Ottoman siege of Constantinople in 1453, the Islamic forces were quite incapable of building cannon with which to assault the walls of the city, and had to rely on the services of a Transylvanian defector: this in spite of the fact that both firearms and gunpowder were originally an Asiatic (Chinese) invention.

The rejection of rationalism and of reason itself is inherent even in Averroes, whose ideas, after all, were predicated on the notion that faith and reason were ultimately irreconcilable. His position has often been described, inaccurately, as the doctrine of the double truth: what is false in theology could be true in philosophy and vice versa, and that contradictory statements could therefore both be true depending on whether they were considered from the point of view of religion or philosophy. What he actually taught was more subtle. He believed that Aristotle's ideas on many issues (such as the eternal existence of the earth) were the results of sound reasoning, and that no fault could be found in the logical process that led to them. Yet these views contradicted divine revelation, as found in the Koran. As a philosopher, Averroes argued, he had to follow the results of reason wherever they led, but since the conclusions they reached contradicted divine revelation, they could not be true in any absolute sense. After all, what was feeble human reason against the omnipotence of God, who transcended it? It is difficult to see in this the beginnings of a scientific revolution on the lines of that which took place in Europe from the fifteenth and sixteenth centuries. Those who claim such have quite misunderstood the science of the Renaissance, which was most assuredly *not* based on the separation of faith and reason. If we doubt this, we need only

---

[245] Bertrand, op cit., p. 58

143

look at the life and thinking of the Renaissance scientist *par excellence*, Isaac Newton, whose guiding principle and *raison d'être* was the examination of the physical universe in order to reveal the majesty of God's design.

Islamic Attitude to War

It is perhaps superfluous to state that Islam is a militant religion, and that Muhammad himself preached the necessity of war and participated in violent conflict. Indeed, he is said to have ordered at least 60 raids and wars often involving massacres and personally participated in 27 of them. It is thus a modern myth that *jihad*, the duty of every Muslim, is an "inner, spiritual struggle." If words and facts have any meaning at all, then *jihad* means primarily physical violence and war directed against outside opponents, specifically "unbelievers." Gibbon, as unbiased an authority as may be found, attributed the spectacular success of Muhammad's faith to the promise of plunder. "From all sides the roving Arabs were allured to the standard of religion and plunder; and the apostle sanctified the licence of embracing female captives as their wives and concubines; and the enjoyment of wealth and beauty was a feeble type of the joys of paradise prepared for the valiant martyrs of the faith. 'The sword,' says Mahomet, 'is the key of heaven and of hell: a drop of blood shed in the cause of God, a night spent in arms, is of more avail than two months of fasting or prayer: whosoever falls in battle, his sins are forgiven ...'" (*Decline and Fall*, Ch. 50) And it cannot be stressed too strongly that all of the early spread of Islam involved the sword. Contrast this with the growth of Christianity, or Buddhism, for that matter. In fact, Islam is virtually unique among world religions in that its primary scriptures advocate the use of military force and its early expansion – indeed its expansion during the first six or seven centuries of its existence – invariably involved military conquest and the use of force.

In 1993 Samuel P. Huntington famously noted that "Islam has bloody borders."[246] He might have added that Islam has always had bloody borders. Before he died, Muhammad told his followers that he had been ordered to "fight

---

[246] Samuel P. Huntington, "The Clash of Civilizations?" *Foreign Affairs*, (Summer, 1993)

with the people till they say, none has the right to be worshipped but Allah." (*Hadith*, Vol. 4:196) In this spirit, Islamic theology divides the world into two parts: the *Dar al-Islam*, "House of Islam" and the *Dar al-Harb*, "House of War." In short, a state of perpetual conflict exists between Islam and the rest of the world. There can thus never be a real and genuine peace between Islam and the *Dar al-Harb*. At best, there can be a temporary truce, to allow Muslims to recuperate and regroup. In the words of Bat Ye'or, "the *jihad* is a state of permanent war [which] excludes the possibility of true peace." All that is allowed are "provisional truces in accordance with the requirements of the political situation."[247] And this is precisely what we find: In the long stretch of time since the life of Muhammad, it is doubtful if there has been a single year in which Muslims, in some part of the world, have not been fighting against Infidels. In the history of relations between Europe and the House of Islam alone, there was continual and almost uninterrupted war between Muslims and Christians since the first attack on Sicily in 652 and on Constantinople in 674. In the great majority of these wars, the Muslims were the aggressors. And even the short periods of official peace were disturbed by the "unofficial" activities of privateers and slave-traders. For centuries, Muslim pirates based in North Africa made large parts of the Mediterranean shore-line uninhabitable for Christians, and it is estimated that between the sixteenth and nineteenth centuries alone they captured and enslaved something in excess of a million Europeans.

At the opposite end of the Islamic sphere, in India and the Far East, war was equally endemic, and the horrors committed by successive Muslim invaders of India would need a volume in themselves to enumerate. Suffice to say that, lacking the limited protection extended to followers of religions "of the Book" (Christianity and Judaism), the Hindus and Buddhists of the Subcontinent suffered merciless slaughter and enslavement. This was violence on a completely unprecedented scale. Nothing like it had been seen before. It is true that by the sixteenth century Islamic rule was somewhat ameliorated under the wise and tolerant Mughals; but for centuries earlier this was not the case.

The seventeen incursions of Mahmud were particularly devastating. In the words of one historian; "Though the court chronicler Utbi clearly exaggerated his sultan's prowess when he claimed that ten thousand Hindu

---

[247] Bat Ye'or, op cit., p. 46

temples were destroyed in Kanauj [district of northern India] alone by Mahmud's sword, it is not difficult to appreciate the legacy of bitter Hindu-Muslim antipathy left by raids that may have taken even 1 percent of that toll."[248] In one of his most notorious attacks, Mahmud assaulted Somnath, whose inhabitants "stood calmly watching the advance of Mahmud's fierce army ... confident that Shiva, whose 'miraculous' iron *lingam* hung suspended within a magnetic field inside Somnath's 'womb-house,' would surely protect his worshippers from harm. Here, too, the chronicler probably exaggerated, for he wrote that fifty thousand Hindus were slain that day and that over two million dinars' worth of gold and jewels were taken from the hollow *lingam* shattered by Mahmud's sword. Yet the bitter shock of such attacks, whatever the factual sum of their deadly impact, was even more painfully amplified in the memories of those who had watched helplessly as friends and family were slain or enslaved by invaders who came to kill, rape, and rob in the name of God."[249]

One long-term consequence of these invasions was the virtual disappearance from India of the hitherto prevalent and pacifist Buddhism and its replacement by a form of Hinduism whose militancy is summed-up in the fact that its central scripture, the Bhagavad Gita, is an account of how the *avatara* Krishna urges his devotee (Arjuna) to take part in a bloody battle – in spite of the pacifist arguments advanced by the latter. The impact of Islam also saw the rise, in Northern India, of the even more militantly-inclined Sikh movement.

The centrality of war in Islamic theology is expressed succinctly by Ibn Abi Zayd al Qayrawani, who died in 966:

> Jihad is a precept of Divine institution. Its performance by certain individuals may dispense others from it. We Malikis [one of the four schools of Muslim jurisprudence] maintain that it is preferable not to begin hostilities with the enemy before having invited the latter to embrace the religion of Allah except where the enemy attacks first. They have the alternative of either converting to Islam or paying the poll tax (*jizya*), short of which was will be declared against them. The *jizya* can only be accepted from them if they occupy a territory where our laws

---

[248] Stanley Wolpert, *A New History of India* (Oxford University Press, 1982) p. 107
[249] Ibid.

can be enforced. If they are out of our reach, the *jizya* cannot be accepted from them unless they come within our territory. Otherwise we will make war against them ...

It is incumbent upon us to fight the enemy without inquiring as to whether we shall be under the command of a pious or depraved leader.

It is not prohibited to kill white non-Arabs who have been taken prisoner. But no one can be executed after having been granted the *aman* (protection). The promises made to them must not be broken. Women and children must not be executed and the killing of monks and rabbis must be avoided unless they have taken part in battle. Women also may be executed if they have participated in the fighting. The *aman* granted by the humblest Muslim must be recognized by other [Muslims]. Women and young children can also grant the *aman* when they are aware of its significance. However, according to another opinion, it is only valid if confirmed by the *imam* (spiritual leader). The *imam* will retain a fifth of the booty captured by the Muslims in the course of warfare and he will share the remaining four fifths among the soldiers of the army. Preferably, the apportioning will take place on enemy ground.[250]

Because the present study focuses primarily on Islam's impact upon Europe and European thinking, it behoves us to look at Islam's record in that part of Europe that came under Islamic domination: Spain. We need not repeat the assertion made, *ad nauseam*, that the Caliphate of Cordoba was a haven of peace and tolerance in a Europe benighted by ignorance and violence. It is doubtful if there exists, in any other area of world history, such a radical untruth which has achieved such wide currency. In reality, from the very start, Islamic rule in Spain was marked by the appearance of a barbarism and savagery such as Europe had not experienced since pre-Christian and even pre-Roman times. Louis Bertrand mentions an incident early in the conquest of a type that was to become all-too characteristic: "After the capture of Seville and Toledo, when Mousa met his lieutenant Tarik, whom he accused of peculation, he received

---

[250] Ibn Khaldun, *The Muqaddimah: An Introduction to History* Vol. 1 (Trans. Franz Rosenthal, Bollingen Series 43: Princeton University Press, 1958) p. 163. Cited from Bat Ye'or, op cit., p. 161

him with blows of a whip and ordered his head to be shaved. ... Later, when booty was being divided, he wanted to deprive another of his lieutenants of an important prisoner, the Christian governor of Cordova. 'It was I who made this man prisoner,' cried the officer, who was called Moghit, flying into a passion; 'they want to deprive me of him; very well, I will have his head cut off!' And he did so on the spot."[251] "Never," says Bertrand, "were these brutal habits to disappear completely from Musulman Spain. From one end to the other, the history of the Spanish Caliphate is strewn with severed heads and crucified corpses."

Bertrand describes some of the savage and inveterate feuding that characterized the first two or three years of Muslim rule. In his words, "the first part of this period, that of the Emirs dependent upon the Caliphate of Damascus ... is nothing but a long series of intestinal struggles, slaughterings, massacres, and assassinations.

"It was anarchy in all its horror, fed by family hatreds and the rivalry of tribe against tribe – Arabs of the North against Arabs of the South, Yemenites against Kaishites, Syrians against Medinites. All these Asiatics had a common enemy in the nomad African, the Berber, the eternal spoiler of cities and the auxiliary of all invaders."[252]

Executions, normally following torture, were most often by crucifixion. This was the fate even of the ninety year-old Abd el-Malik, who was beaten, slashed with swords and then crucified between a pig and a dog. "After that, Bertrand continues, "Yemenites and Kaishites ... came to blows among themselves. The Kaishites, under the leadership of their chief, Somail, routed their adversaries in the plain of Secunda, the Roman town on the other side of the Guadalquiver opposite Cordova. The victorious Somail had the Yemenite chiefs beheaded in the square in front of the Cathedral of Saint Vincent, which as yet was only half turned into a mosque.

"Seventy heads had already fallen when one of the chiefs in alliance with Somail protested against this horrible butchery, not in the name of humanity, but in the name of Musulman solidarity. Somail, nevertheless, went on with his

---

[251] Bertrand, op cit., p. 35
[252] Ibid., p. 36

executions until his ally, indignant at his excessive cruelty, threatened to turn against him."[253]

Again, "Nothing emerges from this perpetual killing but the savagery, the brutality, and the cruelty of the new-comers. Under their domination ... Spain got used to being ridden over and devastated periodically, in a way that soon became as regular as the alteration of the seasons."[254] This pattern, set at the beginning, continued throughout the Muslim period. The savagery inflicted upon fellow Muslims was but a pale reflection of the atrocities committed against the Christian unbelievers in the North, whose territory was raided twice a year by every Muslim ruler.[255] And to top all of this, Islamic Spain became the hub, as we saw, of a vast new slave-trade. Hundreds of thousands of European slaves, both from Christian territories and from the lands of the pagan Slavs, were imported into the Caliphate, there to be used (if female) as concubines or to be castrated (if male) and made into harem guards or the personal body-guards of the Caliph. According to Bertrand, "This army of Slavs [eunuchs] ... was the main instrument of the Caliph's authority. His power was a military dictatorship. He maintained himself only thanks to these foreigners."[256]

In such circumstances, the historian can surely be permitted a wry smile at the popular politically-correct definition of Islam as a "religion of peace."

Islamic Attitude to Slavery and to Women

In Chapter 2 we noted how by the sixth and seventh centuries Christianity had almost succeeded in bringing the institution of slavery to an end throughout the Mediterranean world. We found, however, in Chapter 3, that the invasions of Muslims and Vikings in the seventh to tenth centuries reinvigorated this ancient and repressive institution. And it needs to be stressed that here, once again, Islamic custom and practice was diametrically opposed to that of Christianity: For whereas Christianity acted to emphasize the equality of all before God and to alleviate the conditions of slaves, whose bodies were certainly not open to the

---

[253] Ibid., pp. 37-8
[254] Ibid., p. 37
[255] Ibid., p. 45
[256] Ibid.

sexual exploitation which was frequently the fate of the slave in classical antiquity, Islam had no problem whatsoever with slavery. Indeed, the taking of comely captives seems to have been seen, from the very beginning, as a legitimate bonus owed to the warriors fighting to spread the faith. Thus for example after the slaughter of the male members of the Jewish tribe of Banu Quraiza (of which more will be said shortly) Muhammad took one of the female captives as a concubine; whilst other successful military exploits of the Prophet invariably involved his procuring of slaves. And this behavior is fully sanctioned, for later generations, by the authority of the Koran. Thus, we read, in Sura 23: 5-6: "...abstain from sex, except with those joined to them in the marriage bond, or (the captives) whom their right hands possess - for (in their case) they are free from blame." See also Sura 4:24.

In the words of Robert Spencer, "The Qur'an says that the followers of Muhammad are 'ruthless to the unbelievers but merciful to one another' (48:29), and that the unbelievers are the 'worst of created beings' (98:6). One may exercise the Golden Rule [do unto others as you would have them do unto you] in relation to a fellow Muslim, but according to the laws of Islam, the same courtesy is not to be extended to unbelievers. That is one principal reason why the primary source of slaves in the Islamic world has been non-Muslims, whether Jews, Christians, Hindus, or pagans. Most slaves were non-Muslims who had been captured during jihad warfare."[257]

And, as we have seen, the Muslim advance meant the re-establishment, on a massive scale, of the slave trade, a trade which the Christian rulers of the late Roman Empire, particularly Justinian, had effectively ended. Historian Bat Ye'or says: "When Amr conquered Tripoli (Libya) in 643, he forced the Jewish and Christian Berbers to give their wives and children as slaves to the Arab army as part of their *jizya*. From 652 until its conquest in 1276, Nubia was forced to send an annual contingent of slaves to Cairo. Treaties concluded with the towns of Transoxiana [Iranian central Asia], Sijistan [eastern Iran], Armenia, and Fezzan (Maghreb) under the Umayyads and Abbasids stipulated an annual dispatch of slaves from both sexes. However, the main sources for the supply of slaves remained the regular raids on villages within the dar-al-harb [non-Islamic

---

[257] Spencer, *Religion of Peace,* p. 95

regions] and the military expeditions which swept more deeply into the infidel lands, emptying towns and provinces of their inhabitants."[258]

The most prized of slaves captured by the Muslim jihadis, from the very beginning, were female. Add to this the full acceptance and sanctification of the institution of polygamy, and we can readily understand how the position of women was adversely affected by the advent of Islam. Quite apart from the fact that huge numbers of women, both in the Middle East and in Europe, were enslaved and sold into harems, the fate even of women who voluntarily embraced Islam was dismal. Early Muslim travelers to Europe were astonished at the freedoms European women enjoyed – even in the non-Christian Scandinavian north. As Bernard Lewis says, "The difference in the position of women was indeed one of the most striking contrasts between Christian and Muslim practice, and is mentioned by almost all travelers in both directions. Christianity, of all churches and denominations, prohibits polygamy and concubinage. Islam, like most other non-Christian communities, permits both.... Muslim visitors to Europe speak with astonishment, often with horror, of the immodesty and forwardness of Western women, of the incredible freedom and absurd deference accorded to them, and of the lack of manly jealousy of European males confronted with the immorality and promiscuity in which their womenfolk indulge."[259]

As with war, it was the example of Islam's founder himself which set the pattern for the treatment of woman and slaves. And these two categories were closely connected: For one of the principal forms of booty derived from Muhammad's wars of conquest, were female slaves. Muhammad's favorite wife Ayesha once proclaimed, "I have not seen any woman suffering as much as the believing women [Muslim women]."[260] Although Muhammad himself had about sixteen wives (sources vary), Muslim law itself grants any man as many as four: "If ye fear that ye shall not be able to deal justly with the orphans, marry women of your choice, two or three or four." (Koran 4:3) The conditions in which these

---

[258] Bat Ye'or, *The Decline of Eastern Christianity under Islam: From Jihad to Dhimmitude* (Fairleigh Dickinson University Press, Madison, NJ, 1996), p. 108
[259] Lewis, loc cit.
[260] Al-Bukhari, Vol. 7, book 77, no. 5825

wives exist has always been one of profound insecurity. If a polygamous Muslim man is unhappy with any of his wives, he is under no obligation to put up with her. He is free to divorce her simply by saying "I divorce thee" three times. Women have no such power over husbands. Furthermore, any children of a divorcing couple normally go with the father, and he owes his wife no financial or any other kind of support.[261]

If all this were not bad enough, violence against wives is sanctified in Islamic law. Thus the Koran teaches that a husband may beat his wife as the third stage of a disciplinary process that begins with a verbal warning and follows by sending the woman to a separate bed:

> Men are in charge of women, because Allah hath made the one of them to excel the other, and because they spend their property [for the support of women]. So good women are the obedient, guarding in secret that which Allah hath guarded. As for those from whom ye fear rebellion, admonish them and banish them to beds apart, and scourge them. Then, if they obey you, seek not a way against them. Lo! Allah is ever High, Exalted, Great. (Koran 4: 34)

It goes without saying that these precepts have been adhered to throughout Islamic history; as have the precepts prescribing death for adultery. These, it is true, are not found in the Koran; yet Muhammad himself ordered the stoning of a woman for this "crime." Following from the example of the Prophet, Caliph Omar thus enshrined the custom in law; where it remains to this day.

Islam and the Jews

It is an oft-repeated charge that anti-Semitism, or hatred of the Jews, was implicit in Christianity. Yet even the most vociferous enemies of Christianity, and there are very many currently putting pen to paper, concede that there is little evidence for the existence of widespread anti-Semitism in Europe prior to

---

[261] Spencer, *Religion of Peace*, p. 183

the First Crusade. The one important exception to this, apparently, is the century of Visigoth rule in Spain between circa 612 and 711. Yet even here, it is admitted that anti-Jewish measures never went so far as violence against the person, and the truthfulness of many of the reports emanating from this epoch is questionable, to say the least. Certainly, the majority of the edicts said to have been issued by the Visigothic kings against the Jews seem to find strange echoes in the very real edicts against that people issued by the Spanish kings of the fourteenth and fifteenth centuries; and there are very good grounds for believing that much of the "history" of the Visigoth state of the seventh century was a forgery composed in the thirteenth and fourteenth centuries. More will be said on this topic in due course.

In fact, the first serious acts of violence ever committed against the Jews by Christians occurred at the inception of the First Crusade; and this rather sudden and dramatic change of attitude towards Jews, as we shall see, was intimately connected with the struggle against Islam. Indeed, it was from Islam itself, I shall argue, that Christians first learned the virulent form of Jew-hatred that became characteristic of the Middle Ages.

Anti-Jewish sentiment had of course existed even before the appearance of either Christianity or Islam. We need only take a look at the writings of Cicero, Diodorus Siculus,[262] Dion Cassius,[263] Tacitus,[264] or Justin[265] to be convinced. The Jewish concept of themselves as a "Chosen People" and their self-imposed segregation from other nations and peoples goes some way, or perhaps the whole way, in explaining the prejudice. Yet early Christianity, conspicuously enough, did not participate in this. Some Christian writers, it is true, criticized the Jews; but what they said about them was mild in comparison with what they said about Christian heretics, such as Gnostics, Manicheans, Donatists, etc. And criticism in a theological treatise can hardly be described as persecution. Indeed, as we saw in Chapter 2, such measures as were taken against the Jews by the Christian Emperors, especially Justinian, had an essentially political rather than religious motivation: The Jews had habitually allied themselves with the Persians against the Romans, both before and after

---

[262] Diodorus Siculus, xl.
[263] Dion Cassius, xxxvii, 121
[264] Tacitus, *Historia*, v, 1-9.
[265] Justin, xxxvi, 2, 3.

the Christianization of the Empire. Yet even in face of this, sanctions imposed by Christian Emperors tended to be no more severe than forcing the Jews to celebrate Passover at the same time as Easter and refusal to allow the construction of new synagogues. At no time were Jews subjected to violence, either by mobs or by Imperial sanction. One rather isolated instance of this occurred during the period of Cyril in Alexandria, when some Jews were killed by a mob, after several Christians had been killed by a Jewish mob. Thus in Christendom, and certainly in Europe, until the First Crusade there is little hint of anti-Semitism in any of its more virulent forms.

The same most certainly cannot be said of Islam.

From the very beginning, Islam was violently anti-Semitic. Anti-Semitism was a prejudice enshrined in both the actions and words of Muhammad. It would perhaps be superfluous to enumerate all the anti-Jewish pronouncements in the Koran and the Haditha, where they are portrayed as the craftiest, most persistent and most implacable enemies of the Muslims. In the Koran (2: 63-66) Allah transforms some Jews who profaned the Sabbath into apes: "Be as apes despicable!" In Koran 5: 59-60, Allah directs Muhammad to remind the "People of the Book" about "those who incurred the curse of Allah and His wrath, those whom some He transformed into apes and swine, those who worshipped evil." Again, in 7: 166, we hear of the Sabbath-breaking Jews that "when in their insolence they transgressed (all) prohibitions," Allah said to them, "Be ye apes, despised and rejected."

From the same sources we know that Muhammad's first action against the Jews involved the Qaynuqa tribe, who dwelt at Medina, under the protection of the city. Muhammad "seized the occasion of an accidental tumult," and ordered the Qaynuqa (or Kainoka) to embrace his religion or fight. In the words of Gibbon, "The unequal conflict was terminated in fifteen days; and it was with extreme reluctance that Mahomet yielded to the importunity of his allies and consented to spare the lives of the captives." (*Decline and Fall*, Chapter 50) In later attacks on the Jews, the Hebrew captives were not so fortunate.

The most notorious of all Muhammad's attacks against the Jews was directed at the Banu Quraiza tribe. This community, which dwelt near Medina, was attacked without warning by the Prophet and his men, and, after its defeat, all the males over the age of puberty were beheaded. Islamic authorities claim that Muhammad did not personally order the slaughter, but promised to abide by the decision of one of his commanders. When this man ordered the killing, Muhammad declared it to be the will of Allah, and permitted the slaughter to proceed. The doomed men and boys, whose numbers are estimated at anything between 500 and 900, were ordered to dig the trench which was to be their communal grave. All of the women and children were enslaved, with Muhammad personally taking for himself one of the prisoners. He also confiscated the communitiy's property. These deeds are mentioned in the Koran as acts carried out by Allah himself and fully sanctioned by divine approval. Thus in Koran 33:26-27, we read:

> And he brought those of the People of the Book [Jewish people of Banu Quraiza] who supported them from their fortresses and cast terror into their hearts, some of them you slew (beheaded) and some you took prisoners (captive). And he made you heirs of their lands, their houses, and their goods, and of a land which ye had not frequented (before). And Allah has power over all things.

The killing of the Jewish prisoners is sanctioned in Koran 8:67:

> It is not fitting for an Apostle that he should have prisoners of war until He thoroughly subdued the land...

The Massacre of Banu Quraiza was followed soon after by the attack on the Khaybar tribe. On this occasion, the Prophet ordered the torture of a Jewish chieftain to extract information about where he had hidden his treasures. When the treasure was uncovered, the chieftain was beheaded. This chieftain was the husband of the beautiful Safiyah, whose family members had been killed by the Prophet and his followers at the Banu Quraiza massacre. Now having beheaded her husband, the Prophet took Safiyah as his concubine. The story is told thus by Sahih al-Bukhari, whose compilation of the acts and deeds attributed to Muhammad was written in the ninth century, and forms one of the two pillars of Islamic jurisprudence. (Volume 5, Book 59, Number 512):

> The Prophet offered the Fajr Prayer near Khaybar when it was still dark and then said, "Allahu-Akbar! Khaybar is destroyed, for

155

whenever we approach a (hostile) nation (to fight), then evil will be the morning for those who have been warned." Then the inhabitants of Khaybar came out running on the roads. The Prophet had their warriors killed, their offspring and woman taken as captives. Safiya was amongst the captives, She first came in the share of Dahya Alkali but later on she belonged to the Prophet. The Prophet made her manumission as her 'Mahr'. Muhammad was sixty when he married Safiyyahh, a young girl of seventeen. She became his eighth wife.

The distribution of the booty is described thus in al-Bukhari Hadiths No.143, page-700:

> Sulaiman Ibne Harb…Aannas Ibne Malek (ra) narrated, "in the war of Khayber after the inhabitants of Banu Nadir were surrendered, Allah's apostle killed all the able/adult men, and he (the prophet) took all women and children as captives (Ghani mateer maal).. Among the captives Safiyya Bint Huyy Akhtab was taken by Allah's Apostle as booty whom he married after freeing her and her freedom was her Mahr."

It is said that at first Dihyah al-Kalbi, one of Muhammad's followers, asked for Safiyah. But when Muhammad saw her exquisite beauty, he chose her for himself and gave her two cousins to Dihyah.

In the massacre of the Jewish Settlement of Bani Mustaliq, Muhammad captured their women and took twenty-year-old Jewish girl, Juwayriya as his personal slave. [Al-Bukhari 3.46.13.717, p431-432]. Sahih Muslim (2.2349, p.520) says that Mohammed attacked the Banu Mustaliq tribe without any warning while they were heedlessly grazing their cattle. Juwairiya was a daughter of the chief. Sahih Muslim 3.4292, p.942 and Abu Dawud 2.227, p.728 and al-Tabari 39, p.182-183 also say Juwairiya/Juwairiyyah was captured in a raid on the Banu Mustaliq tribe. She had been married to Musafi' bin Safwan, who was killed in battle.

We need go no further into the details of these events, as they have already been examined by numerous writers and their veracity denied by no one. What we need to emphasize is the attitude these actions betray, as well as the

HOLY WARRIORS

fact that they became the model for the behavior of all future followers of the Prophet.

What caused Muhammad's seemingly implacable hatred of the Jews? According to Gibbon, it was their refusal to recognize him as their long-awaited Messiah that "converted his friendship into an implacable hatred, with which he pursued that unfortunate people to the last moment of his life; and, in the double character of apostle and conqueror, his persecution was extended into both worlds." (*Decline and Fall*, Ch. 50)

As noted above, it is a widely-held fiction that, aside from the Prophet's persecution of the Jews of Arabia, Muslims in general and Islam as a rule was historically tolerant to this People of the Book, who were generally granted *dhimmi* ("protected") status in the Islamic *Umma*, or community. *Dhimmi* status, also accorded to Christians, did not, as we have stressed, imply equal rights with Muslims. The truth is that the Jews, both under Muhammad himself and among his successors, were invariably the subjects of violence, exploitation and enslavement. The violence was not continuous, but the exploitation was. In their march of conquest across the Near East and North Africa, the Muslim armies in general treated the Jews appallingly; and the pattern established in the seventh and eighth centuries was repeated throughout history. It is a fact, for example, that the first massacres of Jews in Europe took place in Spain; but they were carried out by Muslims, not by Christians. The first recorded was in Cordoba, in 1011, and the second was fifty-five years later in Granada. The latter was the more serious. We are told that on December 30 1066, a Muslim mob stormed the royal palace in Granada, then part of Al-Andalus, assassinated the Jewish vizier Joseph ibn Naghrela and massacred most of the Jewish population of the city. "More than 1,500 Jewish families, numbering 4,000 persons, fell in one day."[266]

As shall be explained towards the end of the present volume, I am convinced that dates of the tenth and eleventh centuries need very substantial revision; and I will present evidence to suggest that the above massacres happened much closer to the lifetime of Muhammad. Yet even without a chronological readjustment, there is an evident line of continuity between the killings of Jews carried out in Arabia by Muhammad himself in the seventh

---

[266] Bernard Lewis, *The Jews and Islam* (Princeton, 1987) p. 54

157

century, and those carried out later by his followers. Anti-Jewish violence was therefore continuous and in itself sanctioned by Islamic law. Indeed, in Muslim eschatology, the End Times would be marked by a war of annihilation against the Jews. Thus Bukhari (Vol. 4, book 56, no. 2925), quotes Muhammad as saying, "The Hour [of the End Times] will not be established until you fight with the Jews, and the stone behind which a Jew will be hiding will say, 'O Muslim! There is a Jew hiding behind me, so kill him.'"

One of the most humiliating and noxious measures taken right from the start by Muslims against the *dhimmi* Jews was the requirement of wearing distinctive clothing by way of identification. This is enshrined in decrees first emanating from Caliph Umar, in the seventh century. Thus he wrote to an officer that:

> You have succeeded in forbidding any of them [dhimmi Jews and Christians] to resemble a Muslim by his dress, his mount, his appearance; that all should wear a belt (zunnar) at the waist similar to a coarse string, which each must knot in the middle; that their bonnets be quilted; that their saddles carry, instead of a pommel, a piece of wood like a pomegranate; that their footwear be furnished with double straps. That they avoid coming face to face with Muslims; that their womenfolk do not ride on padded saddles ...[267]

These discriminatory laws persisted as long as Islamic Sharia law survived, in some places into the second half of the twentieth century; and the demands made of Jews in particular to wear badges of identification were chillingly echoed in rules enforced by the Nazis during the 1930s and early 40s.

Early Islamic Culture: the Judgement of Archaeology

Until the nineteenth and twentieth centuries scholars were compelled to rely entirely on written sources for their knowledge of the ancient and medieval worlds. The competent historian of course always had the critical faculty with

---

[267] Bat Ye'or, *The Dhimmi*, p. 169

which to differentiate between fact and fable, between propaganda and honest reporting. There was also, from the seventeenth and eighteenth centuries, a more sophisticated form of textual criticism. Yet no matter how discerning the scholar, in the end all he had to work with was the written word. But this all began to change in the nineteenth century. From then on, scholars had something independent with which to check the claims of the chroniclers and annalists of old: the science of archaeology.

By the mid-twentieth century, archaeologists had begun to put together a fairly comprehensive picture of the archaeology of Europe and the Near East. Indeed, several areas of the Near East, such as Egypt, Palestine and Iraq, were and remain among the most thoroughly excavated regions of the earth.

Medievalists had of course been very interested in throwing light on the somewhat romantic though apparently fabulously wealthy and cultured Islamic world of the seventh, eighth and ninth centuries. Strange and wonderful tales were told of this epoch, though all agreed it was an age of high civilization. Indeed, the seventh to tenth centuries, as we saw, were regarded as the Islamic Golden Age. This was the age of the Omayyad and Abbasid Caliphs; the romantic epoch of Scheherazade and Harun Al-Rashid, the fabulously opulent Caliph of Baghdad, who is said to have donned the disguise of a commoner and wandered by night through the dimly-lit streets of the metropolis – a city of reputedly a million people. This epoch, and this alone, is said to have marked the age of Islam's cultural ascendancy. Consider the following description from an English historian of eighth-tenth century Cordoba, typical of the genre: "In Spain ... the foundation of Umayyad power ushers in an era of unequalled splendour, which reaches its height in the early part of the tenth century. The great university of Cordova is thronged with students ... while the city itself excites the wonder of visitors from Germany and France. The banks of the Guadalquivir are covered with luxurious villas, and born of the ruler's caprice rises the famous Palace of the Flower, a fantastic city of delights."[268] All are agreed that in later years, from the eleventh century onwards, the Islamic world began to fall rapidly behind the West

On the word of the written histories, then, archaeologists expected to find, from Spain to eastern Iran, a flourishing and vibrant culture; an Islamic world of

---

[268] H. St. L. B. Moss, *The Birth of the Middle Ages; 395-814* (Oxford University Press, 1935) p. 172

enormous cities endowed with all the wealth of antiquity and the plunder gathered in the Muslim wars of conquest. They hoped to find palaces, public baths, universities and mosques; all richly decorated with marble, ceramic and carved stone.

In fact, they found nothing of the sort.

The archaeological non-appearance of the Islamic Golden Age is surely one of the most remarkable discoveries to come to light in the past century. It has not achieved the sensational headlines we might expect, for the simple reason that a non-discovery is of much less interest to the public than a discovery. Then again, as archaeologists searched in vain through site after site, they imagined they had just been unlucky; that with the next day's dig the fabulous palaces and baths would be uncovered. And this has been the pattern now for a hundred years. In fact, the entire Islamic world is a virtual blank for roughly three centuries. Normally, we find one or two finds attributed to the seventh century, then nothing for three centuries, then a resumption of archaeological material in the mid- or late-tenth century. Take for example Egypt. Egypt was the largest and most populous Islamic country during the Early Middle Ages. The Muslim conquest of the country occurred in 638 or 639, and we should expect the invaders to have begun, almost immediately, using the wealth of the land to begin building numerous and splendid places of worship – but apparently they didn't. Only two mosques in the whole of Egypt, both in Cairo, are said to date from before the eleventh century: the Amr ibn al-As, AD 641 and the Ahmad ibn Tulun, AD 878. However, the latter building has many features found only in mosques of the eleventh century, so its date of 878 is controversial. Thus, in Egypt, we have a single place of worship, the mosque of Amr ibn al-As, dating from three years after the Muslim conquest, then nothing for another three-and-a-half centuries. Why, in an enormous country with up to perhaps five million inhabitants, should the Muslims wait over 300 years before building themselves places of worship?

And it is the same throughout the Islamic world. No matter where we go, from Spain to Iran, there is virtually nothing between circa 650 and 950. Spain, as we have seen, is supposed to have witnessed a flowering of Islamic culture and civilization in the two centuries after the Arab conquest of 711; and the city of Cordoba is said to have grown to a sophisticated metropolis of half-a-million people or more. We recall the description of a flourishing and vastly opulent metropolis painted by the writer quoted above. Yet the same author admitted that "Little remains of the architecture of this period." Little indeed. As a matter of fact, the only Muslim structure in the whole of Spain dating from before the eleventh century is the so-called Mosque of Cordoba; yet even this, strictly-speaking, is not an Islamic construction: It was originally the Visigothic Cathedral of Saint Vincent, which was converted, supposedly in the days of Abd er-Rahman I, to a mosque. Yet the Islamic features that exist could equally belong to the time of Abd er-Rahman III (latter tenth century) whom we know did conversion work on the Cathedral, adding a minaret and a new façade.[269] Most of the Islamic features in the building actually come after Abd er-Rahman III, and there is no secure way of dating anything in it to eighth century.

The poverty of visible Islamic remains is normally explained by the proposition that the Christians destroyed the Muslim monuments after the city's re-conquest. But this solution is inherently suspect. Granted the Christians might have destroyed all the mosques – though even that seems unlikely – but they certainly would not have destroyed opulent palaces, baths, fortifications, etc. Yet none of these – none at least ascribed to the eighth to early tenth centuries – has survived. And even assuming that such a universal and pointless destruction did take place, we have to assume that at least under the ground we would find an abundance of Arab foundations, as well as artifacts, tools, pottery etc. Indeed, in a city of half a million people, as Cordoba of the eight, ninth and tenth centuries is said to have been, the archaeologist would expect to find a superabundance of such things. They should be popping out of the ground with almost every shovel-full of dirt.

Now Cordoba has been extensively excavated over the past seventy years or so, often specifically to search for Arab/Moorish remains. What then has been found?

According to the prestigious *Oxford Archaeological Guide*, the city has revealed, after exhaustive excavations: (a) The south-western portion of the city wall, which was "presumably" of the ninth century; (b) A small bath-complex, of the 9th/10th century; and (c) A "part" of the Umayyad (8th/9th century) mosque.[270] This is all that can be discovered from two-and-a-half centuries of the history of a city of supposedly half a million people. And the rest of Spain,

---

[269] Bertrand, op cit., p. 54
[270] *The Oxford Archaeological Guide* (Collins, 1998) pp. 73, 119, 120

4: CONDITIONS UNDER ISLAM

which has been investigated with equal vigor, can deliver little else. A couple of settlements here and a few fragments of pottery there, usually of doubtful date and often described as "presumably" ninth century or such like.

The sheer poverty of these remains makes it clear that the fabulously wealthy Cordoba of the eighth, ninth and early tenth centuries is a myth; and the elusive nature of all material from these three centuries, in every part of the Islamic world, makes us wonder whether the rise of Islam has been somehow misdated: For the first real mark left (in archaeological terms) by Islam in Spain is dated to the mid-tenth century, to the time of Abd er-Rahman III, whose life bears many striking comparisons with his namesake and supposed ancestor Abd er-Rahman I, of the eighth century. Again, there are strange and striking parallels between the major events of Islamic history of the seventh and eighth centuries on the one hand and of the tenth and eleventh centuries on the other. Thus for example the Christian *Reconquista* in Spain is supposed to have commenced around 720, with the great victory of Don Pelayo at Covadonga; but the real *Reconquista* began three hundred years later with the victories of Sancho of Navarre around 1020. Similarly, the Islamic invasion of northern India supposedly commenced around 710-720 with the victories of Muhammad bin Qasim, though the "real" Islamic conquest of the region began with the victories of Mahmud of Ghazni, roughly between 1010 and 1020.

What then does all this mean?

The lack of Muslim archaeology from before the tenth and eleventh centuries (with the exception of two or three monuments such as the Dome of the Rock in Jerusalem and the Amr ibn al-As mosque in Cairo, usually of the mid-seventh century), would indicate that the rise of Islam has been misdated, and that some form of error has crept into the chronology. But error or not, the fact that virtually nothing from before the mid-tenth century has been found means that Islam was not a flourishing, opulent and cultured civilization whilst Europe was mired in the Dark Ages. By the late tenth century Europe was experiencing her own "renaissance", with a flowering of art and architecture, much of it strongly reminiscent of the Late Classical work of the Merovingian and Visigothic period.

The meaning of this archaeological "dark age", of central importance to our understanding of European and Islamic history, will be discussed again briefly in the Appendix.

162

CHAPTER 5

RESISTANCE ANDTRANSFORMATION

Christendom Besieged

he war Islam unleashed upon Christendom in the 630s was to continue unabated for centuries. To recapitulate briefly, the conquest of Egypt in 638 or 639 was followed by a general assault on the west, including North Africa and Mediterranean Europe. By the mid-600s, southern Italy and Byzantium had been attacked, and by 700 all of North Africa was subdued. Spain was next in the jihadis' sights, and the Straits of Gibraltar were crossed in 711. The Iberian Peninsula was quickly overrun, and shortly thereafter Muslim armies crossed the Pyrenees and penetrated into the heart of France. The whole of Europe was now in the utmost peril. A Frankish leader called Charles, the Martel, or "Hammer", famously halted them at Tours in 732. This gave Europe a breathing space, but it did not mean that the danger had gone away.

From the perspective of hindsight, of course, we now know that the Islamic tide had, for the moment, reached its high-point, and was afterwards, for some time, doomed to recede. But in the eighth century no one could have predicted that. The terror of the Islamic name, which had swept all before it in the preceding century, must have made Christians wonder whether the end time had come. We must bear in mind that, since its emergence from the Arabian Peninsula in the 630s, Islamic arms had been unstoppable, carrying, within a space of ninety years, the faith and the fanaticism of its followers from the borders of Jerusalem to the middle of France. And the Battle of Tours, though justly celebrated, did not mark the first or the last Islamic incursion into Gaul. It was not even the first Islamic reverse north of the Pyrenees. That is said to have occurred at Toulouse in 721, when an invading force from Spain was destroyed by Odo the Great, Duke of Aquitaine. Nor did the defeat at Tours bring Muslim incursions into France to an end. At the time, it must have seemed like only a temporary respite.

But if moderns fail to grasp the sense of terror and foreboding that must have gripped Europe at the approach of the Islamic armies, historians at least have recognized significance (mainly symbolic) of Charles Martel's victory. It is regularly listed as one of the pivotal battles of history; an event which change the course of civilization. According to Gibbon, an Islamic victory at Tours may well have led to the invasion and occupation of the rest of Europe, as far, at least, as the Rhine or Elbe, and the Islamicization of the continent. And an Islamic Europe must inevitably have led to an Islamic world.

Thus the battle to save Christendom itself was joined at the invasion of Spain, and the war for the Iberian Peninsula was to become a real clash of civilizations. From this point on, there was continual and incessant hostilities between the Muslims, ensconced in central and southern Spain, and the Christians of northern Spain and France. This great war of the civilizations was to last several centuries and was to see countless engagements between the two sides. These engagements, and the events surrounding them, had, from the very beginning, an especially brutal nature. The Muslim invaders saw Christian Europe as a bountiful source of booty and slaves; and the Islamic armies collected slaves both from the already subdued Christian populations of central and southern Spain and from the unsubdued populations of northern Spain and France. They also imported, from Viking slave-traders, vast numbers of Christian captives from further north, from northern France, England, Scotland and Ireland.

It is the contention of the present writer that the epic movement which we have come to know as the Crusades had its roots in this Muslim aggression. This is not, of course, the opinion now prevailing, which tends to see the Crusades as an unprovoked attack by a barbarous Europe against a quiescent and cultured Islamic world. One reason for this is the time-lag. Apparently four centuries had passed since the initial Muslim push into Europe and the European response. More will be said on this important topic in the Appendix. The other reason is political correctness; which sees only barbarism and aggression on the part of Christian Europeans. But this consensus is now increasingly challenged. Thus recently Bernard Lewis, himself no friend of medieval Christianity, has remarked: "We are now expected to believe that the Crusades were an unwarranted act of aggression against a peaceful Muslim world. Hardly. The first call for a crusade occurred in 846 CE, when an Arab expedition to Sicily sailed up the Tiber and sacked St Peter's in Rome. A synod in France issued an appeal to Christian sovereigns to rally against 'the enemies of Christ,' and the pope, Leo IV, offered a heavenly reward to those who died fighting the Muslims. A century and a half and many battles later, in 1096, the Crusaders actually arrived in the Middle East. The Crusades were a late, limited, and unsuccessful imitation of the jihad – an attempt to recover by holy war what was lost by holy war. It failed, and it was not followed up."[271]

For Lewis then "Holy War" was an idea copied by the Christians from the Muslims. We have already seen other ideas copied by Christians from Islam; the most important of which was the destruction of sacred art (iconoclasm). Now we see this other, and most portentous, concept imported into Europe from the Islamic world.

Conditions in Spain

We have noted that historians, especially those of the English-speaking world, tend to romanticize Islamic Spain and to demonize Christian, or more accurately, Catholic Spain. There are sound historical reasons reaching back to the Reformation why historians of the Anglosphere should do this, though to these has recently been added the politically-correct viewpoint that sees only barbarism and backwardness among Christians and among Europeans.

---

[271] Bernard Lewis, "2007 Irving Kristol Lecture," delivered to the American Enterprise Institute, Washington, DC. (March 7, 2007).

5: RESISTANCE AND TRANSFORMATION

The reality of Islamic Spain was of course quite contrary to this myth.

Even the most Islamophile of scholars have been forced to concede that, after the establishment of the Cordoba Caliphate by Abd er-Rahman III, Spain fell under the control of the intolerant and brutal Almoravids and Almohads. What is not spelled out so often is that conditions were almost as bad under Abd er-Rahman and his predecessors. According to Richard Fletcher, as Islamophile a writer as may be found, "The period of maximum turbulence and dislocation in the peninsula as a whole seems to have been the half-century or so after the outbreak of the Berber revolt in 740. Breakdown of public order, disruption of administrative structures and legal routines, faction fighting and vendettas, the forcible transfer of communities from one place to another, random slave-raiding and cattle-rustling – all the things to which Theodulf referred in one of his poems, perhaps with an inward shudder, as 'overwhelming disaster' – all of these must have had the gravest social and economic consequences, at which we can only guess. In some areas these would last for centuries. In the *tierras despobladas* olive groves and vineyards would go untended, grass and scrub would encroach on road and threshing floor, squatters in the abandoned towns would look round in alarm for their children at the thud of collapsing masonry. Cities like Salamanca would not rise from their rubble until the twelfth century."[272] This description of the country is restrained in the extreme and glosses over or ignores the horrific reality on the ground. For the war brought to Iberia by the Arabs and Berbers was like no other. According to Louis Bertrand, rapine and destruction was the order of the day from the very beginning: "To keep Christians in their place it did not suffice to surround them with a zone of famine and destruction. It was necessary also to go and sow terror and massacre among them. Twice a year, in spring and autumn, an army sallied forth from Cordova to go and raid the Christians, destroy their villages, their fortified posts, their monasteries and their churches ..."[273]

This raiding and pillaging, which continued throughout the entire period of Muslim domination, had terrible consequences: "If one bears in mind that this brigandage was almost continual, and that this fury of destruction and extermination was regarded as a work of piety – it was a holy war against the

---

[272] Fletcher, op cit., pp. 31-2
[273] Bertrand, op cit., p. 91

infidels – it is not surprising that whole regions of Spain should have been made irredeemably sterile."

As always, it was the war carried out against the non-combatants that was to be the most disruptive and shocking: "... the really lucrative part of the operation was the booty and the sale of slaves. Thousands of women and children, whole populations, were sold by auction."[274]

Inevitably, the Christians began to respond in kind: "... the Christians devoted themselves to similar extermination, as soon as they got the chance. Eye for eye, tooth for tooth – they replied to carnage with carnage, to executions with executions. Ordono II, King of Leon, had the head of the Musulman general nailed to the walls of the castle of Saint Etiennne de Gormaz, side by side with a boar's head. In both camps they spoke of each other mutually as 'dogs' and 'sons of dogs.'"[275]

The Christians thus began, at an early stage, to emulate the savagery of their foes. This was a phenomenon that was to continue and would eventually work a profound transformation on the Spanish character. And contact with Islam would produce the same result in all of the Christian nations whose shores were washed by the Mediterranean. At the same time, the savagery of the Viking wars in northern Europe, elicited also by the coming of Islam, would have a similar impact on the peoples of those regions. And the war to save Christendom and repel Muslims and Vikings would, in a very short time, transform the peoples of Europe in a fundamental way.

Islam's second Age of Conquest

According to conventional ideas, the seventh and eighth centuries constitute the great age of Islamic expansion. By the eleventh century – the time of the First Crusade – we are told that the Islamic world was quiescent and settled and that, by implication, the Crusaders were the aggressors. Indeed, the Crusaders are routinely portrayed as a horde of barbarians from a backward and superstitious Europe irrupting into the cultured and urbane world of the eleventh century Near East.

---

[274] Ibid., p. 92
[275] Ibid.,

5: RESISTANCE ANDTRANSFORMATION

This at least is the populist language often employed on television and in newspaper articles. Academia tends to be more circumspect. Nonetheless, the general consensus is the same: The threat of Islam had very little, if anything, to do with the Crusades; the Muslims were simply the convenient targets of a savage and brutal Europe, mired in a culture of habitual violence and rapine. The "energies" of Europe's warrior-class, it is held, were simply directed by the Papacy away from internal destruction onto the convenient targets of the Islamic world. This, for example, is the line taken by Marcus Bull in his examination of the origins of the Crusades in *The Oxford History of the Crusades*. In an article of almost ten thousand words, Bull fails to consider the Muslim threat at all. Indeed he mentions it only to dismiss it: "The perspective of a Mediterranean-wide struggle [between Islam and Christianity] was visible only to those institutions, in particular the papacy, which had the intelligence networks, grasp of geography, and sense of long historical tradition to take a broad overview of Christendom and its threatened predicament, real or supposed. This is a point which needs to be emphasized because the terminology of the crusades is often applied inaccurately to all the occasions in the decades before 1095 when Christians and Muslims found themselves coming to blows. An idea which underpins the imprecise usage is that the First Crusade was the last in, and the culmination of, a series of wars in the eleventh century which had been crusading in character, effectively 'trial runs' which had introduced Europeans to the essential features of the crusade. This is an untenable view."[276]

With what justification, we might ask, does Bull dissociate the earlier Christian-Muslim conflicts of the eleventh century in Spain, Sicily, and Asia Minor from the First Crusade? The answer can hardly be described as convincing. "There is plenty of evidence," he says, "to suggest that people regarded Pope Urban II's crusade appeal of 1095-6 as something of a shock to the communal system: it was felt to be effective precisely because it was different from anything attempted before."[277] Of course it was different: the Pope had called a meeting of all the potentates and prelates of Europe to urge the assembly of a mighty force to march to Constantinople and eventually to retake the Holy Land. It was new because of its scale and its ambition. But to

---

[276] Marcus Bull, "Origins," in Jonathan Riley-Smith (ed.) *The Oxford History of the Crusades*, p. 19
[277] Ibid.

168

thus dismiss the connection with what went before in Spain and Sicily – and Anatolia – is ridiculous. Such a statement can only derive from a mindset which somehow has to see the Crusaders as the aggressors and to thereby detach them from the legitimate defensive wars which Christians had been fighting in Spain and throughout the Mediterranean in the decades immediately preceding 1095.

The fact is, in the twenty years before the First Crusade, Christendom had lost the whole of Asia Minor and Anatolia, an area greater than France, and a region right on the doorstep of Europe. The ordinary peasants of Europe may not have been fully cognizant of the danger from the east, but the ruling classes and the Church could not have been anything but alarmed. Yet even if the peasantry and artisans of Europe knew little about Anatolia, they would certainly have had some knowledge of the Muslim threat. It is Bull's suggestion that they did not which is untenable. The advances of Abd er-Rahman III and Al-Mansur through northern Spain in the latter years of the tenth century would have sent a flood of Christian refugees into southern France; and the raids even into southern France which continued well into the eleventh century would have sent refugees from there fleeing into central and northern France.[278] These people would have spread knowledge of the danger throughout western Europe. Granted, peasants and manual laborers would have had a very imperfect understanding of Islam and what Muslims actually believed; but that is not the point: They knew enough to know that Muslims were enemies of Christ; that they waged war against non-combatants and enslaved women and children, and that they had conquered all of Spain and threatened France.

And this is a point that needs to be stressed repeatedly: The reality is that, far from being quiescent and peaceful, by the latter years of the tenth century Islam was once again on the march. Muslim armies waged wars of conquest against non-believers from one end of the Islamic world to the other; from Spain in the west to India in the east. Furthermore, this new aggression was not confined to the eastern and western extremities, for by the middle of the eleventh century Islamic armies were also on the move in the Near East, against the Christian kingdoms of Armenia, Georgia and Byzantium. Many aspects of this new Islamic thrust, particularly those which occurred around the beginning of the eleventh century in Spain and India, are strangely reminiscent of the

---

[278] Regarding Christian refugees from Spain to France, see Richard Fletcher, op cit., p. 31

5: RESISTANCE AND TRANSFORMATION

earlier Islamic expansion in the eighth century, and cause us to wonder, yet again, whether the birth of Islam has been misdated and moved into the past by several centuries. So, for example, we are told that the main Islamic invasion of India began with the conquests of Mahmud of Ghazni, a Turkish-speaking prince based in Afghanistan, who launched a series of 17 campaigns into Northern India. These began in 1001 and ended in 1026, just four years or so before his death; a series of campaigns, we should note, which caused immense destruction and loss of life in the country. By the 1020s Mahmud ruled an empire that included much of the Indus Valley, Afghanistan and Persia. Yet these conquests, at the start of the eleventh century, seem to echo those of Muhammed bin Qasim, three centuries earlier, who created an Islamic Empire in roughly the same region (circa 710).

It is strange too that Mahmud of Ghazni's name differs little from that of his predecessor. Only the "n" in Ghazni differentiates it from Qasim, a word which could equally well be written as Qasmi. And even more astonishingly, tradition seems to place Mahmud of Ghazni only five generations after Muhammad. We are told that his father Sebektagin was "the slave of the slave of the slave of the Commander of the Faithful [Muhammad]."[279]

In the western end of the Islamic world we encounter the same phenomenon. "In the tenth century," says Runciman, "the Moslems of Spain represented a very real threat to Christendom."[280] Under Abd er-Rahman III (912-961) the followers of Muhammad found a leader who promised to repeat the successes of the eighth century. As founder of the Cordoba Caliphate, he presided over a new age of splendour and military power. His forces battled the Christians to the north, and the boundary between the two religions was marked by the battles he fought. The most decisive of these were at Simancas (939), between Salamanca and Valladolid on the Duoro River, where he was stopped. These were areas that had been overrun by the Muslims two centuries earlier, though the Christians had apparently retaken them in the interim. In many ways then Abd er-Rahman III resembles his ancestor and namesake Abd er-Rahman I, who conquered these areas in the eighth century. And this new conquering impulse continued under Al-Mansur (980-1002), whose career was to see

---

[279] See Gibbon, Chapter 57
[280] Steven Runciman, *The History of the Crusades,* Vol. 1 (Cambridge, 1951) p. 89

Muslim power once again enveloping all of Spain, including the far north. He burned Leon, Barcelona and Santiago de Compostela, and, copying his Muslim predecessors almost three centuries earlier, advanced over the Pyrenees. We are told that in Al-Mansur's time, "Never had the Christians found themselves in such a critical position."[281]

It was the attacks of Al-Mansur that finally roused Christian Europe into undertaking the *Reconquista*, which commenced with the campaigns of Sancho III (called the Great) of Navarre and the Norman Baron Roger de Tony in the 1020s. Yet these events recall the earlier beginning of the *Reconquista* with the victory of Don Pelayo at Covadonga around 718.

Whether or not Islamic history needs to be shortened by three centuries, which seems to the present author a distinct possibility, there can be no doubt that by the end of the tenth and the beginning of the eleventh century Islam experienced a new epoch of expansion. Above all, in the middle of the Islamic world, a newly-converted race of nomads, the Turks, were about to launch a decisive episode in the war against Byzantium.

Re-establishment of the Western Empire

The most dramatic political consequence of the appearance of Islam was the re-establishment of the Western Roman Empire. Henri Pirenne rightly saw the crowning of Charlemagne by Pope Leo III on Christmas Day 800 as Emperor of the West as a defining moment in the history of Europe. This represented, symbolically at least, the final break between the West and the East, between the world of Latin Christendom and Greek Christendom. And the fact that this must have been a direct consequence of the growth of Islamic power is rather obvious, when we think of it. The Germanic kings who ruled western Europe during the fifth, sixth and early seventh centuries, regarded themselves (on the whole) as officers of the Empire, that is, officers of the Byzantine Empire. We recall that they bore titles like consul, and struck coins bearing the image of the Eastern Emperor. Only in the seventh century did the Merovingian kings dare to issue coins emblazoned with their own portraits. This occurred, as we saw,

---

[281] Bertrand, op cit., p. 57

during the time of Heraclius, the first Emperor to come into conflict with the Arabs. Here then we have unmistakable evidence of the beginning of the final rift between East and West and a vital clue as to its cause. Yet even then no one, not even the most powerful of the Merovingians, presumed to assume the title of Emperor. The power and prestige of Byzantine was as yet simply too great. Even if she did not possess the armies to crush such a usurper, she possessed the wealth to finance the enemies of her enemies – a wealth she used to great effect against opponents in Italy, Gaul, Spain and North Africa during the sixth and early seventh centuries.

The re-establishment of the Western Empire, with some or other of the Germanic kings of the region assuming the Imperial Purple, is therefore something we should almost expect after Islam brought Byzantium to her knees. And by the middle of the seventh century she was most assuredly in that position. All of Syria and North Africa had been irretrievably lost, her economy was ruined and, as we shall see, her cities (in the small portion of territory that remained to her) almost completely abandoned. Constantinople itself now stood in the greatest peril. The time was ripe for a new Emperor in the West. But such did not appear for another 150 years, or so we're told. Why did Charles the Great and his apparently very Germanic Franks wait such an enormous period of time before doing what commonsense would have dictated should have occurred around 650?

There are other problems with this "Carolingian Empire", the most pressing of which is the fact that hardly a single artifact or structure attributed to it can be assigned to the eighth and ninth centuries. Indeed, it can be shown that everything described as Carolingian belongs to a later epoch, mostly to the time of the Saxon Ottonian kings of the tenth century and their successors in the eleventh. Even the greatest of Charlemagne's monuments, the wonderful Aachen Cathedral, has been proved beyond reasonable doubt to belong to the mid-eleventh century.[282]

Now it is well-recognized that the Ottonian kings had much – very much – in common with the Carolingians, and we know that they were extremely active in promoting the "cult" of Charlemagne. Indeed, the cult of this king, the whole myth surrounding him, was an Ottonian creation; and the fact that

---

[282] For a detailed discussion of this topic, see. Heribert Illig, *Das erfundene Mittelalter* (Ullstein, Berlin, 2005)

virtually all artifacts described as "Carolingian" belong to the Ottonian period (tenth and eleventh centuries) makes us wonder whether the entire Carolingian Empire was an invention, for propaganda purposes, of the Ottonians. In this regard we note that the most striking parallel between the Ottonians and the Carolingians is also the most politically controversial: Both lines of Germanic rulers claimed the title of Emperor. And it was the Ottonians rather than the ephemeral or semi-legendary Carolingians who, in co-operation with the Papacy, definitively revived the Western Empire – the new Roman Empire which, in the time of Frederick Barbarossa, would be named the Holy Roman Empire. This, and not mythic reign of a king Charles, marked the definitive turning away from the East; the final break with Constantinople which was to produce a quite separate Latin Christendom in the West.

So, by the mid-tenth century, and after the epoch-making defeat of the Magyars at the Lechfeld, Otto I did what no German king had dared do before: He made himself Emperor. This step, three centuries after we would expect it (and three centuries after the Germanic kings of the West had ceased to emblazon the image of the Byzantine Emperor on their coinage), was designed specifically to protect Western Christendom from the enemies who threatened its destruction. The events surrounding Otto's assumption of the Imperial Purple strikes one, at first, as almost accidental. In 962, Pope John XII, at the mercy of Berenger II, appealed to Otto, then Duke of Saxony, for help. Otto had recently married the widow of Berenger's predecessor, and was the strongest power in northern Italy. He hurried to Rome, where John hastily crowned him Emperor. Berenger surrendered soon afterwards, leaving Otto supreme, and the Empire of the West reborn. This was an institution that was "to continue virtually uninterrupted to the age of Napoleon."[283] We are told that Otto's overriding ambition was "to restore his empire to the power and prosperity it had enjoyed under Charlemagne."[284] He spent a great deal of his eleven-year reign in Italy, where the idea of a German Emperor was still evidently unpalatable – especially in Rome. In 966 he was faced with serious riots in the city, which he quelled only after he had hanged the prefect of the city by his hair from the equestrian statue of Marcus Aurelius in front of the Lateran.[285]

---

[283] John Julius Norwich, op cit., p. 95
[284] Ibid.
[285] Ibid. pp. 95-6

5: RESISTANCE ANDTRANSFORMATION

Notwithstanding the problems Constantinople faced with the Saracens, the Byzantines were by no means happy with the revival of the Western Empire – the whole territory of which they evidently saw as still rightfully theirs. In the ensuing conflict, Otto attempted to seize Apulia and Calabria, but the Greeks' hold on their Italian provinces was too strong for him. Having failed by war, he tried diplomacy, and married his son and heir to the Byzantine princess Theophanou. She came with a generous dowry which did not, however, include southern Italy.

Otto's son Otto II endeavored to continue his father's policy of building a strong and united Western Europe (under him of course) and thereby preparing for the repulse of Christendom's enemies. He undertook campaigns against the Danes and Bohemians, and reasserted the Empire's unity by subduing insurgent Bavaria, which he reduced in size and partitioned. To further strengthen Imperial authority, he successfully invaded France and shortly thereafter attempted to unite Italy under his authority by a campaign against both Muslims and Byzantines in the south. Here however he suffered a crushing defeat at Cotrone (982), news of which induced the Slavs and Danes to rebel. He died of malaria shortly thereafter while preparing another Italian campaign, and was the only German Emperor to be buried in Rome. His son by Theophanou, Otto III, "proved a strange contrast to his forebears, combining the ambitions of his line with a romantic mysticism clearly derived from his mother and forever dreaming of a great Byzantinesque theocracy that would embrace Germans, Italians, Greeks and Slavs, with God at its head and Pope and Emperor His twin viceroys."[286]

Notwithstanding his enthusiasm for the recreating of the glories of Rome, the young German theocrat was still evidently not acceptable to his Roman subjects. He had barely left Rome after his coronation than the city rose once again in revolt. He returned in strength two years later, restored the German visionary Gregory V to the Papacy, and built himself a magnificent palace on the Aventine. "Here he passed the remaining years of his life in a curious combination of splendour and asceticism, surrounded by a court stiff with Byzantine ceremonial, eating in solitude off gold plate, occasionally shedding his purple dalmatic in favour of a pilgrim's cloak and trudging barefoot to some

---

[286] Ibid., p. 96

174

distant shrine."[287] We know that in 999 he elevated his old tutor Gerbert of Aurillac to the Papacy under the name of Sylvester II. "Gerbert was not only a distinguished theologian; he was also the most learned scientist and mathematician of his time, and is generally credited with having popularized Arabic numerals and the use of the astrolabe in the Christian west. For a Pope of such caliber the Romans should have been grateful to their Emperor, but Otto tried their patience too hard and in 1001 they expelled him from the city. He died the following year, leaving, as might have been expected, no issue. He was twenty-two."[288]

If Otto's tutor Gerbert introduced Arabic numerals, then he himself was responsible for the equally portentous introduction of the *anno domini* system of dating the calendar. But his method of counting the number of years back to the birth of Christ left much to be desired, and has had far-reaching consequences, as we shall see at a later stage.

The Western Empire was thus re-established with a German, for the first time, wearing the purple. The time was ripe for a major counterattack against Islam.

The *Reconquista* and the Beginnings of Crusading

Whilst these momentous events were occurring at the centre of Europe, the war for the possession of Spain raged unabated. By the start of the eleventh century the conflict reached a turning-point, and from then on the Christians began the long process of driving the Muslims back. This war, known as the *Reconquista*, was a true clash of civilizations. It became, not just among the Spaniards and southern French, but throughout Europe, a *cause célèbre*. As soon as the Viking and Magyar menace began to subside, that is, by the first decades of the eleventh century, knights from England and from the Empire (mainly Germany and Italy) and above all France, rallied to the cause. The last great shrine of northern Spain free from Islamic control, the Shrine of Saint James in Asturias – Santiago de Compostela – became a center of pilgrimage for the pious of all Europe. The struggle was, from the beginning, of transnational significance. The

---

[287] Ibid.
[288] Ibid.

pilgrimage to the Shrine became, as well as an act of personal piety, a political act of defiance against the infidel enemy to the south.

The Crusades then, properly speaking, began with the *Reconquista* in Spain. Yet here again we encounter a curious chronological anomaly: For according to the history books, the *Reconquista* began in the eighth century with the victory of Don Pelayo at Covadonga. This earlier Reconquista, commencing around 720, roughly three centuries before the real thing in the eleventh century, also began in the extreme north of the country, when Spain was in danger of being completely overwhelmed by the Muslims. Nevertheless, it was only in the 1020s, with the victories of the Norman Roger de Tony, that the real *Reconquista* got going; and by 1085 the fall of Toledo to the Christians proved to be a watershed in the protracted struggle. This strange 300-year gap between the start of the *Reconquista* around 720 and the "second" start around 1020 is a phenomenon we have already encountered in other areas of the Early Middle Ages: Events of the seventh and eighth centuries finding an "echo" three hundred years later in events of the tenth and eleventh centuries. Here then is one more vital clue to a great distortion of history caused apparently by a faulty chronology; a distortion which has twisted our perception of this whole epoch. We repeat, it is universally held that the Crusades were launched by a barbarous and aggressive Europe against a settled and quiescent Islamic world. If however the chronology is wrong (and there is much evidence to suggest that it is), then the Crusades were part of a general European response to an aggressive Islam whose onslaught against Christendom had not yet reached its high water mark.

Ignoring for the present the chronological question, let us take up the story in the tenth century, when it is known that the war for possession of the Iberian Peninsula raged throughout the land. And it was in this century too that the Viking raids reached a peak of intensity, whilst the Magyars were launching their devastating incursions into the West. Just as in the seventh century, it seemed that Christendom was on the verge of collapse. Whilst the Muslims pushed northwards towards the Pyrenees and beyond (supposedly repeating the progress they had made three centuries earlier), the Vikings, incited by the prospect of Muslim gold, brought devastation to the coastlands of north-western Europe. And now their ambitions reached new heights. In 911 a huge territory in northern France was granted by the French king to a group of Norwegian Vikings under Rollo, with the aim of establishing them as a buffer against other

HOLY WARRIORS

Viking raiders, whilst in England the Vikings of Denmark seized half the country and fought hard to possess the remainder.

The struggle to save the surviving remnants of Christendom grew more intense.

All during this time the war for possession of Spain continued unabated. The whole of Europe, indeed, was engulfed in war – a war of the most brutal and total variety imaginable. This was war waged specifically against non-combatants, peasants and village folk, who were themselves the main prize of victory; the main booty sought by both the Muslims and Vikings. A new brutality, a new callousness, entered European life; a callousness which not even Christianity could fully ameliorate. It is a cliché that violence begets violence, and yet, like all clichés, it contains more than a germ of truth. Christian warriors, knights from France and Germany, who fought and repulsed the Vikings and the Moors, began with increasing frequency to take vengeance on their enemies in like manner. As these wars dragged on, this tit for tat violence only intensified in ferocity.

Yet all the while, the military situation did improve. By the end of the tenth century, and following the conversion of many Danish and Norwegian rulers to Christianity, the Viking threat began slowly to abate. There still however remained the threat of the Muslims, whose advance through Spain towards the Pyrenees and beyond showed no signs of interruption. Their raids too, both by land and by sea – in search of slaves – remained an urgent problem.

As we have seen, the North of Spain was the one part of the Peninsula that had never succumbed to the armies of Islam. Now, at the beginning of the eleventh century, the Christians of the West signaled their intention of making the region a base for the re-conquest of all Iberia and a symbol of the endurance of Christianity. It was alleged that the tomb of Saint James, one of the apostles of Jesus, who is said to have ended his days in Spain, was discovered in a remote part of Galicia. The establishment of a shrine at the spot made him in a very real sense the inspiration for the Re-conquest, and the saint himself became known as *Santiago Matamoros* ("Saint James the Moor-Slayer"). Pilgrimages were organized from all over Europe to the shrine, with a well-defined route, supplied with hostels, leading south from Paris through Aquitaine, across the Pyrenees and along the Cantabrian Mountains. Many, indeed most, of the

5: RESISTANCE ANDTRANSFORMATION

pilgrims were warriors, who would subsequently take part in the struggle against the Muslims.

These were the first crusaders.

While the *Reconquista* was raging in Spain, other theatres of combat with Islam were not lacking. Muslim pirates and slave-traders were continually being confronted all along the southern coastlands of France and the shores of Italy. In 1057 things were taken a stage further by the arrival in southern Italy of the Norman adventurer Robert Guiscard. First he captured the "toe of Italy", Calabria, from the Byzantines, a territory that provided him with a base for the invasion and conquest of the Muslims in Sicily. Meanwhile the maritime states of Pisa, Genoa and Catalonia were all actively fighting Islamic strongholds in Majorca and Sardinia, freeing the coasts of Italy and Catalonia from Moorish raiders.

It is known and recognized that following the end of the wars with the Vikings and Magyars in the eleventh century, huge numbers of men remained in arms throughout Europe, and the energies of these warriors were often misplaced fighting one another and terrorizing the local population. The Church tried to stem this violence with the so-called Peace and Truce of God movements. These were partially successful, but trained soldiers always sought an outlet for their skills, which were, with the end of the Magyar and Viking threats, becoming scarcer in northern Europe. Spain and southern Italy provided important exceptions, where the wars against the Muslims continued unabated and with increasing ferocity. All the major battles between Christians and Muslims in Spain during the eleventh century involved large numbers of knights and foot-soldiers from all over Western Europe, but especially from France and Germany. At the taking of Toledo, for example, the Burgundians played a pivotal role.[289]

It cannot be emphasized too strongly that, unlike the wars against the Vikings and Magyars, these battles were specifically about religion. They had been thus defined by the Muslims themselves. Their conquests all over North Africa and Asia had been motivated specifically to spread the faith. Now Christians began to think of their own endeavors in similar terms; and it is now

---

[289] Trevor-Roper, op cit., p. 119

widely accepted amongst professional historians that the Christians of this time derived the concept of "Holy War" from Islam.[290]

The official religious sanction for the concept came in 1063, when Pope Alexander II gave his blessing to the Iberian Christians in their struggle, granting both a papal standard (*vexillum sancti Petri*) and an indulgence to those who fell in battle.

We should note that there was much soul-searching in the minds of Christian theologians and lay people at this time. The concept of fighting – and killing – for Christ was something quite new. It had of course long been taken for granted that defensive war was permitted – though even this, in an earlier age of Christianity, had been the subject of much controversy. For centuries, however, Christians had had to accustom themselves to using the sword in defense of their homes and families. And the arrival in Western Europe if the Germanic peoples in the fourth and fifth centuries had seen the appearance of a new ruling class thoroughly steeped in warrior culture. This had, over the next two or three centuries, been modified by the Christian ethos, though somewhat more than a trace of the Germanic warrior ideal survived in the medieval institution of the knight. The knight represented a mildly Christianized version of the Teutonic warrior-hero; and his transformation into a Crusading Holy Warrior cannot have been too difficult.

Nonetheless, the idea of fighting and killing for Christ still sat uneasily with Christian teaching – and this held good right throughout the Crusader period. In Runciman's words, "The Christian citizen had a fundamental problem to face: is he entitled to fight for his country? His religion is a religion of peace; and war means slaughter and destruction. The earlier Christian Fathers had no doubts. To them war was wholesale murder."[291] Runciman goes on to note that the rise of the Germanic kingdoms brought with it the glamorization of the warrior-hero and the knight, against which "the church could do little." Nonetheless, there was still resistance, especially in the East. Saint Basil, for example, maintained that anyone guilty of killing in war should refrain for three

---

[290] See above, Bernard Lewis, "2007 Irving Kristol Lecture," delivered to the American Enterprise Institute, Washington, DC. (March 7, 2007).
[291] Runciman, op cit., p. 83

years from taking communion as a sign of repentance.[292] In fact, as Runciman notes, the Byzantine soldier was not treated as a murderer; but his profession brought him no glamour. "Byzantine history was remarkably free of wars of aggression. ... Justinian's campaigns had been undertaken to liberate Romans from heretic barbarian governors, Basil II's against the Bulgars to recover imperial provinces and to remove a danger that menaced Constantinople. Peaceful methods were always preferable, even if they involved tortuous diplomacy or the payment of money. ... The princess Anna Comnena, one of the most typical of Byzantines, makes it clear in her history that, deep as was her interest in military questions and much as she appreciated her father's success in battle, she considered war a shameful thing, and a last resort when all else had failed, indeed in itself a confession of failure."[293]

The western point of view was less enlightened, and there is no question that Western Christendom, after having had to absorb the warrior ideals of the Goths, Franks and Vandals, and having then to fight a life-and-death struggle against Muslims, Vikings and Magyars, was more amenable to the idea of fighting for Christ. In Runciman's words, "the military society that had emerged in the West out of the barbarian invasions inevitably sought to justify its habitual pastime. The code of chivalry that was developing, supported by popular epics, gave prestige to the military hero; and the pacifist acquired a disrepute from which he has never recovered. Against this sentiment the Church could do little."[294]

The Seljuks and the First Crusade

The end result of the First Crusade was the establishment of a series of Christian kingdoms along the coastal regions of Syria and Palestine; and the taking of Jerusalem in 1098 marked the definitive point of the campaign. Perhaps because of this, the idea has entered popular culture that the conquest of the Holy Land was always the primary goal. But this was not the case. In fact, the First Crusade

---

[292] J. P. Migne, *Patrologiae Graeco-Latina*, Part II of *Patrologiae Cursus Completus*, (Paris, 1857-66), Letter no. 188, Vol. XXXII, col. 681
[293] Runciman, op cit., pp. 83-4
[294] Ibid., p. 84

was originally designed as a defensive measure to halt the westward encroachment of Islam. The two decades preceding 1095 had seen the loss of virtually all of the Eastern Empire's Asiatic territories, and Muslim forces now stood ready at the fortress of Nicaea, threatening the very existence of Constantinople itself.

And this is a crucial point to remember: Islam in the eleventh century was an aggressive and expansionist force; and the proselytizing energy of the faith, which seemed to spend itself in the eighth century, now, three hundred years later, reawakened.

It is not the place here to go through the story of how the nomadic Turks of Central Asia were converted to Islam and how, upon the death of Mahmud of Ghazni – the Islamic conqueror of India – they seized the kingdom of Persia and became, *de facto*, the rulers of the entire Islamic world from the borders of Egypt to the Indus Valley. In 1038 they appointed as their Sultan a warrior called Togrul Beg, grandson of Seljuk, from whom the dynasty derived its name. In 1050, with all the enthusiasm of the recent convert, Togrul Beg undertook Holy War against the Christians of Anatolia, who had thus far resisted the power of the Caliphs. We are told that 130,000 Christians died in the war, but that, upon Togrul Beg's death in 1063 the Christians reasserted their independence and freedom. This was however to be of short duration, and no sooner had Togrul Beg's nephew Alp Arslan been proclaimed Sultan than the war was renewed. In 1064 the old Armenian capital of Ani was destroyed; and the prince of Kars, the last independent Armenian ruler, "gladly handed over his lands to the [Byzantine] Emperor in return for estates in the Taurus mountains. Large numbers of Armenians accompanied him to his new home."[295] Indeed, at this time, the entire Armenian nation was effectively transplanted hundreds of miles to the south and west.

But the Turkish attacks continued. From 1065 onwards the great frontier-fortress of Edessa was assaulted yearly. In 1066 they occupied the pass of the Amanus Mountains, and next spring they sacked the Cappadocian metropolis of Caesarea. Next winter the Byzantine armies were defeated at Melitene and Sebastea. These victories gave Alp Arslan control of all Armenia, and a year

---

[295] Ibid., p. 61

5: RESISTANCE ANDTRANSFORMATION

later he raided far into the Empire, to Neocaesarea and Amorium in 1068, to Iconium in 1069, and in 1070 to Chonae, near the Aegean coast.[296]

These events make it perfectly clear that the Turks now threatened all the of Empire's Asiatic possessions, with the position of Constantinople herself increasingly insecure. The imperial government was forced to take action. Constantine X, whose neglect of the army was largely responsible for the catastrophes which now overwhelmed the Empire, had died in 1067, leaving a young son, Michael VII under the regency of the Empress-mother Eudocia. Next year Eudocia married the commander-in-chief, Romanus Diogenes, who was raised to the throne. Romanus was a distinguished soldier and a sincere patriot, who saw that the safety of the Empire depended on the rebuilding of the army and ultimately the reconquest of Armenia.[297] Within four months of his accession, Romanus had gathered together a large but unreliable force and set out to meet the foe. "In three laborious campaigns," writes Gibbon, "the Turks were driven beyond the Euphrates; in the fourth, and last, Romanus undertook the deliverance of Armenia." (Ch. 57) Here however, at the seminal battle of Manzikert (1071), he was defeated and captured and all of Anatolia was irretrievably lost.

Any honest reading of these events leaves us in no doubt whatsoever that the aggressor was Alp Arslan and his Turks, and that Romanus Diogenes' march into Armenia was a last-ditch counter-attack by the Byzantines to prevent the loss of all of Anatolia and Asia Minor. Yet observe how the battle is described in the recently-published *Chambers Dictionary of World History*: "The Byzantine Emperor, Romanus IV Diogenes (1068/71), tried to extend his empire into Armenia but was defeated at Manzikert near Lake Van by the Seljuk Turks under Alp Arslan (1063/72), who then launched a full-scale invasion of Anatolia."[298]

We see in the above a graphic example of the disinformation disseminated by the mentality of political correctness, where the victim is transformed into the aggressor and the aggressor portrayed as the victim.

Alp Arslan was killed a year later, and the conquest of Asia Minor, virtually all that was left of Byzantium's Asiatic possessions, was completed by

---

[296] Ibid.
[297] Ibid.
[298] Bruce Lenman (ed.) *Chambers Dictionary of World History* (2000) p. 585

his son Malek Shah (1074 – 1084). These conquests left the Turks in possession of the fortress of Nicaea, on the southern shore of the Sea of Marmara, and the survival of Constantinople in question.

These then are the major political events which prefigured the First Crusade. Within a space of thirty-five years the Turks had seized control of Christian territories larger than the entire area of France, and they now stood poised on the very doorstep of Europe. We are accustomed to think of the Crusades as first and foremost an attempt by Christians to retake the Holy Land and Jerusalem; but this is a mistake. The Emperor Alexius Comnenus now made his famous plea to the Pope, not to free Jerusalem, but to drive the Turks from his door, to liberate the huge Christian territories in Asia Minor and Anatolia that had so recently been devastated and annexed by the followers of the crescent. It is true, of course, that the Turks, who had also assumed control of Syria/Palestine, now imposed a barbarous regime in that region; and that the sufferings of Christian pilgrims in that region, described so vividly by Peter the Hermit and others, provided a powerful emotional impetus to the Crusading movement among ordinary Europeans; but the relief of pilgrims was not – to begin with at least – the primary goal of the Crusaders. Nonetheless, the barbarous nature of the Turkish actions in Palestine was a microcosm of their behavior throughout the Christian regions which they conquered, and the nature of their rule in the entire Near East is described thus by Gibbon in his usual vivid manner:

"The Oriental Christians and the Latin pilgrims deplored a revolution, which, instead of the regular government and old alliance of the caliphs, imposed on their necks the iron yoke of the strangers of the north. In his court and camp the great sultan had adopted in some degree the arts and manners of Persia; but the body of the Turkish nation, and more especially the pastoral tribes, still breathed the fierceness of the desert. From Nicaea to Jerusalem, the western countries of Asia were a scene of foreign and domestic hostility; and the shepherds of Palestine, who held a precarious sway on a doubtful frontier, had neither leisure nor capacity to await the slow profits of commercial and religious freedom. The pilgrims, who, through innumerable perils, had reached the gates of Jerusalem, were the victims of private rapine or public oppression, and often sunk under the pressure of famine and disease, before they were permitted to salute the holy sepulcher. A spirit of native barbarism, or recent zeal, prompted the Turkmans to insult the clergy of every sect; the patriarch was dragged by the hair along the pavement and cast into a dungeon, to extort a ransom from the sympathy of his flock; and the divine worship in the church of the Resurrection was often disturbed by the savage rudeness of its masters." (Chapter 57)

Crusaders and Jews

The First Crusade began, notoriously, with a massacre of Jews in Germany and Bohemia. This was the first, though sadly not the last, violent attack against the Jews of Europe by Christians. During the pogroms of 1096, which were led by three robber-barons named Emich, Volkmar and Gottschalk, Jews were given the choice of Christian baptism or death. Many chose death. In all, perhaps three thousand were killed. Christian churchmen and princes made attempts to save the persecuted communities, and several were also rescued by the payment to the "Crusaders" of a huge bribe. Of these massacres, Gibbon states that the Jews had received no such blow since the days of Hadrian, though in this he is mistaken: for he neglects to mention the atrocities carried out by the Muslims in Cordoba in 1011, when about two thousand perished; in Fez (Morocco) in 1033, when between five and six thousand Jews lost their lives; and again in Granada (Spain) in 1066, when an estimated three thousand were murdered.[299] Still, the massacres in Germany were the first carried out by Christians, and they were to become the blueprint for future persecutions of the Jews. As such, they deserve our close attention.

It goes without saying that the commonly-accepted view is that Christians, raised in a dark and bigoted creed, viewed the Jews as the murderers of Christ and therefore their natural enemies. And indeed it is true that the murderous savages who followed Emich, Volkmar and Gottschalk, did hurl the accusation of Christ-killers against their victims. Yet we cannot ignore the fact that this was the first such attack on Jews in Christian Europe in a thousand years. And this, together with the fact that the assaults occurred at the beginning of a war against Muslims, makes us wonder what could have provoked such novel behavior.

---

[299] Bat Ye'or, *The Dhimmi*, p. 61

HOLY WARRIORS

Here we need to be very clear. Novel this behavior certainly was. Although, as we saw in Chapter 2, there were historical reasons for the antipathy between Christians and Jews, and discriminatory laws against Jews were enacted in the Eastern Empire under Justinian, there are no grounds for supposing that the Jews of western Europe suffered persecution of any serious nature in the centuries prior to the First Crusade. Indeed, the evidence speaks quite to the contrary: By the eleventh century both France and Germany were home to large and prosperous Jewish communities. Steven Runciman notes that, "Jewish colonies had been established for centuries past along the trade routes of western Europe."[300] These colonies "kept up connections with their co-religionists in Byzantium and in Arab lands, and were thus enabled to play a large part in international trade, more especially the trade between Moslem and Christian countries." Runciman notes that, "Except long ago in Visigothic Spain they had never undergone serious persecution in the West. ... The kings of France and Germany had always befriended them; and they were shown particular favour by the archbishops of the great cities of the Rhineland."[301]

We shall presently examine the persecution by the Visigoths alluded to above, and will argue strongly that it is a fiction. But if there was no prior persecution of the Jews, whence, we might ask, did this hatred arise?

Before answering that question it is important to bear in mind an obvious fact; one so obvious that it might indeed be overlooked: The rise of anti-Semitism in Europe coincides precisely with the beginning of crusading. In short, hatred and persecution of the Jews is intimately connected to the war against Islam. And that war, as we have seen, began in Spain – a land with a very large Jewish community. This cannot have been coincidental. It is an acknowledged fact that it was in Spain that the warriors who later joined the First Crusade learnt their dislike of the Jews. In Runciman's words, "Already in the Spanish wars there had been some inclination on the part of Christian armies to maltreat the Jews."[302] Runciman notes that at the time of the expedition to Barbastro, Pope Alexander II had written to the bishops of Spain to remind them that there was all the difference in the world between Muslims and Jews. The former were irreconcilable enemies of the Christians, but the latter were ready to

---

[300] S. Runciman, op cit., p. 134
[301] Ibid.
[302] Ibid. p. 135

185

work for them. However, in Spain "the Jews had enjoyed such favour from the hands of the Moslems that the Christian conquerors could not bring themselves to trust them."[303] This lack of trust is confirmed by more than one document of the period.[304]

The idea that the Jews had been favored by the Muslims needs further comment – especially in view of the fact that ferocious massacres of Jews had been carried out both by Muhammad himself and by Muslims in North Africa and Spain in the eleventh century. How then were the Jews seen as favored?

In fact, from the very beginning, the Muslim conquerors had employed learned and able Jews in many areas of trust, including finances and public administration. One at least, Joseph ibn Naghrela, was even made vizier. The skills of Jewish mathematicians and doctors were freely used; and they were generally favored to Christians, who were numerically superior and whose co-religionists were actively involved in war against the Muslims. Furthermore, Christians tended to be less qualified to undertake the tasks required. We cannot fail either to mention the international connections of the Jews and their mastery of languages. As such, they were used by the Muslims as intermediaries between themselves and the Christians. Again, we cannot pass over the role of Jewish merchants in supplying Muslim Spain with all its essentials – including slaves from northern and north-eastern Europe.[305]

Of course, the great mass of the Jewish population in Spain was treated no better than the Christians, and was subject to periodic violent attack, as the pogroms in Granada and Cordoba in 1011 and 1066 illustrate only too clearly. Yet for the embattled Christians of northern Spain, involved at the beginning of the eleventh century in a life and death struggle against an expanding Islam, these must have seemed insignificant. Muslim attacks against Christians, both in Spain and elsewhere, were just as bloody, or even moreso. This, combined with the fact that so many high officials in the employ of the Caliphs were Jews, could easily have turned the Christians against the latter.

Bat Ye'or, who has made an extensive study of conditions experienced by Jews and Christians under Islam, comes to a similar conclusion. "It may well

---

[303] Ibid.
[304] J. P. Migne, *Patrologiae Latina*, Part I of *Patrologiae Cursus Completus*, (Paris, 1844-55), Letter in Vol. CLXVI, col. 1387
[305] Trevor-Roper, op cit., p. 143

be," she says, "that the role that some Jews assumed as intermediaries for the Muslims accounts for the extreme forms of anti-Jewish persecution in the period of the *Reconquista* in Spain …"[306] Nor should we neglect to mention that the Muslim authorities actually encouraged this Jewish-Christian hostility, on the old and well-known principle of "divide and rule". Far better that the oppressed communities should expend their energies attacking each other than that they should unite against their common oppressor. This too is acknowledged by Bat Ye'or: "The [Arab] invaders knew how to take advantage of the dissensions between local groups in order to impose their own authority, favoring first one and then another, with the intention of weakening and ruining them all through a policy of 'divide and rule.'"[307]

Having said all that, we must acknowledge that not all the savages who attacked the Jews in Germany in 1096 had fought in Spain. Indeed, it is unlikely that more than a handful had. We cannot then attribute the barbarous behavior of these people simply to habits learned there. The leaders of these pogroms, Emich, Gottschalk and Volkmar, were members of minor nobility (Volkmar, or Folkmar, was a priest), classic representatives of feudal society, a system which we have already traced to the Viking epoch. They were local potentates, thoroughly steeped in a culture of violence and vendetta. As we have seen, most of these lords and barons were virtually beyond the control of both Church and King, and their attitudes were to shape the Middle Ages in a profound way. The lack of central control, and with it the culture of feuding and raiding, prevented the development of a more settled and also more humane civilization in Europe. The Church could and usually did condemn the excesses of these people, but she was powerless to punish their brutalities. Only the monarchy was capable of such, but its hands were tied by its own dependency on the barons.

As noted, we have already traced the development of feudalism and the feudal system following the demise of Classical Civilization in the mid-seventh century. This ended, as Pirenne noted, with the Muslim invasions. Yet it is possible that Classical Civilization need not have developed into feudal Medievalism had not the Vikings made their mark in northern Europe. The incessant raiding and pillaging of these people necessitated the development of localized defensive forces; and these formed the basis of the feudal aristocracy.

---

[306] Bat Ye'or, *The Dhimmi*, p. 90
[307] Ibid. p. 87

5: RESISTANCE ANDTRANSFORMATION

In the Age of the Vikings men became used to violence and counter-violence; to slave-raiding and the torture of prisoners. The Christian faith, which had been working to soften the attitudes of the Gothic and Frankish rulers of the West, had to begin again from the start. The native ferocity of the peoples of Germany was now reinforced by the barbarism of the Viking Wars, as well as by the endemic warfare which began to take root throughout the West in the tenth century.

In addition to this we cannot ignore the fact that when trying to understand the attacks against the Jews, there was a residual anti-Jewish sentiment present in most of Europe, which, although it had not been manifest in a violent way until the First Crusade, had always existed: For it is true that a historical antipathy had long existed between Christians and Jews. It is commonly believed that this antipathy earlier revealed itself in Europe – not admittedly in a violent way – in the writings of Christian authors and in the laws passed by several Christian kings and prelates. What are we to make of these claims?

Origins of European Anti-Semitism

We have already seen that in the centuries which preceded the First Crusade, the Jews of western Europe had prospered and increased, and had found especial favor with the kings and prelates of France and Germany. It is true, of course, that in an earlier age, in the time of the Roman Empire, Christians and Jews had been antagonistic: the Jews had been inveterate enemies of the Christians when they were a persecuted sect; and there is evidence that they would, as Gibbon puts it, "gladly have extinguished the dangerous heresy [Christianity] in the blood of its adherents." (Ch. 16) It is pointless to go through the various animosities that existed at this time between the two groups, yet there is clear evidence that, well into the third century, Jewish religious leaders agitated in favor of persecuting Christians, and harbored much hatred towards them.[308] This needs to be said, for early Christian writers are frequently attacked for their

---

[308] Gibbon notes (Ch. 16) in a footnote that "The acts of the martyrdom of Polycarp exhibit a lively picture of these tumults, which were frequently fomented by the malice of the Jews."

animosity towards the Jews. There currently exists on the internet, for example, a website named "Religious Tolerance" which, in a page titled "Anti-Judaism: 70 to 1200 CE", lists a series of anti-Jewish pronouncements by early Christian writers such as Saint John Chrysostom, Saint Hilary of Poitiers, Saint Augustine and Saint Jerome. Now, there is no question that these men, and many others beside, did make statements which nowadays would be regarded as straightforwardly anti-Semitic, in a religious sense. Yet these are the statements of individuals, not imperial policy. Furthermore, it should be stressed that John Chrysostom's attack, which he launched when he was a priest in Antioch (386), was designed to put an end to the practice among Christians of going to synagogues and participating in their services. As one historian notes, "the fact that Christian attendance in synagogues was widespread in late fourth-century Antioch indicates that neither anti-Semitism nor anti-Judaism were dominant among Christians at the time, many of whom understood that there was a bond between Christianity and Judaism."[309] We note too that what John Chrysostom and the rest said about the Jews is mild in comparison with the attacks they made against heretics such as Manicheans and Donatists; and Jewish writers of the time were equally vociferous in their condemnation of Christians; and whilst Christians had suffered death – often on a large scale – simply for being Christian, Jews had not.

Perhaps as a result of Jewish antipathy, Christians reciprocated; and, when the control of the Empire had passed into their hands, they did enact several anti-Jews laws. None of these however were severe, and none of them, that we know of, resulted in the deaths of any Jews. Furthermore, they were gradually rescinded as the memory of the persecution suffered by the Christians under the pagan emperors receded; and the proof of their mildness is in the great increase in the numbers and the prosperity of the Jewish people in the centuries that preceded the First Crusade.

There is said however to have been one exception to this general rule; and that was in the land of Spain. We are told that under the Visigothic kings, beginning with Sisebur (612-620), and continuing for almost a century, Catholic monarchs of Spain enacted decree after decree against the Jews; robbing them of property rights, forcibly converting them to Christianity, and expelling from the

---

[309] Spencer, *Religion of Peace?* p. 113

country those who refused. Some of these decrees, recorded and sanctified in an astonishing thirteen church councils (4th to 16th Councils of Toledo), prefigure and indeed predict the decrees enacted against the Jews in the fourteenth and fifteenth centuries by the rulers of Castile: namely, forced conversion, confiscation of property, and mass expulsion. As such, and knowing the well-recognized medieval custom of forging documents (usually to set a legal precedent or accord the authority of ancient practice to a new law), we must question the authenticity of the material relating to these Councils. We shall find, in fact, in the Appendix, that a great deal of evidence exists to show that all events normally attributed to the seventh, eighth and ninth centuries might well be fictitious, and that documents said to date from these years were actually forged in the later Middle Ages (normally the twelfth to fourteenth centuries).

Now, there is no question that, as one historian has put it, "Forgery of documents was a favourite mediaeval pastime,"[310] The most notable example of this was the so-called Donation of Constantine, supposedly written in the eighth century, but now widely recognized as originating at a later date. Another famous, or rather infamous, example of this *genre* are the so-called Pseudo-Isidorean Decretals. These constitute the most extensive and influential set of forgeries in medieval Canon Law. Some collections of them included, for good measure, copies of the Donation of Constantine. Supposedly dating from the time of Isidore of Seville (seventh century), are now known to have been forged in north-eastern France centuries later. We should note that "Immense labor and erudition went into creating this work, and a wide range of genuine sources were employed."[311] Like the Donation of Constantine, the forgers' main object was to empower the Church.

Document forgery then was something of an industry during the Middle Ages. These, as noted above, were not produced by amateurs, but by men of immense erudition, who employed, to make matters worse, a wide range of genuine sources. Over the past few years it has become increasingly obvious that a great many of the Early Medieval documents still regarded as genuine have an "anticipatory" nature. In other words, they set a legal or moral precedent which, at the supposed time of writing, was useless or redundant, but which later, during the twelfth, thirteenth and fourteenth centuries, became very useful

---

[310] Painter, op cit.
[311] http://en.wikipedia.org/wiki/Pseudo-Isidore

indeed. Now the documents of the Councils of Toledo, of the seventh and eighth centuries, are prime examples of Early Medieval texts with an "anticipatory" character. They set legal and moral precedents for the treatment of Jews which, during the thirteenth, fourteenth and fifteenth centuries, were in fact enacted against that people. And it should be noted that the documents of the Toledo Councils deal with a period of time very close to the life of Isidore of Seville, whose epoch is also the setting for the forged Pseudo-Decretals.

I contend then that the persecution of the Jews in seventh century Spain is a fiction, and that it was a fiction invented to justify the persecution undertaken by the kings of Castile in the fourteenth and fifteenth centuries.

Yet it is true that European anti-Semitism, as it appeared in the time of the First Crusade, originated in Spain. We have already examined some of the reasons for this. Spain, at the time of the Arab conquest, had a very large Jewish population, almost certainly the largest in Europe. The Jewish people had prospered and flourished here in the centuries since they arrived there following their expulsion from Israel by the emperor Hadrian. When the Arabs arrived, the latter were confronted, as they always were, with the problem of controlling a non-Muslim population infinitely greater numerically than the Muslim conquerors. By the time they arrived in Spain, the Arabs had become masters of the principle of "divide and rule". This they employed in Spain to great effect. The Jews of course, though numerous, were numerically inferior to the Christians. It was therefore in the interests of the Arabs to separate the Jews from the Christians as quickly as possible, and to foment as much mistrust and mutual hatred between the two as possible.

This they managed to do with quite masterly skill.

One of the most dangerous myths from this time, and one whose origin lay probably at least partly in Arab propaganda, was the story that the Jews had assisted the Muslims in the conquest of Spain. This source of this claim is unclear, though it seems to have been widely accepted by all parties, including the Jews. Christian accounts of the conquest are fragmentary and are heavily dependent upon Muslim sources. The Arabs claim Jewish assistance, but it was not an organized and full-scale assistance. There was no Jewish rebellion against the Visigoths in support of the incoming Arabs. In general, the "assistance" amounted to little more than a few individual Jews co-operating with the invaders. People of this faith, it seemed, were in general more willing to co-operate than Christians. This hardly amounted to a fifth-columnist conspiracy.

Commonsense alone suggests that any organized and large-scale Jewish co-operation with the Muslims is highly improbable. It just does not make sense. Hitherto no Christian king had ever seriously persecuted the Jews simply for being Jews. Laws had been passed against them, especially under Justinian, which may have been a temporary nuisance. But no Jew was ever killed for being a Jew. The contrast with Islam and the Arabs could not have been greater. Right from the beginning, from the time of Muhammad, Jews had been killed by Muslims on a large scale; and Jewish women had been enslaved by Arab conquerors within Arabia itself and later in Syria and North Africa. The Jews were *par excellence* travelers and communicators. Their communities kept in close touch with each other all around the Mediterranean and beyond. Intelligence on the killings of the Jews in Arabia in the time of Muhammad would have been swiftly transmitted throughout the Mediterranean. In short, the Jews of Spain can have been under no illusions about the Muslims. They would have viewed with trepidation the approach of Muslim armies across North Africa. Many of their co-religionists – and probably close relations – would only recently have been victims of Muslim actions in that region. Many, very many, of their women and children had been enslaved. The idea of Jewish co-operation with the Arabs was thus, as far as I can see, nonsense. If they co-operated, it was purely out of fear.

As I shall explain in the Appendix, there is good reason to question much about the timetable and circumstances of the first Arab/Muslim expansion. I am convinced that the great sweep of conquest across the Middle East and North Africa in the seventh century was accomplished primarily through the military strength of the Persians, who became allies of the Arabs in Syria. Now, as we saw in Chapter 2, the Jews of Syria/Palestine did indeed co-operate with the Persians in the great conflict between Heraclius and Chosroes II which erupted in 613. Jewish forces helped the Persians capture Jerusalem, and together they carried out a massacre of the city's Christian inhabitants. Yet, although I am convinced the Persians converted to Islam a good deal earlier than is generally supposed, I cannot believe they had become Muslim at this stage. If they had, the Jews would certainly not have co-operated with them.

HOLY WARRIORS

Yet the knowledge of what the Jews had done in Palestine would no doubt have reached Spain shortly thereafter, and would have contributed to suspicions about their loyalties. These would have increased as the Muslim armies crossed North Africa in a seemingly irresistible march of conquest, and the inhabitants of Spain began to feel vulnerable. There is no question too that the abiding belief among Christian Europeans that the Jews could not be trusted owed its origins to the events on the Byzantine/Persian frontier.

Whether or not there was substantial Jewish collaboration during the Muslim conquest, there is no doubt that afterwards the Jews of the region were employed by the Islamic authorities as administrators, technical experts, and as suppliers of merchandise from abroad. The Jewish involvement in this trade alone would have incited Christian suspicions, since, to begin with, no Christians at all ventured across the boundaries of the Muslim-controlled territory. Yet Jewish merchants were involved in one enterprise which did their reputation much damage. This was the selling of European slaves into bondage in the Islamic world. This trade, we have seen, was conducted at the height of the Viking onslaught, and there can be no doubt that it really existed. It seems likely that some Jewish entrepreneurs were involved in the commerce – an enterprise that on occasion involved the sale of Christian (as well as Slavic) captives to Muslims. The involvement of the Jews is explained by the fact that slaving would have been condemned as sinful by the church and therefore debarred from Christian participation: this type of commerce, like money-lending, would have been left to Jews (though Christian rulers, hypocritically, would have profited from it through taxation).[312] And the Jews, as Trevor-Roper emphasizes, with their contacts all across Europe and the Near East, would have more easily moved across international and religious boundaries.

Jewish involvement in the slave trade, irrespective of its extent and intensity, would undoubtedly have added fuel to the suspicion of collusion with the Muslims.

One of the charges against the Jews, throughout the centuries, was that they were involved in some form of criminal conspiracy; either to dominate the

---

[312] It has been suggested, reasonably, that some of those who participated in the massacres that preceded the People's Crusade were seeking to cancel debts owed to Jewish money-lenders.

world, or to subvert the societies of the Gentiles among whom they dwelt. The most notorious example of this idea, in recent history, was the so-called *Protocols of the Elders of Zion*, a document composed in 19th century Russia. Other manifestations of the theory, which appeared throughout the centuries in Europe after the First Crusade, was that the Jews had poisoned wells, stolen or murdered Christian children, etc. There is no question that much of this paranoid idea can be traced back to the supposed Jewish treachery during the Muslim invasion of Spain. And yet, once again, this is an idea that may very plausibly be traced to seventh-century Arabia. In the Koran and Haditha the Jews are listed among those who are "treacherous" and "enemies of God". It is but a small step from describing a people as treacherous and enemies of God, to accusing them of poisoning wells and murdering babies. And this was a step taken very early by Muslims. The massacres in Spain in 1011 and 1066 were prompted by such accusations. From the Muslim areas of Spain, the rumors and calumnies would easily have spread to the Christian lands, first of Spain and France, and then beyond. And these rumors would have found fertile ground in which to incubate. Both Spain and France had been ravaged continuously, for very many years, by Viking and Muslim raiding-parties and slave-traders. The prevailing mood, for as long as anyone could have remembered, would have been one of fear, insecurity and paranoia; a paranoia that would have been reinforced by the knowledge that some of the Jews, people who lived in their own communities, had actually profited by the slave-trade with the Spanish Muslims. It would have mattered little that most of the slaves carried to Cordoba and Damascus were heathen Slavs: the very fact that Jewish traders had been involved in the commerce would have been held as evidence of collusion. And this would have reinforced the rumor – a rumor encouraged by the Arabs themselves – that the Jews had actually helped the Muslims conquer Spain.

It was rumor and paranoia of this type that led to the massacres of the Jews in Germany at the start of the First Crusade: the first act in a tragedy that was to last for centuries.

CHAPTER 6

IMPACT OF ISLAM

The Spread of Islamic Ideas

n the foregoing pages we saw that Crusading, properly speaking, began in the eighth century; and it was one of the phenomena which most signally marked the transformation of European civilization into the "medieval" one familiar to all historians. We have argued that this transformation was a direct result of contact with Islam; and we have hinted that it was within Islam that the medieval mindset first appeared, whence it transmitted itself to Europe. Indeed, everything we have seen demonstrates that Islam's impact upon Europe was much greater than has hitherto been imagined. So far, we have examined two dimensions of that:

(a) The closure of the Mediterranean by war and piracy in the seventh century meant the impoverishment of Europe, the decline of cities, a fall in literacy, and an increasingly rural economy.

(b) The almost perpetual war and banditry experienced in the South and on the shores of the Mediterranean meant a militarization of these regions and their cultures. The Viking raids produced the same result in the North.

These two factors explain a great deal. Yet in themselves they do not account for everything. A society might be rural, illiterate and warlike without becoming what medieval Europe became. Whence came the intolerance of other faiths; the fanatical devotion to the literal word of the Bible; the distrust of reason and rationality; as well as more lethal things, such as violent persecution of the Jews and judicial use of torture?

It is of course the conventional view, in some quarters, to see in these things the natural outgrowth of Christian ideology, as preached by the Church. And there is no doubt that the Church cannot be exonerated from all guilt. Yet, from what we have already seen, there is no reason why these things should naturally have occurred in Christianity, even the official version, which many moderns now regard as not quite true to the original teachings of Christ. We have seen, for example, that the animosity between Christians and Jews during the first seven centuries of the faith's existence never resulted in lethal violence against the latter. Yes, there was animosity; but that was at least as much the fault of Jewish religious leaders as it was of Christians. And when any kind of vandalism was perpetrated against Jewish property, as when several synagogues of Ravenna were burnt in 519, the authorities took decisive action against the vandals. In the latter case king Theodoric compelled the citizens of the city to rebuild the synagogues, at their own expense.[313] What a contrast with the attacks on the Jews that preceded the First Crusade. Here, too, the violence was perpetrated by mobs who acted on no authority but their own. Yet they were not, as far as we are aware, punished. Their behavior was condemned and criticized, but not punished: thus making future attacks almost certain. In the time of Theodoric, the ringleaders would have been put to death. Now, the civil and ecclesiastical authorities were content to "condemn". Clearly, some change of a fundamental nature had come about.

It is a simple matter of fact that all the attitudes which we now consider to be typically "medieval" made their appearance first in Islam. And it is a virtual certainty that it was from Islam that these attitudes transmitted themselves to Europe. In the following pages we shall see that Islamic ideas, including ideas about theology and spiritual matters, as well as on warfare and jurisprudence,

---

[313] www.en.wikipedia.org/wiki/Theodoric_the_Great

began to influence European thinking almost from the beginning, and by the eighth century had made a major impact upon Christendom.

It is of course widely accepted nowadays that Islam had an enormous ideological impact upon Europe. Historians tend to focus, as we saw, on certain scientific and philosophical concepts. It is well-known, for example, that Muslim scholars, beginning with the Persian Avicenna (Ibn Sina) in the late tenth and early eleventh century, had made extensive commentaries upon the works of Aristotle, which they attempted to integrate, with a very limited degree of success it must be noted, into Islamic thought. In the second half of the twelfth century Avicenna's work was taken up by the Spanish Muslim Averroes (Ibn Rushd), who made his own commentaries and writings on the Greek philosopher. By that time European scholars were very much aware of Arab learning, and men like John of Salisbury even had agents in Spain procuring Arabic manuscripts, which were then translated into Latin. "Soon the commentaries of Averroes were so well known in Europe that he was called 'the Commentator,' as Aristotle was called 'the Philosopher.'"[314] At a slightly earlier stage, Christian Europeans had found their way into Muslim-controlled regions such as Sicily, often in disguise, in order to avail themselves of the scientific and alchemical knowledge they discovered there. No less a person than Gerbert of Aurillac, the genius of the tenth century, on whom the figure of Faust was based, had journeyed into the Muslim regions to acquire knowledge. The profound influence exerted by Islam upon the philosophical and theological thinking of Europeans at this time cannot be stressed too much. Thus, at one stage, Briffault notes how, "The exact parallelism between Muslim and Christian theological controversy is too close to be accounted for by the similarity of situation, and the coincidences are too fundamental and numerous to be accepted as no more than coincidence. ... The same questions, the same issues which occupied the theological schools of Damascus, were after an interval of a century repeated in identical terms in those of Paris."[315] Again, "The whole logomacy [of Arab theological debate] passed bodily into Christendom. The catchwords, disputes,

---

[314] Painter, op cit., p. 303
[315] Briffault, op cit., p. 217

vexed questions, methods, systems, conceptions, heresies, apologetics and irenics, were transferred from the mosques to the Sorbonne"[316]

Europeans could not, of course, fail to be impressed by what they found in Islamic Spain and southern Italy. They themselves lived in a culturally and economically impoverished environment. It is quite beside the point that it was Islam itself and Muslim piracy which had created that poverty. Such considerations would not have prevented the northern travelers being overawed by the luxury, wealth and knowledge they encountered amongst their Saracen foes. Crucial technologies began to creep into Europe at this time, often via Jewish traders and scholars, who were, for a while, the only class of people able to safely cross the Christian-Islamic frontiers. To these Jewish travelers, some of whom were physicians, alchemists and mathematicians, Europe almost certainly owes the acquisition of such things as the "Arabic" numeral system, knowledge of alcohol distillation, and probably algebra and a host of other information. "Muhammedan philosophy and theology had, we know, been carried to the Benedictine monasteries through the Jews, and the metropolitan house of Monte Cassino."[317] The Spanish Jews in particular "supplied Arabic versions of Greek writers to Christendom."[318] Indeed, so important was the influence of these Jewish traders and scholars that we might even say that, at a crucial moment, the Jews delivered to Europe the knowledge that helped her survive the Muslim onslaught. And we know how Europe later thanked them!

We encounter here again that curious chronological dichotomy met at every turn in our examination of this epoch. Having appeared in the seventh century, we would expect the ideological impact of Islam to have occurred then or shortly thereafter, say in the late seventh and throughout the eighth centuries. Yet the real impact of Islamic ideas is only felt in the tenth and eleventh centuries, almost exactly three hundred years later. Or, should we say, almost all of the impact is felt then: For in reality, the arrival of Islamic ideas is divided into two phases, separated from each other by three centuries: The great majority of those arrived in the tenth and eleventh centuries, but at least one – of fundamental importance in our understanding of Islam – arrived in the eighth century. And this was a concept which illustrates very clearly the darker side of

---

[316] Ibid. p. 219
[317] Ibid. p. 217
[318] Trevor-Roper, op cit., p. 143

HOLY WARRIORS

Islam and Islamic influence, the side that modern historians, chained by the bonds of political correctness, do not like to mention. The real ideological impression of Islam was not the enlightened thinking of Avicenna and Averroes, who were in any case rejected and expelled from the Muslim canon, but the darker thinking found in the Koran and the Haditha: the doctrines of perpetual war against non-believers; of holy deception (*taqiyya*); of death for apostates and heretics; of judicial torture; of slave and concubine-taking as a legitimate occupation. These were the teachings, and not those of the philosophers, which left an indelible imprint on medieval Europe. And this began right at the beginning.

The first Islamic (or Koranic) idea to find followers in Europe, and the one most obvious and recognized, was the impulse to iconoclasm, to the destruction of religious imagery. As we noted in Chapter 3, Iconoclasm began sometime between 726 and 730 when the Byzantine Emperor Leo III ordered the removal and destruction of all sacred statues and images throughout the Empire. His justification for doing so came from the Old Testament denunciation of idol-worship, yet it is evident that the real inspiration came from Islam.

The question of the Iconoclast episode is one of primary importance. Above all, we must ask ourselves: What could have prompted Byzantine Emperors to go against one of the most fundamental tenets of their faith (the honoring of sacred images) and start destroying these in a manner reminiscent of Oliver Cromwell? Such action can only have been prompted by a crisis of the most profound kind. We have seen that in the early years the advance of Islam seemed unstoppable. The Empire suffered defeat after defeat. Within little more than a decade she had lost all her Middle Eastern possessions outside Anatolia. These included the most prosperous and populous provinces, Egypt and Syria; core areas of the Empire, and part of Imperial territory for seven hundred years. The Empire was experiencing its darkest days; and the fall of Constantinople must surely have seemed inevitable. It is precisely crises of such type – those which threaten our very existence – that lead human beings to question fundamentals. The Empire's losses had been so great that Constantinople began to think the unthinkable. Perhaps God is angry with us; perhaps we've been doing something wrong that the Muslims have been doing right! A central tenet of Islam is the rejection of images, which are regarded as idols and their

199

honoring condemned as idolatry. Perhaps the Saracens are right, and we are idolaters. Perhaps the Empire is offending Heaven, and our fortunes will improve once this is put right.

If this was the psychology behind Byzantine Iconoclasm, then it is clear that Constantinople did not willingly and enthusiastically adopt Islamic thinking. Rather, the success of the new faith from Arabia was such that the Byzantines began to believe that it might enjoy God's favour. Islamic ideas were therefore considered as a way of resolving a profound crisis. Yet, it is important to remember that, for whatever reason, Islamic ideas were copied. The whole of Christendom, East and West, was threatened by Islam; and, one way or another, ideas derived from Islam itself began to be considered by Christians as an answer to that very crisis.

Iconoclasm caused great divisions within the Empire, and was firmly rejected by the West – creating, it seems, some of the conditions leading to the final break between the Pope and Constantinople. Yet the very fact that a Roman Emperor could introduce a policy so obviously inspired by the beliefs of Islam tells us eloquently the extent to which the influence of Islamic ideology now began to make itself felt throughout Europe.

The Theocratic State

One of the most outstanding characteristics of the Middle Ages, and one that above all other perhaps differentiates it from Classical Antiquity, was its theocracy. The Middle Ages were, *par excellence*, the age of priestly power. In the West, the influence of the Church was immense, reaching much further than it ever had under the Christian Roman Emperors or the Germanic kings of the fifth and sixth centuries. The Papacy now stood in judgment of kings and Emperors, and had the power to choose and depose them. "By me kings reign" was the proud boast of the medieval papacy.[319]

How did this come about? We have seen that the refounding of the Western Empire under Otto the Great was intimately connected with the attempt to defend Western Christendom. This was a project undertaken jointly by Otto

---

[319] Trevor-Roper, op cit., p. 133

and Great and Pope John XII. In years to come, the Empire would be renamed the Holy Roman Empire – a singularly appropriate title, for the Empire represented a symbiotic union, at the heart of Europe, of spiritual and temporal authorities. The crowning of the Emperor – for which the inauguration of Charlemagne became the model – was an event loaded with religious significance and symbolism. Otto was ruler *Dei gratis*, and he made the Church the main instrument of royal government. His authority would henceforth not simply be derived from his own military and economic strength, as it had been under the Caesars and Germanic kings of the fifth and sixth centuries, but ultimately upon the sanction and approval of the Church.

We have already identified several factors in this crucial development. Pirenne, as we saw, noted that, with the decline in literacy and urban life in the seventh century – following the closing of the Mediterranean – kings were forced to look to the Church to supply the educated functionaries needed to run the apparatus of the state. Again, the loss of much of their tax revenue after the termination of the Mediterranean trade meant that the position of the monarch was weakened *vis a vis* the barons and minor aristocrats. These now gained in power and independence. The kings desperately needed a counterbalance to this, and the support of the Church carried great weight indeed. With the Church on their side the kings could – just about – keep the barons under control. But there was necessarily a trade-off. The Church might keep the king on his throne, but it gained in return an unheard-of power and influence. Eventually the kings of Europe became, quite literally, subordinate to the Pope, who could even, in extreme cases, dethrone them. Everything a medieval ruler did, or proposed to do, he had to do with the sanction of the Church. Even powerful and independent warriors, such as William of Normandy, could only proceed with a project like the invasion of England after gaining papal approval.

The Ottonian Emperors thus laid the foundations of the medieval theocracy; yet in their time (tenth century), the papacy was still relatively weak. It was, remember, to elicit the support of Otto I against his Italian opponents, that Pope John XII revived the dignity of Emperor in the West. Here we see that in the tenth century, supposedly at the end of a 300-year-long Dark Age, there existed conditions remarkably similar to those pertaining in the sixth and early seventh centuries: Germanic kingdoms that were essentially secular in character, where Popes and prelates were subordinate to the monarchs. Yet conditions had changed. Otto I and his successors staffed their administrations with churchmen, who by then clearly had a monopoly on learning and even literacy. The old, Roman world, was very definitely a thing of the past. From this point on, the power of the Church would grow and grow.

Yet even now the Church had to fight for supremacy, a struggle which commenced in the tenth century, with the aid of the Ottonians, and which ended in the eleventh, with papal victory. "They [Church reformers] fought to secure ultimate control of a self-contained, independent, dominant, monarchical Church. Such a contest was a frontal challenge to the old system of the Roman Empire. It was a frontal attack on the kings who presumed that they had inherited the rights of the Roman emperors. It was an indirect attack on the emperor of Constantinople who, in the East, continued to maintain the old system [of secular supremacy] and was now called schismatic for his pains."[320]

The very peak of the medieval Church's power came a century later in the age and in the person of Innocent III (1198 – 1216). This man judged between rival Emperors in Germany and had Otto IV deposed. He laid England under an interdict and excommunicated King John for refusing to recognize Stephen Langdon as Archbishop of Canterbury. His two most memorable actions however were the establishment of the Inquisition and the launching of the notorious Albigensian Crusade, which led to the elimination of the Cathar movement. Innocent III then, the most powerful of medieval theocrats, was a proponent of Holy War, and an enforcer of absolute doctrinal conformity. Apostasy under Innocent III became a capital offence. During his time too the other Crusades, against Islam in Spain and in the Middle East, continued to rage.

Ironically, Innocent's attitude to apostasy and doctrinal conformity – as well as to "Holy War" – is completely in accord with Islamic notions, and we must consider to what extent these extreme positions of the European theocracy derived ultimately from the Islamic one.

Islam itself was, of course, from the very beginning, theocratic in nature. In it, there was no "render unto Caesar the things that are Caesar's, and unto God the things that are God's". Right from the start, in the person of Mohammed, spiritual and temporal power was united. After Mohammed, under the Caliphs, the same situation pertained. Every Caliph was, first and foremost,

---

[320] Trevor-Roper, op cit., p. 137

a "commander of the faithful". For all that, we cannot judge that the founding of theocracy in Europe was a result of deliberate imitation of Islamic notions, as was iconoclasm and Holy War. Islam's contribution to the European theocracy was real enough, but rather more accidental, or rather, inferential As we saw, the impoverishment of Europe and her monarchs caused by Islam's blockade of the Mediterranean, left them little option but to turn to the Church for support. Also, the fight for the defense of Europe, because of the very nature of the enemy, took on a religious dimension (all faiths gain in strength when faced with opposition), and this too would have increased the power and prestige of the Church.

So, whilst the medieval European theocracy was not the result of direct imitation of Islamic ideas, Islam was still instrumental in giving birth to it. Furthermore, the type of theocracy which took shape in Europe, and some of the underlying ideas associated with it, very definitely derived from Islam.

Intolerance of Heretics and Apostates

We have seen that, from its inception, Islam regarded apostasy and heresy as capital offences.[321] The most notorious, though by no means the only, example of this is found in the fate of Mansur Al-Hallaj (858 – 922), the Persian mystic, whose death mimicked that of Christ – though before being crucified Al-Hallaj was first, it is said, blinded and otherwise tortured. And the killing of political and religious opponents, or those who deviated in any way from orthodox Islam, occurred at the very start and was continuous throughout Muslim history. So it was with infidels such as Christians and Jews who, though theoretically *dhimmi*, or "protected," were in fact always the subject of violent attack. We know, for example, that in 704 or 705 the caliph Walid (705-715) "assembled the nobles of Armenia in the church of St Gregory in Naxcawan and the church of Xrain on the Araxis, and burned them to death. Others were crucified and decapitated and their wives and children taken into captivity. A violent persecution of Christians in Armenia is recorded from 852 to 855."[322] There even existed, as we have

---

[321] Muhammad said, "If anyone changes his religion, kill him." (Bukhari, Vol. 9, book 84, no. 57).
[322] Bat Ye'or, *The Dhimmi*, pp. 60-1

6: IMPACT OF ISLAM

seen, in Spain and North Africa, at least from the time of the Almohads (early twelfth century), a commission of enquiry, a veritable "inquisition", for rooting out apostates. We are told that the Jews, who had at this time been forced to accept Islam, formed a mass of "new converts" who nevertheless continued to practice their own religion in secret. But the "Almohad inquisitors, doubting their sincerity, took away their children and raised them as Muslims."[323]

Medieval Christianity, beginning in the late twelfth/early thirteenth century, adopted the same attitude. Christians now had their own Inquisition for rooting out heretics, and the death penalty was now prescribed for such miscreants. The judicial use of torture too, "a novelty in Europe" at the time, became accepted practice.[324] All of these practices were in fact novel in Europe: There is no evidence of the lethal intolerance which marked the foundation of the Inquisition before Innocent III's time. It is true, as we have already seen, that in the early centuries, the Church was involved in a series of prolonged and bitter disputes over the correct interpretation of Christ's words. Those who disagreed with the mainstream dogmas, as laid down by various Councils, were decreed to be heretics, and fairly severe condemnation of these people and groups was common: indeed, it was almost endemic. Yet it has to be repeated that, intemperate as was the language used in these disputes, they rarely turned violent; and even when they did, the violence was on a very small scale and invariably perpetrated by those with no official sanction or approval. And the use of force to enforce orthodoxy was condemned by all the Church Fathers. Thus Lactantius declared that "religion cannot be imposed by force; the matter must be carried on by words rather than by blows, that the will may be affected." He wrote,

> Oh with what an honorable inclination the wretched men go astray! For they are aware that there is nothing among men more excellent than religion, and that this ought to be defended with the whole of our power; but as they are deceived in the matter of religion itself, so also are they in the manner of its defense. For religion is to be defended, not by putting to death, but by dying; not by cruelty, but by patient endurance; not by guilt, but by good faith. ... For if you wish to

---

[323] Ibid. p. 61
[324] Trevor-Roper, op cit., p. 159

204

defend religion by bloodshed, and by tortures, and by guilt, it will no longer be defended, but will be polluted and profaned. For nothing is so much a matter of free will as religion; in which, if the mind of the worshipper is disinclined to it, religion is at once taken away, and ceases to exist.[325]

Later, St. John Chrysostom wrote that "it is not right to put a heretic to death, since an implacable war would be brought into the world."[326] Likewise, St. Augustine was to write of heretics that "it is not their death, but their deliverance from error, that we seek."[327] In spite of these and many other such admonitions, incidents of violence against heretics did occur; but they were isolated and it was never sanctioned by Church authorities. Such, for example, was the case with the suppression of the so-called Priscillian Heresy in Spain in the latter years of the fourth and early years of the fifth century. Several followers of Priscillian were put to death, and the sect was persecuted in other ways. Yet the killing of Priscillian and his immediate associates (about seven? in all) had no Church sanction, and was thoroughly condemned by the ecclesiastical authorities.

The same was true of another, and more famous, case – the murder of Hypatia. This incident, in the early fifth century, has achieved, in some quarters, almost legendary status, and is seen as the example *par excellence* of Christian bigotry and obscurantism. From what little we know of this incident, it is clear that, like the killing of the Priscillians, the murder had no official sanction, and was carried out by a group of lawless fanatics. From the few sources we have, it is evident that Hypatia, daughter of the philosopher Theon, was a major figure in Alexandria during the latter years of the fourth and early years of the fifth centuries. She famously refused to embrace Christianity and remained a pagan, a

---

[325] Lactantius, "The Divine Institutes, in "Fathers of the Third and Fourth Centuries," in *The Ante-Nicene Fathers*, 156-7.

[326] John Chrysostom, Homily XLVI, in George Prevost, trans. "The Homilies of St. John Chrysostom" in Philip Schaff, ed. *A Select Library of the Nicene and Post-Nicene Fathers of the Christian Church*, Vol. X (Eedermans, Grand Rapids, MI, 1986) p. 288

[327] St Augustine, Letter C, in "Letters of St. Augustine," in J. G. Cunningham, trans. in A Select Library of the Nicene (etc as above)

6: IMPACT OF ISLAM

Neoplatonist. She freely discussed her ideas with many, including not a few Christian theologians, with whom she was on friendly terms.

But being such a prominent figure, she attracted enemies. Rumor spread that she was a factor in the strained relationship between Bishop Cyril and the Prefect Orestes, and this attracted the ire of some elements in the Christian population, eager to see the two reconciled. One day in March 415, during the season of Lent, her chariot was waylaid on her route home by a Christian mob, possibly Nitrian monks led by a man identified only as "Peter". She was stripped naked and dragged through the streets to the newly christianised Caesareum church and killed. Some reports suggest she was flayed with *ostrakois* (literally, "oyster shells", though also used to refer to roof tiles or broken pottery) and set ablaze while still alive, though other accounts suggest those actions happened after her death.

In view of the differing and contradictory accounts of this incident, we should perhaps quote the earliest, that closest to the event, which stands the best chance of accuracy. In the words of Socrates Scholasticus (5th century):

> Yet even she [Hypatia] fell a victim to the political jealousy which at that time prevailed. For as she had frequent interviews with Orestes, it was calumniously reported among the Christian populace, that it was she who prevented Orestes from being reconciled to the bishop. Some of them therefore, hurried away by a fierce and bigoted zeal, whose ringleader was a reader named Peter, waylaid her returning home, and dragging her from her carriage, they took her to the church called Caesareum, where they completely stripped her, and then murdered her by scraping her skin off with tiles and bits of shell. After tearing her body in pieces, they took her mangled limbs to a place called Cinaron, and there burnt them.

Although this was a horrific manifestation of religious bigotry, it was not sanctioned by Church leaders. Furthermore, it occurred in Egypt, a land with a long tradition of religious fanaticism. During the time of Julius Caesar, for example, an Egyptian mob lynched a Roman centurion (an act which could have brought upon them a terrible retribution) for having the temerity to kill a cat. Such isolated acts of fanaticism have occurred in all faiths at all periods of history. Even that most pacifist and tolerant of religious ideologies, Buddhism, is not entirely free of it. So, in itself, the murder of Hypatia cannot tell us much. That the Christian writer Socrates Scholasticus, in the fifth century, regarded it as a deplorable act of bigoted zeal, is very significant. Remember however what John of Nikiu, another Christian commentator, this time of the eighth century (about a century after the Muslim conquest), says. He described Hypatia as "a pagan" who was "devoted to magic" and who had "beguiled many people through Satanic wiles." And whilst Socrates Scholasticus condemned her killing, John of Nikiu approved it, speaking of "A multitude of believers in God" who, "under the guidance of Peter the magistrate ... proceeded to seek for the pagan woman who had beguiled the people of the city and the prefect through her enchantments."

John of Nikiu's attitude is clearly that of a medieval bigot and obscurantist, who regards all dissent from orthodox Christianity as the work of Satan. His thinking would not have been far removed from that of Innocent III, yet it was a world away from that of Socrates Scholasticus, his fellow-countryman. And whilst we might plausibly blame the medieval outlook on the general poverty and illiteracy of Europe after the termination of the Mediterranean trade in the late seventh and eighth centuries, we cannot attribute John of Nikiu's attitudes to the same cause. He, after all, lived in a land that was not cut off from the great centres of learning of the Orient. He came from a land which, supposedly, remained wealthy and prosperous, and which was moreover ruled by Caliphs friendly towards science and learning. The supply of papyrus was never cut off from Egypt! Whence, then, came John of Nikiu's dark and unenlightened view? And if his attitude had been confined to him alone, it would hardly be significant. Yet, the fact is, by the beginning of the eighth century, shortly after the Muslim conquest, all writers in Egypt and throughout the Near East, both Christian and Muslim, took the same view. This is a crucial point: If the medieval outlook were simple the product of the illiteracy and poverty that prevailed in Europe after the closing of the Mediterranean (as one interpretation of Pirenne's ideas might have it), then we should not expect to find it in Muslim-controlled lands. Yet find it we do – and it occurs here even *before* it appears in Europe.

The view of the world we call "medieval" was one in which the reason and humanism of the classical world had all but disappeared. Dark fantasies and superstitions took its place. Belief in the power of magicians and sorcerers, a belief associated with the most primitive type of mind-set, made a comeback. In the most backward of modern societies we still find perfectly innocent people accused of "witchcraft" and brutally put to death for a crime which they never committed and which does not even exist. By the end of the Middle Ages this mentality had returned to Europe; and in 1487 a papal Bull named *malleus maleficarum* ("hammer of the witches") pronounced the death of witches and Satanists. Even in Innocent III's time the "heretics" of the age, the Cathars and Waldensians, were believed to be under the inspiration of Satan.

Yet Europe, as she emerged from the so-called Dark Age in the tenth century, still bathed in the light of reason and humanitarianism. Thus a tenth century canon of Church Law criticized and condemned the belief among country folk that "certain women" were in the habit of riding out on beasts in the dead of night and crossing great distances before daybreak. According to the canon, anyone who believed this was "beyond doubt an infidel and a pagan." Somewhat earlier, Saint Agobard, Bishop of Lyons, declared it was not true that witches could call up storms and destroy harvests. Nor could they devour people from within nor kill them with the "evil eye".[328] "Only a few generations later," note Colin Wilson and Christopher Evans, "any person who did not believe in night flying and witches as the Church defined them was in danger of being burned as a heretic."[329] What, ask these two authors, had happened in the intervening years to change the Church's attitude?

In answer to that question, let us recall the comments of Lious Bertrand, who noted how, in the eleventh and twelfth centuries inquisitive young men from northern Europe flocked to Islamic Spain to study their knowledge and learning. But it was not so much the "science" of the Moors that attracted them as the pseudo-science: the alchemy, the astrology and the sorcery. Largely deprived of books and the urban society which fostered them, Islamic Spain and Islamic North Africa became the teachers of Medieval Europe. But what these regions taught was a far cry from the learning now so widely praised in the politically-correct textbooks that fill our libraries and bookshops.

---

[328] Colin Wilson and Christopher Evans, eds. *Strange but True* (Parragon Books, 1995) p. 285
[329] Ibid. p. 285

Sorcery and alchemy were not the only things learned by the Europeans from the Muslims. We know, and this is admitted by all, that European theology was profoundly influenced at this time by Islamic. But it was not just Avicenna and Averroes that the Christians took from their Muslim teachers. They took also ideas directly from the Koran and the Haditha; ideas about how heretics, apostates and sorcerers should be treated. And it is scarcely to be doubted that in establishing his own Inquisition Innocent III was directly imitating the example of the Almohads in Spain, who had set up their own commission for investigating heretics and apostates fifty years earlier.

Innocent III is viewed by the enemies of Christianity as the *bête noir*, the living embodiment of everything that was and is wrong with Christianity. Yet the fact that his attitudes were profoundly influenced by Islam is never mentioned. And there is another point to consider: whilst we do not seek to minimize the enormity of Innocent's actions, we must never forget that in the 12th and 13th centuries the Muslim threat had by no means receded: it remained as potent and dangerous as ever. In such circumstances – indeed, in any war situation – internal dissent (such as the Cathars represented) is liable to be viewed as representing a fifth column working for the enemy. And it is well-known fact that all wartime dissent is suppressed with a thoroughness and ruthlessness much more severe than would normally be the case. The later Spanish Inquisition, which implemented draconian measures against dissenters in the Iberian Peninsula, must be seen in the same light. The threat of Islam was ever present, and we can be reasonably certain that the severe repression of Muslims at this time was directly attributable to the fear of a renewed Muslim invasion of the Peninsula (by the Ottomans) and the possibility that the native Muslims would form a fifth column in support of the invaders.

An Enduring Legacy

We have found that in the years after 600 Classical civilization, which was by then synonymous with Christendom, came into contact with a new force, one that extolled war as a sacred duty, sanctioned the enslavement and killing on non-believers as a religious obligation, sanctioned the judicial use of torture, and provided for the execution of apostates and heretics. All of these attitudes, which, taken together, are surely unique in the religious traditions of mankind, can be traced to the very beginnings of that faith. Far from being manifestations of a degenerate phase of Islam, all of them go back to the founder of the faith himself. Yet, astonishingly enough, this is a religion and an ideology which is still extolled by academics and artists as enlightened and tolerant. Indeed, to this day, there exists a large body of opinion, throughout the Western World, which sees Islam as in every way superior to, and more enlightened than, Christianity.

By around 650 almost half the Christian world was lost to this new and "enlightened" faith; and by 715 the remainder was in serious danger. These events had an enormous impact. The closure of the Mediterranean meant the impoverishment of Western Europe, which was then thrown back on its own resources. The lack of papyrus forced the use of the immensely expensive parchment, leading naturally to a serious decline in literacy. The Viking Wars, which the Islamic Invasions solicited, brought enormous disruption also to Northern Europe. Desperate for a unifying force that could bring together all the Germanic kingdoms of the West for the defense of Christendom, the Western Empire was re-established. Constantinople, fighting for her very survival, could do little about this.

Western culture began to change radically. For the first time, Christians began to think in terms of Holy War, and the whole theology of the faith began to alter beyond recognition. This great transformation began in the years after 650, and the phenomenon we call "Crusading" began, properly speaking, in southern Italy and more especially Spain, during the seventh and eighth centuries, as Christians fought a desperate rearguard action to save what they could of their culture. This action was to develop into a protracted struggle that was to last for centuries, and was to have a profound and devastating effect upon European culture and civilization. Above all, it meant, by sheer impact of force and time, the gradual adoption by the Christians of many of the characteristics of their Muslim foes. Thus we note that, by the eleventh and twelfth centuries Christian kings in Spain and southern Italy reigned over arabized courts and began to adopt Muslim customs, such as polygamy. The most famous, or infamous, example of this was the Emperor Frederick II, "the baptized sultan of Sicily," who kept an expensive harem guarded by eunuchs.[330]

---

[330] Trevor-Roper, op cit., p. 147

HOLY WARRIORS

As well as this direct influence, there was the barbarizing effect of the continual war into which the whole Mediterranean littoral was now plunged. The arrival of Islam brought to a definitive end the peace of the Mediterranean, the *pax Romana* that had even survived the fall of Rome. With the arrival of Islam, the Mediterranean was no longer a highway, but a frontier, and a frontier of the most dangerous kind. Piracy, rapine, and slaughter became the norm – for a thousand years! And this is something that has been almost completely overlooked by historians, especially those of northern European extraction. For the latter in particular, the Mediterranean is viewed in the light of classical history. So bewitched have educated Europeans been by the civilizations of Greece and Rome, that they have treated the more recent part of Mediterranean history – over a thousand years of it – as if it never existed. The visitor to Mediterranean lands, perhaps on the Grand Tour, was shown the monuments of the classical world: here Caesar fought a battle; there Anthony brought his fleet, etc.

This distorted and romanticized view of the Mediterranean and its past, which ignored the savagery and fear of the past millennium, was particularly characteristic of those of Anglo-Saxon origin, with whom there was the added problem of religious antagonism. With the reign of Elizabeth I, England became the mortal enemy of Catholic Europe; and the Catholic power of the time was of course Spain. From this point on, English-speaking historians tended to be heavily biased against Catholic Spain and, unsurprisingly, extremely favorable towards Spain's Muslim enemies, who were romanticized and portrayed as cultured and urbane. It was then that the myth of the "golden age" of the Spanish Caliphate was born – a myth which, as we have seen, still has a very wide circulation.

Yet the reality was quite different: With the Muslim conquest of North Africa and Spain, a reign of terror was to commence that was to last for centuries. The war in Spain dragged on until the fifteenth century. By then, a new front was opened in Italy, as the rising power of the Ottoman Turks, having already engulfed Greece and the Balkans, threatened to penetrate Italy. This danger remained active and alive for the next three centuries, until the Turks were finally beaten back at the gates of Vienna in 1683. In the interim, the Pope was ready to flee from Rome on more than one occasion, as Ottoman fleets scoured the Adriatic and Ionian Seas. After the fall of Constantinople in 1453, it seemed that all of central Europe, including Hungary and Austria, was about to be overwhelmed; and though the imminent danger was averted by the victory of John Hunyadi at Belgrade (1456), it was renewed again in the sixteenth century, when an enormous Turkish invasion force was stopped by the Holy League at the naval battle of Lepanto (1571). And it is worth noting here that the Turkish losses at Lepanto, comprising 30,000 men and 200 out of 230 warships, did not prevent them returning the following year with another enormous fleet: Which speaks volumes for their persistence and the perennial nature of the threat they posed. A short time before this, in the 1530s, the Turks had extended their rule westwards along the North African coast as far as Morocco, where they encouraged an intensification of slaving raids against Christian communities in southern Europe. Fleets of Muslim pirates brought devastation to the coastal regions of Italy, Spain, southern France, and Greece. The Christians of the islands, in particular, Sicily, Sardinia, Corsica and the Balearics, had to get used to savage pirate raids, bent on rape and pillage.

Hugh Trevor-Roper was at pains to emphasize that the epoch we now call the Renaissance, which we view as an age of artistic and intellectual achievement, as well as exuberant optimism, seemed very different to the inhabitants of Europe at the time. Even as Cortes and Pizarro conquered the vastly wealthy lands of Mexico and Peru in his name, the Emperor Charles V gloomily awaited the dissolution of Christendom. "We set out to conquer worthless new empires beyond the seas," lamented Busbequius, the Belgian whom the King of the Romans sent as ambassador to the Sultan of Turkey, "and we are losing the heart of Europe."[331] Christendom, he wrote, subsided precariously by the good will of the king of Persia, whose ambitions in the east continually called the Sultan of Turkey back from his European conquests.[332]

These events had a profound effect on the character of the Christian peoples of the Balkans and of the Mediterranean, a fact which has never been fully appreciated by Northern Europeans. From the vantage-point of London or Paris, the Ottomans and the Barbary Pirates do not loom large. From Rome however things looked quite different. Rome, the very seat of the Catholic faith, was for centuries on the front line of this never-ending war. Viewed from central

---

[331] Trevor-Roper, op cit., p. 17
[332] Ibid.

HOLY WARRIORS

Italy, the paranoia of Medieval Popes about heresies and internal enemies becomes somewhat more understandable.

And the people of Spain, who held the front line of the bloody boundary for centuries, were transformed. The war against Islam became the *raison d'être* for many, even most, Spanish kings. It was a perennial project: Not an obsession, more like a normal part of life. It was taken for granted that there could never be peace with the Islamic world. How could it be otherwise, when making wear against the infidel world was a religious duty for every Muslim? Jihad was a state of permanent war which excluded the possibility of a true peace. Christians had understood this centuries earlier, and it was reiterated in the fourteenth century by the Islamic historian Ibn Khaldun:

> In the Muslim community, the holy war is a religious duty, because of the universalism of the [Muslim] mission and [the obligation to] convert everybody to Islam either by persuasion or by force. Therefore, caliphate and royal authority are united [in Islam], so that the person in charge can devote the available strength to both of them [religion and politics] at the same time.
>
> The other groups did not have a universal mission, and the holy war was not a religious duty to them, save only for purposes of defense. It has thus coma about that the person in charge of religious affairs [in other religious groups] is not concerned with power politics at all. [Among them] royal authority comes to those who have it, by accident and in some way that has nothing to do with religion. It comes to them as a necessary result of group feeling, which by its very nature seeks to obtain royal authority, as we have mentioned before, and not because they are under obligation to gain power over other nations, as is the case with Islam. They are merely required to establish their religion among their own [people].
>
> This is why the Israelites after Moses and Joshua remained unconcerned with royal authority for about four hundred years. Their only concern was to establish their religion (1: 473).
>
> Thereafter, there was dissensions among the Christians with regard to their religion and to Christology. They split into groups and sects, which secured the support of various Christian rulers against

each other. At different times there appeared different sects. Finally, these sects crystallized into three groups, which constitute the [Christian] sects. Others have no significance. These are the Melchites, the Jacobites, and the Nestorians. We do not think that we should blacken the pages of this book with discussion of their dogmas of unbelief. In general, they are well known. All of them are unbelief. This is clearly stated in the noble Qur'an. [To] discuss or argue those things with them is not up to us. It is [for them to choose between] conversion to Islam, payment of the poll tax, or death.[333]

Ibn Khaldun was a native of Andalusia, but what he wrote about jihad would have been understood by every monarch of Spain, Christian and Moor. Thus for the kings of Castile the survival in the Iberian Peninsula of any region from which Islam could launch attacks was seen as a real and ever present threat, and the reduction of Islamic Spain to the southern strongholds of Andalusia did not make Christians feel any more secure. Now the threat was not from North Africa but from Turkey. The existence of Granada threatened the existence of Christian Spain, for the Ottomans could at any moment use it as a beach-head for a second conquest of the Peninsula. Thus Granada had to be reduced, no matter what the cost. And even after that, the Spaniards did not feel secure. The war against Islam would continue, as it always had. The Ottomans were now threatening Italy and the entire western Mediterranean, Spain herself could be next. Indeed, that was the primary reason for the effort Ferdinand and Isabella invested in the siege of Granada: to deny the Turks a port by which they might launch an invasion and a new conquest. Even the voyages of discovery were undertaken with the struggle against Islam in mind. Columbus' first voyage, for example, had as its object the discovery of a direct route to the East Indies, bypassing Muslim territory, "so as to take Islam in the rear," says Louis Bertrand, "and to effect an alliance with the Great Khan – a mythical personage who was believed to be the sovereign of all that region, and favourable to the Christian religion …"[334] Bertrand was very insistent on this point, which he

---

[333] Ibn Khaldun, *The Muqaddimah: An Introduction to History* Vol. 1 (Trans. Franz Rosenthal, Bollingen Series 43: Princeton University Press, 1958) p. 480. Cited from Bat Ye'or, *The Dhimmi*, p. 162
[334] Bertrand, op cit., p. 163

emphasized in half a dozen pages. The voyage of discovery was to begin a new phase, he says, in "the Crusade against the Moors which was to be continued by a new and surer route. It was by way of the Indies that Islam was to be dealt a mortal blow."[335]

So certain was Bertrand of the connection between the exploits of the Conquistadores in the Americas and the war against Islam that he actually describes the conquest of America as the "last Crusade."

The record of the Conquistadores in the New World needs no repetition here: It is one of cruelty and greed on a truly monumental scale. Yet the habits of the Spaniards here, habits which gave rise to the "Black Legend," were learned at the school of the Caliphs. In Bertrand's words: "Lust for gold, bloodthirsty rapacity, the feverish pursuit of hidden treasure, application of torture to the vanquished to wrest the secret of their hiding-places from them – all these barbarous proceedings and all these vices, which the conquistadores were to take to America, they learnt at the school of the caliphs, the emirs, and the Moorish kings."[336]

Indeed all of the traits associated with the Spaniards, for which they have been roundly criticized by Anglo-Saxon historians, can be traced to the contact with Islam.

"The worst characteristic which the Spaniards acquired was the parasitism of the Arabs and the nomad Africans: the custom of living off one's neighbour's territory, the raid raised to the level of an institution, marauding and brigandage recognized as the sole means of existence for the man-at-arms. In the same way they went to win their bread in Moorish territory, so the Spaniards later went to win gold and territory in Mexico and Peru.

"They were to introduce there, too, the barbarous, summary practices of the Arabs: putting everything to fire and sword, cutting down fruit-trees, razing crops, devastating whole districts to starve out the enemy and bring them to terms; making slaves everywhere, condemning the population of the conquered countries to forced labour. All these detestable ways the conquistadores learnt from the Arabs.

"For several centuries slavery maintained itself in Christian Spain, as in the Islamic lands. Very certainly, also, it was to the Arabs that the Spaniards

---

[335] Ibid.
[336] Ibid., p. 159

owed the intransigence of their fanaticism, the pretension to be, if not the chosen of God, at least the most Catholic nation of Christendom. Philip II, like Abd er Rahman or El Mansour, was Defender of the Faith.

"Finally, it was not without contagion that the Spaniards lived for centuries in contact with a race of men who crucified their enemies and gloried in piling up thousands of severed heads by way of trophies. The cruelty of the Arabs and the Berbers also founded a school in the Peninsula. The ferocity of the emirs and the caliphs who killed their brothers or their sons with their own hands was to be handed on to Pedro the Cruel and Henry of Trastamare, those stranglers under canvas, no better than common assassins."[337]

The undoubted negative influence of Islam upon the character and culture of Spain and the other Mediterranean lands should not blind us to the fact that the Christian message was never completely lost nor the church as an institution completely corrupted. We have seen that, following the rise of the Germanic kingdoms in the fifth century, the church worked hard to uphold the rights of slaves and the peasants against the cupidity and passions of the fierce warrior-class which now ruled Spain, Gaul and Italy. This continued during the period of the Muslim and Viking invasions and afterwards. "The tenth and eleventh centuries saw a struggle between the lords and the church over the rights of these people [the peasants]. The lords wanted to deprive the serfs of all the rights of human beings, to say that they had no souls and to refuse to call their unions marriages."[338] The church, notes the above writer, won this battle, but not without fierce resistance on the part of the nobles. This struggle on behalf of the poor continued right throughout the Middle Ages and beyond, and we have already noted how the monasteries, for example, provided free medical care, as well as alms and shelter, to the poor and destitute all throughout this epoch. And the church further protected the poor by ensuring the enactment of laws against speculation, such as the fixed price of bread and grain, and the various rules which governed the business of the guilds. Even war was regulated by the church, and Medieval conflicts, at least within Europe, were not nearly as violent as many imagine. As Sidney Painter notes; "Even when kings and feudal princes fought supposedly serious wars in the early Middle Ages, they were not

---

[337] Ibid., p. 160
[338] Painter, op cit., p. 100

bloody. At the great and decisive battle of Lincoln in 1217, where some 600 knights on one side fought 800 on the other, only one knight was killed, and everyone was horrified at the unfortunate accident."[339]

There is no question that the Medieval custom of ransoming important hostages provided an economic motive for this remarkable unwillingness to use lethal force; but it is equally clear that the idea of chivalry, with its strongly Christian overtones, exerted a powerful moderating influence.

Nor should we forget that during the centuries which followed the First Crusade, when we might imagine Christians in Europe to have become thoroughly accustomed to the idea of fighting and killing for Christ, there is much evidence to show that this did not happen. The idea of violence in the name of Christ was, in the words of Jonathan Riley-Smith, "without precedent" when it was first promoted in the eleventh century.[340] "So radical was the notion of devotional war," says Riley-Smith, that it is surprising that there seem to have been no protests from senior churchmen"[341] Be that as it may, Christians could never be fully at ease with the idea, and enthusiasm crusading soon waned. Riley-Smith notes that, following the success of the First Crusade, the supply of new recruits immediately dried up, even among those groups and families who had been its strongest supporters. These reverted, instead, to the traditional non-military pilgrimage to the Holy Land.[342] We should note too individual statements like that of the English Franciscan Roger Bacon in the 1260s, who criticized the very idea of Crusading, arguing that such military activities impeded efforts to peacefully convert Muslims.[343] Contrast this with the attitude in Islam, where all warriors who died in the *Jihad* were "martyrs" and guaranteed an immediate reward of 72 virgins in Paradise. And the contrast is seen very clearly in the words of Gregory Palamas, an Orthodox metropolitan, who was a captive of the Turks in 1354: " ... these infamous people, hated by God and infamous, boast of having got the better of the Romans [Byzantines] by

---

[339] Ibid., p. 119

[340] Jonathan Riley-Smith, "The State of Mind of Crusaders to the East: 1095-1300," in Jonathan Riley-Smith (ed.) *Oxford History of the Crusades*, p. 79

[341] Ibid., p. 78

[342] Ibid., pp. 80-2

[343] Alan Forey, "The Military Orders, 1120-1312," in Jonathan Riley-Smith (ed.) *Oxford History of the Crusades*, p. 205

their love of God. ... They live by the bow, the sword, and debauchery, finding pleasure in taking slaves, devoting themselves to murder, pillage, spoil ... and not only do they commit these crimes, but even – what an aberration – they believe that God approves of them."[344]

And when the Spaniards began the conquest of the New World, one should not forget that the great majority of the excesses carried out were by individual and unregulated adventurers, over whom the royal and church authorities had little control. Nor should we neglect to mention that it was owing to the enormous and sustained pressure of many humane and courageous churchmen that the custom of enslaving the native inhabitants of the New World was finally abandoned.

Thus it would be a mistake to imagine, amidst the Crusades, the Inquisition, and the colonization of the Americas, that the original spirit and teaching of the Carpenter of Galilee was irretrievably lost. Nonetheless, the violent world in which the church found itself put many strains upon it; and the message of Christ was undeniably diluted.

What makes a Civilization?

Civilizations are the product of a complex interplay of physical, cultural and ideological factors. On an obvious level, urban civilizations cannot form without a large population, and a large population means agriculture. The more effective the agriculture – the more surplus food produced – the greater the population: The greater the population, the greater the technical and scientific advance. Put simply, the more people, the more knowledge and innovation. Furthermore, a civilization's geographical location is important. If the core of the civilization is at a cultural crossroads, such as was classical Greece, then the greater will be the technical and scientific advancement. Coming into contact with other peoples, learning how they do and view things, obviously has the effect of stimulating new enquiry and development.

Yet, as we have demonstrated in the present volume, the general culture and security of a society is crucial. It is a fact that has never been given the

---

[344] Robert Irwin, "Islam and the Crusades: 1096-1699," in Jonathan Riley-Smith (ed.) *Oxford History of the Crusades* pp. 251

attention it deserves that those societies which are most peaceful, and in a sense most civilized, are also those which are most secure. India, safe for centuries behind the barrier of the Himalayas, had the time and the tranquility to develop a civilization based upon the pacifist principles of Buddhism. In the same way, Tibet, protected by the ramparts of those same peaks, could evolve its own humane culture. In more modern times, the nations of Scandinavia, famous for their pacifism, have also been spared the horrors of war for several centuries. China never quite developed in the same way; for she was always vulnerable to attack by the tribesmen who stalked the steppe lands of Mongolia and Central Asia.

On the other face of the coin, it is a fact that lands that have never known security, never develop a pacifist mentality. We tend to find very few pacifist vegetarians in Viking societies. So for example the Aztecs of Mexico, inhabiting a land wracked by the forces of nature in the form of volcanoes, earthquakes and hurricanes, and open to the attacks of nomads from the north, remained caught in a cycle of incessant war and human sacrifice. And even in modern times, areas that have a history of inter-communal conflict tend to have a more "violent" culture, tend to see violence as an acceptable way of solving problems.

The same, it is clear, holds good for nations and civilizations. Europe, under the protective mantle of the Roman legions, might have developed into a pacifist society like Buddhist India. Yet the removal of Roman power, and the flooding of the western provinces by barbarian armies, produced a revival of the military and warrior spirit which had characterized Rome herself in her earlier days. Even then, however, things could have developed differently: The barbarians became "softened" by the settled lives they began to lead in the western provinces and by the influence of the Christian faith. Even newly-arrived hordes, like the Franks and Langobards in the late fifth and sixth centuries, fell under the civilizing spell of Rome and of Christianity; and the fierce customs of the men who, just a generation earlier had dwelt in the forests and wildernesses of Germany, soon began to be softened in the vineyards of Gaul and the olive-groves of Spain. It was just then, however, at the beginning of the seventh century, when a Christian civilization holding fast to all the teachings of Christ might well have arisen, that there appeared a new enemy: one that could not be placated and could not be Christianized. To the normal horrors of war the Muslim invaders added a new and dangerous element:

religious fanaticism. These were invaders intent not only on plunder and enslavement, but also on the extinction or at the very least subjugation of the Christian faith. Against the barbarians of Germany and Scythia, the Christians of the west might fight for the possession of their homes and their lands. These enemies were not intent on the destruction of the Christian religion. Christians were free to worship as they wished; and indeed many of the barbarians showed, from the very start, that they could be influenced by and even converted to the Christian faith.

With the Muslims, this was never an option. These were the "unconvertibles", men who were driven by their own religious zeal, and who waged war specifically to spread that faith. And this was an enmity that time did not ameliorate: for centuries after the invasions of southern Italy, Spain and the islands of Sicily, Sardinia and Corsica, Muslim freebooters scoured the Mediterranean and the coastlands of southern France and Italy, robbing, killing and enslaving. This last point cannot be emphasized too strongly: With the arrival of Islam, Mediterranean Europe was never again at peace – not until the early part of the nineteenth century, anyway. Hard as it might be to believe, Muslim privateers based in North Africa, the Barbary Pirates, terrorized the Mediterranean until after the end of the Napoleonic Wars. In the centuries preceding that, Muslim armies, first in the form of the Almoravids and later the Ottomans, launched periodic large-scale invasions of territories in southern Europe; and even when they were not doing so, Muslim pirates and slave-traders were involved in incessant raids against coastal settlements in Spain, southern France, Italy, Dalmatia, Albania, Greece, and all the Mediterranean islands. This activity continued unabated for centuries, and the only analogy that springs to mind is to imagine, in northern Europe, what it would have been like if the Viking raids had lasted a thousand years.

It has been estimated that between the sixteenth and nineteenth centuries Muslim pirates based in North Africa captured and enslaved between a million and a million-and-a-quarter Europeans.[345] Although their attacks ranged as far north as Iceland and Norway, the impact was most severe along the Mediterranean coasts of Spain, France and Italy, with large areas of coastline eventually being made uninhabitable by the threat.

---

[345] http//:en.wikipedia.org/wiki/Barbary_pirates

HOLY WARRIORS

The impact of this incessant violence has never, I feel, been either thoroughly studied or fully understood. The Mediterranean coastlands must learn to live in a state of constant alert, with fear never far removed. Populations needed to be ready, at a moment's notice, with a military response. Fortifications must be built and young men trained in the use of arms. There was the development of a semi-paranoid culture in which killing and being killed was the norm, or at least not unusual. Small wonder that some of these territories, particularly Southern Italy, Sicily, Spain, Corsica, parts of Greece and Albania, would in time develop their own violent and relentless cultures; and that it would be above all in Spain that the Inquisition would find its spiritual home. Small wonder too that it would be from this same land that Holy Warriors would set out, in the fifteenth and sixteenth centuries, to conquer the peoples of the New World for Christ.[346]

It is not true, of course, that Christendom and Christianity can be entirely absolved of the guilt for what happened in the decades and centuries that followed the First Crusade. There is no doubt, for example, that at least one aspect of Christian doctrine may have been a contributing factor. I refer to the easy and ready forgiveness of sins. Fundamental to Christian thinking is the idea that Christ took upon himself the guilt of all humanity, and that he washed mankind's sins in his blood. All Christians need do, to obtain this forgiveness, is confess their sins. But the system of the confessional at once conferred great power and a great burden upon the Catholic priesthood. Any miscreant, no matter how heinous his acts, must be granted absolution if he requests it. In many ways, however, this might be taken almost as a license to sin. True, the Church did teach, and insist, that the though the mortal guilt of a murder might be abrogated by the act of confession, the venial guilt remained; and though the penitent might not be condemned to the fires of everlasting Hell for his sins, he might be required to spend a very long time indeed in the equally severe fires of Purgatory. Yet though the priest might teach this from the pulpit, in the eyes of the vulgar and the worldly, the lifting of the threat of Hell must have seemed like absolute and unconditional forgiveness; and the easy manner with which the

---

[346] We should not forget of course that the Conquistadors usually acted without official sanction, and that the Church, often in co-operation with the Spanish Government, worked very hard to control their excesses.

6: IMPACT OF ISLAM

criminal had escaped the ultimate sanction might make him less averse to repeating the offence at a future date.

If we doubt that this was how men actually thought, and think, we need only recall the example of no less a personage than Constantine, who, after a life marred by some very serious crimes, waited till his deathbed to receive Christian baptism and absolute remission of all guilt.

The priests and monks of Buddhism and Hinduism could offer their flocks no such easy remedies. In their system, a man might cleanse his own karma only by suffering or by the performance of good works equal in weight to the bad already committed. A warrior guilty of murder or rapine might approach the monastery or the temple with a heart full of remorse, only to be turned away by this bleak, though profoundly motivating, message.

We need to consider too the fact that Christianity (along with Islam) insisted that each individual has but one life to find the truth. This naturally gave an urgency to those proselytizing on behalf of the faith. Hell, or perhaps Limbo, beckoned for those who had not undergone Christian baptism. Not for them the easygoing Indian notion that if one did not find enlightenment this time round, one could find it in the next incarnation. Thus the rejection of reincarnation by the western faiths simultaneously produced a zealous urgency to convert others and magnified the importance of the Devil and Hell. All those who failed to find the truth this time round became part of Satan's kingdom; thereby assigning, in western minds, an immense empire to the latter. Among the Eastern faiths (Buddhism, Hindiusm, etc), the Devil enjoys no such prominence. In their theologies (as in the Neoplatonic) all creatures, even the devils, are eventually brought back to the godhead.

In the end, however, it was not to any faults in the theology of the Christian faith, or the Church's interpretation of that faith, that led to the rise of a militant and intolerant Christianity. Without the continued and incessant violence directed at the Christians by Islam over a period of many centuries, there seems little doubt that Europe would have developed in a very different way: And it seems certain that the rapacious militarism which characterized Europe from the beginning of the Age of the Crusades would never have appeared

How then, without Islam, would events have unfolded? It is of course impossible to say with certainty, but it seems fairly obvious that the "Medieval"

222

world as we now know it would never have appeared. It is likely that Byzantium would have continued the process, already well under way in the late sixth century, of raising the cultural level of the West. The break between Rome and Byzantium might not have occurred, or been so acrimonious, and there seems little doubt that Western Europe would have experienced its "Renaissance", or rediscovery of classical civilization, much earlier. Basilicas such as those built by Justinian at Ravenna in the middle of the sixth century would no doubt soon have been appearing throughout Gaul, Spain and Germany, and, with the continued availability of papyrus from Egypt, there would have been a rapid development of literature and the arts. The Viking raids would not have occurred, or at least would not have been as destructive as they were. There would certainly have been no Crusades, there being no Islam to launch them against. And the lack of Viking and Islamic influence would have induced the development in Europe of a more pacific culture. Without Islamic influence it is doubtful if anti-Semitism would have arisen; certainly not in the virulent form it eventually took. The lack of an external and dangerous enemy like Islam would have hindered the development of the paranoia that gripped Europe over the issue of heretics and "witchcraft". There would have been no Inquisition. And without the Islamic example of slavery, the contact with the natives of the New World, when it came, would have been very different, as would Europe's relations with the peoples of sub-Saharan Africa.

But these are all what-ifs. History happened, and what happened cannot be changed. Yet if we are not to repeat the mistakes of the past, it is important that we understand exactly what did happen, and why.

APPENDIX

A MYTHICAL DARK AGE?

The Dark Age Problem

Throughout the present volume it has been hinted that the period of history popularly known as the "Dark Age" – namely the early seventh to the early tenth centuries – needs to be re-examined in a fundamental way. It seemed that almost everywhere we looked we uncovered anomalies, enigmas, and echoes. Events of the seventh and eighth centuries, for example, seemed to have reoccurred in the tenth and eleventh. On the one hand, much evidence seemed to suggest that the rise of Islam had been somehow misdated; that it appeared in the tenth century and got backdated into the seventh. This was indicated very strongly, for example, by the archaeology, particularly of Spain, which seemed to be devoid of Muslim remains until the tenth century. On the other hand, events of the tenth and eleventh centuries seemed in many instances to belong to an earlier age, and, were it not for accepted chronology, would most assuredly be placed in the seventh or eighth centuries. Much evidence, for example, suggested that the Viking and Magyar assault against the Christian West, which is supposed to have reached its high point in the tenth century, corresponded with the high point of the Muslim advance from the south, which of course came in the seventh and eighth centuries.

225

APPENDIX: A MYTHICAL DARK AGE?

Could it be then that there is something dramatically wrong with the chronology of this period? At first glance, the idea seems preposterous. Upon closer inspection, however, one begins to wonder.

The term Dark Age, or "dark period", was first introduced into the nomenclature of historians during the fourteenth century by the Italian scholar Petrarch. Although originally not pejorative, it rapidly became so, and was soon employed by Protestant writers to describe everything between Constantine and the Reformation. The term took on new meaning during the Enlightenment, when men such as Voltaire and Kant saw the whole of what we now call the Middle Ages as a period of faith and thus the opposite of "enlightenment".

By the nineteenth century the term became generally confined to the seventh, eighth, ninth and early tenth centuries, a span of three centuries which remained little known and from which time very few architectural structures seemed to have survived. By the start of the twentieth century however, an increasing number of academics began to reject the "Dark Age" nomenclature even for this period. These writers stressed what they saw as a very real cultural continuity from the end of the sixth century through to the tenth and eleventh. It was found that the arts and sciences did not decline to the extent that was previously believed in the intervening centuries. By the beginning of the tenth century, Western culture still looked strikingly Roman. This was illustrated most graphically in the art of the Ottonian period, where illuminated manuscripts and ivory book-covers are executed in a typically late classical style. Some of these look as if they had been created in the sixth or early seventh centuries. (see eg. Figs. 7 and 8) According to one author, "the tenth century produced work as splendid and as technically skilful, even as delicate, as any other age."[347] The kings and prelates of the time evidently – if the evidence of art is anything to go by – still inhabited Roman or at least Roman-style villas and palaces; and the same situation still pertained into the eleventh century, when we again find kings and monarchs ensconced in Roman villas (as in the Bayeux Tapestry).

In accordance with this picture of continuity, it is now increasingly admitted that the monastic settlements preserved the Greek spirit of enquiry and logical thinking far more completely than has hitherto been allowed. We find, for example, that early in the eleventh century a monk named Eilmer flew more

---

[347] Clark, op cit., p. 24

than 600 feet with a glider, an achievement celebrated for centuries afterwards.[348] Other scientific innovations, which seem to prefigure the achievements of Leonardo Da Vinci, there were in plenty. One of the most impressive of these was clock-making. The first clock of which we have any record was built by Gerbert of Aurillac, the future Pope Sylvester II, for the German town of Magdeburg, around the year 996. Gerbert of course studied among the Arabs, and there is no question that much of his knowledge was derived from that source. Yet it seems virtually certain too that he had access to much of the technical knowledge of the Greeks and Romans, who are now known to have constructed sophisticated astronomical clocks (astrolabes) using gears and cog-wheels. After this, Europeans began to surpass the ancients. In Chapter 3 we saw how the Muslim conquerors of Spain, at the start of the eighth century, described the large and opulent Visigothic cities of the region, and how one of their scribes, Ibn Adhari, spoke of Seville as (in his time) "the seat of the Roman adepts of sacred and profane science." Another Arab writer, Merida, mentions Seville's great bridge as well as "magnificent palaces and churches,"[349] whilst Mousa, after completing the conquest, proudly displayed to the Caliph in Damascus the booty he had taken from the Spaniards: "... thirty thousand virgins, daughters of Gothic kings and princes, and an innumerable quantity of merchandise and precious stones." Among these objects there was one named by the Arabs the Table of Solomon: "The edges and the legs were of emeralds. ... These, to the number of three hundred and sixty, were enriched with pearls and coral." And we are told that after a raid as far as France, found in Saragossa "riches incalculable."[350]

The reader will bear in mind that these are contemporary accounts of a country supposedly in the midst of a Dark Age; an epoch during which, according to Bernard Lewis, living conditions in Europe were almost Neolithic.

For those academics who wish to abolish the term Dark Ages there remains, however, the problem of archaeology: or rather, the lack of it. The intensive archaeological investigation which has characterized the last hundred

---

[348] Stanley L. Jaki, "Medieval Creativity in Science and Technology," in *Patterns and Principles and Other Essays* (Bryn Mawr, Pennsylvania: Intercollegiate Studies Institute, 1995), 81.
[349] Bertrand, op cit., pp. 17-8
[350] Ibid. p. 18

years has added virtually nothing to our knowledge of the three hundred years which mark the peak of the "Dark Ages", namely the three centuries between the early seventh century and the early tenth. Three hundred years, it would seem, have left almost no trace in the ground. Truly, it would appear, these years were indeed dark. Not only did men forget how to build in stone, they seem to have lost the capacity even of creating pottery; and the centuries in England that are generally designated Anglo-Saxon have left little or nothing even of this necessary domestic art.[351] Pottery-making does appear again in the tenth century, but what did the Anglo-Saxons use in the ages that preceded it?

Fig. 7. Tenth-century book-covers, showing celebration of the Mass

---

[351] See eg. Boris Johnston, *The Dream of Rome* (London, 2006) p. 198

Fig. 8. Tenth-century book-cover, showing Saint Gregory and scribes. (after K. Clark). The artistic style of portrayal and the background architecture all look typically late Roman, and could equally well be dated to the seventh century.

Fig. 9. Otto III as Christian Roman Emperor, tenth century.

APPENDIX: A MYTHICAL DARK AGE?

Yet the absence of buildings and of archaeology throughout Europe, a situation normally blamed on the depredations of the Germanic Barbarians, is matched in the Arab and Byzantines worlds – two regions never conquered by the Barbarians and therefore two regions which should not have a "Dark Age". Yet a Dark Age there most assuredly is.

The lack of Arab and Byzantine archaeology for this period has only recently come to the attention of the scholarly community, and has caused something of a sensation. We have already (Chpater 2) remarked upon this Byzantine Dark Age and attributed it, in part at least, to the impact of Islam. Byzantium, like Western Europe, was devastated both economically and culturally by the interminable war with Islam and by the closing of the trade-routes to the East. Yet the decline in prosperity, population, and urban life was such that not even war of the most total kind can explain.

In the Byzantine lands archaeologists discovered an unbroken line of development from the foundation of Constantinople through the fifth and sixth centuries. But then, about forty years after the death of Justinian the Great, from the first quarter of the seventh century, there is a total and absolute break. Hardly a house, a church, or artifact of any kind has been recovered from the next three centuries. Cities were abandoned and urban life came to an end. There is no sign of revival until the middle of the tenth century. In his *Byzantium: The Empire of New Rome*, Cyril Mango describes this epoch as a "dark age", and in a chapter entitled "The Disappearance and Revival of Cities", he looks at the vexed question of causes. "The evidence," he notes, "for the collapse of the cities [in the seventh century and after] is largely archaeological."[352] This veritable disappearing act is found throughout the Byzantine realms, both in the Balkans and in Asia. Sirmium, he notes, was "completely deserted" after its surrender to the Avars in 582." South of Sirmium, in Stobi, we find "considerable evidence of building" throughout the fifth century, but "no building activity whatever after the sixth century."[353] Town after town throughout the region "ceased to exist" shortly after circa 600.[354] "The same panorama of abandonment," he notes, "is visible in Greece." This is the case at Athens, Corinth and elsewhere. "In Boeotian Thebes there is no sign of any

---

[352] Mango, op cit., p. 69
[353] Ibid., pp. 69-70
[354] Ibid., p. 70

urban life between the sixth century and the second half of the ninth."[355] "We may add," he says, "that, with the exception of Thessalonica and the island of Paros, not a single Early Christian Church remained standing in all of Greece, and there is no evidence of any building activity between about 600 and the early years of the ninth century."

There seems then to have been a general and complete abandonment throughout all the urban centres of south-eastern Europe. But precisely the same is observed in Asia Minor. "In Bithynia, the Asiatic province closest to Constantinople, only Nicaea appears to have survived. Nicomedia, once a great imperial capital, lay in ruins in the ninth century."[356] Further south the same picture is repeated. Ephesus, according to the documentary sources, did survive into the eighth century, and produced a tax revenue of a hundred pounds of gold; "yet the excavators have found little evidence of any building activity, save for a small church replacing the earlier and much larger basilica of St. Mary."[357] Sardis too was abandoned in the early seventh century, and the same story was repeated at Miletus and Pergamum. "Other sites that have been investigated, like Nysa and Laodicea, tell essentially the same story ..."[358]

Coinage can give a fairly good indication of the economic life of a country. Mango notes, "In sites that have been systematically excavated, such as Athens, Corinth, Sardis and others, it has been ascertained that bronze coinage, the small change used for everyday transactions, was plentiful throughout the sixth century and (depending on local circumstances) until some time in the seventh, after which it almost disappeared, then showed a slight increase in the ninth, and did not become abundant again until the latter part of the tenth."[359] Yet even the statement that some coins appeared in the ninth century has to be treated with caution. Mango notes that at Sardis the period between 491 and 616 is represented by 1,011 bronze coins, the rest of the seventh century by about 90, "and the eighth and ninth centuries combined by no more than 9."[360] And, "similar results have been obtained from nearly all provincial Byzantine cities."

---

[355] Ibid.
[356] Ibid., p. 71
[357] Ibid., p. 72
[358] Ibid.
[359] Ibid., pp. 72-3
[360] Ibid., p. 73

APPENDIX: A MYTHICAL DARK AGE?

It cannot be stressed too strongly that the paltry remains of the eighth and ninth centuries, whether they be in the form of coins or church buildings, are usually of questionable provenance, a fact noted by Mango himself, who remarked that often, upon closer inspection, these turn out to originate either before the dark age, or after it.

It is precisely the same with the Islamic world. Here of course the impact of Islam cannot be blamed for the poverty of remains. The seventh to tenth centuries, after all, were reputedly Islam's Golden Age, when the Muslim world stood at the head of civilization. Yet, as we saw in Chapter 4, the Islamic regions are as devoid of material remains in this epoch as the Christian. Egypt was the largest and most populous Islamic country during the Middle Ages. The Muslim conquest of the country occurred in 638, and we should expect the invaders to have begun, almost immediately, using the wealth of the country to begin building numerous and splendid places of worship – but they didn't. Only two mosques in the whole of Egypt, both in Cairo, are said to date from before the eleventh century: the Amr ibn al-As, AD 641 and the Ahmad ibn Tulun, AD 878. However, the latter building has many features found only in mosques of the eleventh century, so its date of 878 is controversial. Thus, in Egypt, we have a single place of worship, the mosque of Amr ibn al-As, dating from three years after the Muslim conquest, then nothing for another three-and-a-half centuries. Why should the Muslims wait over 300 years before building themselves places of worship? And it is the same throughout the Islamic world. No matter where we go, from Spain to Iran, there is virtually nothing between circa 650 and 950. Spain, for example, is supposed to have witnessed a flowering of Islamic culture and civilization in the two centuries after the Arab conquest of 711; and the city of Cordoba is said to have grown to a sophisticated metropolis of half-a-million people or more. Yet according to the *Oxford Archaeological Guide*, the city has revealed, after exhaustive excavations over the past half-century: (a) The south-western portion of the city wall, which was "presumably" of the ninth century;[361] (b) A small bath-complex, of the 9th/10th century;[362] and (c) A "part" of the Umayyad (8th/9th century) mosque.[363] The poverty of these remains, from a reputedly half-million-strong metropolis, is striking; and we can

---

[361] *The Oxford Archaeological Guide* (Collins, 1998) p. 73
[362] Ibid. p. 119
[363] Ibid. p. 120

only conclude that the evidence shows that such a metropolis never existed. It would appear that we have a "dark age" in regions where there was no collapse of civilization – where no dark age should exist.

What does all this mean? We are accustomed to think in terms of a "dark age" in Western Europe, because we have been told for centuries that the Barbarian peoples of Germany and the East destroyed the Roman world in the fifth and sixth centuries. This of course is flatly contradicted by the literary evidence, highlighted by Pirenne, of which we have had much to say. Even the Islamic sources speak of an opulent and flourishing civilization in Visigothic Spain. Still, archaeology apparently pronounces otherwise; and we are now told that the Anglo-Saxon invaders of Britain for example sank so low that they even forgot how to make pottery for three centuries! Truly a return, as Bernard Lewis described it, to an almost Neolithic existence. Indeed, a Neanderthal existence would be a more appropriate comparison, as Neolithic peoples were well able to make pottery.

A Radical Solution

The lack of archaeology during this epoch has long been an enigma, but it is an enigma for which a novel solution has now been proposed. Since the early 1990s, German writer Heribert Illig has been suggesting that the years between 600 and 900, or, more precisely, between 614 and 911, never actually existed, and that almost three phantom centuries were inserted into the calendar. It was this chronological error, more than anything else, that gave rise to the notion of the Dark Age.

The present writer has been aware of Illig's thesis now for over a decade, and researched it thoroughly before coming out in favour. I was initially attracted to the idea because it seemed to solve many of the riddles and enigmas surrounding the Dark Age. On the other hand, acceptance of the thesis appeared (at first glance) to create almost as many problems as it solved. Copious records, in the forms of chronicles and annals, are known to exist from the Dark Age; and these documents cover the period between 600 and 900 in detail. In addition, they appear to be internally consistent. The Anlgo-Saxon Chronicle, for example, and Bede, will mention the visit of a Anglo-Saxon king to France in a certain year, and the corresponding chronicles of medieval France will confirm the visit. Furthermore, if three hundred years were added to the calendar, how could this error have been transmitted to the Byzantine and Islamic worlds? Do not their records agree in detail with the western calendar? To argue that all these documents are false, we would apparently need to assume that they are in some sense fraudulent and there was thus a vast conspiracy that somehow took in all the nations of Europe and the Middle East. Such a proposition seemed utterly improbable.

Yet evidence seemed to appear again and again which brought Illig's thesis forcefully to mind. The most crucial, for me, and the most decisive, came in the astonishing absence of Byzantine and Islamic archaeology for this period. These regions, as noted above, were never overrun by barbarian tribes and should not, therefore, have experienced any kind of "Dark Age," and yet, in those very areas, from the three centuries between circa 600 and 900, we find precisely the same gap: an almost complete absence of architecture, plus a poverty of smaller artifacts and of original documentation. As with western Europe, the records and chronicles which cover these periods in the Byzantine and Islamic worlds were all written many centuries later.

The conclusion seemed inescapable to me: The "Dark Age," both in the east and the west, was a fiction; a phantom 300 years that have, somehow, slipped into the calendar. But how could such a thing have happened?

This latter question was, for me, the crux of the issue. It is scarcely possible that the Byzantines or Muslims would have co-operated with the western Christians in a deliberate falsification of history. Their histories, it is said, run in an unbroken sequence from the foundation of Constantinople and the life of Muhammad respectively. The Muslims even begin their calendar with Muhammad. How could they have been mistaken about the date of their own founder's lifetime?

Before commenting on this, it is necessary to look at the whole issue of how chronology was calculated in antiquity and the Middle Ages. The Romans, it is well-known, counted their dates from the foundation of the city by Romulus (*ab urbe condita*). This was the system in place during the entire period of the Western Empire – even after most of the inhabitants had become Christian. It was only during the fifth century that the old system was abandoned.

Origins of the *Anno Domini* Calendar

It is generally assumed that, following the Christianization of the Roman Empire in the years after Constantine, the Romans immediately adopted the *anno domini* system. This, however, was not the case. In fact, the old calendar of *ab urbe condita*, which dated the years according to the number that had elapsed since the foundation of the city under Romulus, continued to be used for some time. With the formal abolition of the Western Empire in 476, the centralized Roman bureaucracy, with its records and record-keeping, disappeared. In its place there arose much smaller and localized bureaucracies working for the various Gothic, Vandal, and Frankish kings under whom they labored. These new kingdoms were all, in theory at least, Christian; and they still, as we saw, regarded themselves ultimately as subjects of Rome – though now Rome lay in Constantinople. The new kingdoms each adopted their own calendars and dating-systems. These were, it is true, based upon the Bible; but they were not based on counting the years since the birth of Christ: They were based instead upon counting the years since the creation of the world, as outlined in the Old Testament. Christians of that period were not particularly interested in how long it had been since Christ's birth.[364] What they were interested in – what they were intensely interested in – was the question of how long it would be until Christ returned. The earliest Christians had believed that return to be imminent, owing to the fact that Christ had, in describing the times which would see the return of the Son of Man, said that "this generation" would not pass until these events had taken place.

By the fourth and fifth centuries, Christians no longer saw the Second Coming as imminent, but remained intensely interested in the question of when it would occur. In preparation for this great event, believers were not cremated, like the pagan Romans, but entombed in a vast and growing labyrinth of catacombs under the streets of Rome and the other cities of the Empire. The bodily resurrection was something expected and anticipated. And it was this expectation that turned the attention of Christians to the Old Testament. In the

---

[364] It is true that Dionysius Exiguus (c. 470 – 544) calculated, counting back through consular years, the number that had elapsed since the birth of Christ (525). However, Dionysius' computation was never used for official purposes.

APPENDIX: A MYTHICAL DARK AGE?

Book of Revelation, John had said that, after his return, Christ would rule the world for a thousand years – the millennium – and that after that time, the world would come to an end. Christians theorized endlessly on when this millennium would begin, connected as it was with the second coming of Christ. A clue appeared to be contained in the account of creation in the Book of Genesis. Here it stated that God made the world in six days, and that on the seventh He had rested. In one of Peter's epistles however (2 Peter 3:8), we find the statement that "with the Lord a day is like a thousand years and a thousand years are like a day." Christians began to speculate that the six days of creation might represent six thousand years of ordinary or profane history and that the seventh day, the Holy Day, the day on which God rested, might represent the Millennium, the thousand years during which Christ would reign triumphantly over the world. Gibbon puts it thus: "The ancient and popular doctrine of the Millennium was intimately connected with the second coming of Christ. As the works of the creation had been finished in six days, their duration in the present state, according to a tradition which was attributed to the prophet Elijah, was fixed to six thousand years. By the same analogy it was inferred that this long period of labour and contention, which was now almost elapsed, would be succeeded by a joyful Sabbath of a thousand years; and that Christ ... would reign upon earth till the time appointed for the last and general resurrection." (*Decline and Fall*, Chapter 15)

Thus, if it could be determined exactly how many years had passed since creation, it might be possible to predict when Christ's return might be expected. There arose then, in some quarters, an intense interest in the Old Testament and the Book of Genesis. Educated and sophisticated Romans, of course, trained in the thinking of Plato and Aristotle, could not look upon the Book of Genesis as anything other than myth, or at best allegory. Yet even at its height, the Roman Empire was not a literate society in the modern sense, and the great majority of Christian believers retained a simple and simplistic notion of the sacred scriptures and their interpretation. This would have been true also of the Germanic kings who now controlled the territory of the Western Empire. And even philosophers (and there remained plenty during the fifth and sixth centuries) could view the dates and figures provided in Genesis as, if not real history, at least providentially significant. The belief in science and reason does not automatically exclude the possibility of the supernatural.

Using the Book of Genesis then, and counting the generations of kings and patriarchs back to the time of Adam and Eve, it was possible to date the age of the world. Yet even such a simplistic and fundamentalist exegesis posed great problems, because the Book of Genesis was by no means clear as to when one generation ended and another began. The earlier patriarchs are said to have lived many centuries, and they had children throughout their lives. Using Genesis then as a guide to the Age of the World was thus a very unspecific "science," and it was possible to arrive at many alternative dates. Jewish scholars around the time of Christ generally believed the world to be roughly between 3700 and 4000 years old. Archbishop Ussher of Armagh, famously – using the Latin *Vulgate* Bible – dated the Creation to 4004 BC. Scholars of the early Christian period, using the *Septuagint*, and anxious to "speed-up" the date for the approach of the year 6000, and thus for Christ's return, tended to favour later dates. Thus one school, led by Bishop Eusebius and Saint Hieronymus, placed the birth of Christ just two years short of 5200; whilst another school, led by Saint Hippolytus, placed it in the year 5500. Other schools of thought favored 5300. All agreed, however, that the year 6000 would see the Second Coming of Christ and the beginning of the thousand years of Christ's earthly reign.

Thus Christians of the fifth and sixth centuries were not particularly interested in the time which had elapsed since the birth of Christ, but in the time that had elapsed since the creation of the world. And when a Bible-based chronology was adopted, it was this Age of the Creation, or Age of the World, that was used. Nor would this system be abandoned until the eleventh and twelfth centuries. Only then did Christian Europe begin to count the years as *anno domini*.

The adoption of *anno domini* as a calendar reckoning-point has been traced in great detail by Heribert Illig, who has proved, beyond reasonable doubt, that it was under the Holy Roman Emperor Otto III that the system was devised. By the middle of the tenth century (in reality, the middle of the seventh century), Europe was under sustained attack from north, south, and east; from Muslims, Vikings, and Hungarians. Crucially, by the second half of the seventh century, Byzantium was near to collapse as territory after territory fell to the Muslims. As we saw, ever since the abolition of the Western Empire in 476, the Germanic kings of the occident, who now occupied the territories of the West, continued to give their allegiance to the Emperor in Constantinople. The gold

237

coins they struck all bore the image of the Emperor. No king of the Goths or of the Franks, no matter how powerful, dared to assume the Imperial Purple. The first signs of radical change are seen during the reign of Chlotar II in Gaul (584 – 630) and Heraclius in Byzantium (610 – 641). The latter was the first Eastern Emperor to come into conflict with the Arabs, and it was during his time, according to Illig, that the great and wealthy territories of Egypt and Syria were lost to the Empire. It was in the reign of Heraclius, as we saw in Chapter 1, that the kings of the West ceased to strike the image of the Emperor on their coins. Chlotar II became the first king of the West to put his own image on his coins. This was the beginning of the definitive break between East and West.

With Byzantium fully engaged, and in danger of falling, the time was ripe for a new Emperor in the West; for a German Emperor, no less. Such, by the middle of the tenth century (in reality, middle of the seventh), was the conclusion reached by Otto the Great, Duke of Saxony and son of Henry the Fowler. Yet the idea of a German Emperor was without precedent. Since none existed, one had to be created.

This was not so difficult to do because in those days very few people had any idea of history or of chronology. A half-forgotten or semi-legendary Merovingian king whose nickname was "Carl" or "Carolus" ("the Warrior"), and who may or may not have briefly claimed the title of Emperor (there are some grounds for believing Theodebert I did that in 539-540, as he waged war against Justinian in Italy), could be used as the basis for an earlier Imperial dynasty. Such a dynasty would need its own century or two in which to reign, and this had to be added to the calendar. How could the Ottonians get away with this? Very easily, in fact: It cannot be stressed too strongly that what we moderns call "history", namely a body of literature outlining a more or less agreed picture of the past, along with an agreed chronology, did not then exist. In those days there were no public libraries, newspapers, and almost no education. Even today, after almost 150 years of compulsory education, and with extremely easy access to knowledge, how many people, taken at random in the street, could tell much about the life of Julius Caesar? Nine out of ten might say "a Roman Emperor", (which is in fact wrong), and have no idea when he lived. Perhaps one in twenty might give a few details of his life, including a guess as to when he lived. In a largely illiterate society, such as Ottonian Germany, no one would have known anything about the past. A few, a very few, educated persons, such as churchmen, may have been acquainted with the names of the great persons of the past, such as Alexander, Caesar, etc. But of their lives and when they lived they could probably have said very little. The past therefore was an unknown territory, a foreign region which one might populate with the creations of one's own imagination.

Of course, we cannot invent centuries that never existed, if a firmly-established calendar, starting with a known event of history – such as the birth of Christ – is employed. If the *anno domini* calendar had been introduced when almost everyone believes it was introduced, during the time of Constantine, then the Ottonian kings certainly could not have gotten away with what they did. But the fact is, the *anno domini* system was not introduced until the time of Otto III, and did not become widespread in Europe until the twelfth century.

The motive then for the insertion of phantom centuries (and phantom characters such as Charlemagne) into history, was the revival of the Western Roman Empire. It should be obvious that a revival of the Roman Empire in the tenth century, after centuries during which Roman civilization and even the memory of Rome's existence became dimmed (as we are required to believe by the textbooks) is a nonsense. But if Otto the Great was crowned by Pope John XII in 662 (or 665), rather than 962, everything makes perfect sense. It was then that there was a crying need for a leader who could unite the depleted remnants of Christendom to withstand enemies who seemed on the verge of complete victory. Attacked on the north, east, and above all south, Christendom's days seemed numbered. Emperor and Pope, working together, hand in glove, might just save the day: might rally the peoples of a diminishing Christian Europe in one last effort. And the effort was not in vain. By the time of Otto III, the main thrust of the Magyar and Viking threat had been beaten off, and, towards the end of the tenth century (actually towards the end of the seventh), virtually all of Europe had accepted, or was on the verge of accepting, the Christian faith. Thus Harald Bluetooth had made Denmark a Christian country in 965 (in reality, around 665 or 668), whilst King Steven of Hungary had indicated his willingness to be baptized and to bring his country with him into the Christian fold. This he actually did on Christmas Day 1000 (or New Year's Day 1001), on which occasion he was reputedly crowned as a Christian king with a crown sent to him by Pope Silvester.

APPENDIX: A MYTHICAL DARK AGE?

Poland too had accepted the faith, as had Russia (in its Orthodox form) a short time earlier. Since one of the prophecies of the Gospels was that Christ's return would coincide with the preaching of the Gospel to all nations, and since that prophecy seemed on the verge of fulfillment, Otto III, something of a religious fanatic, conceived the notion that he should be the one to reign at the start of the Millennium; and that he, as Christ's temporal representative, should be the one to rule in his name. And so, working with the co-operation of the Pope, he decreed that New Year's day 701 (or actually, New Year's Day 704, since the error is not exactly three hundred years, but 297), the very day that the ruler of the mighty kingdom of Hungary was also crowned as a Christian monarch, should be celebrated as New Year's Day 1001. He was able to get away with this, we have seen, because of the general ignorance of history among the population, and by the confusion that reigned throughout Europe regarding calendars and dates. Some, as we saw, held that they were living in the Year 5700 of Creation, some that it was 5800 of Creation, and others various other dates. The point was: no one was sure, and confusion was the order of the day. Another element of chaos had been added by the arrival in Germany of Otto's own mother, the Byzantine princess Theophanou, who had wed Otto's father, Otto II. Theophanou came with a very large entourage of scholars and court officials. These brought with them their own Byzantine system of dating. Now, the calendars employed in the Eastern Empire were quite different to those used in the West. The Byzantines reckoned time, till quite a late date, according to a system designated the "Alexandrine Era". This actually counted the years, not since the death of Alexander the Great, but since the visit of the Emperor Augustus to Alexander's tomb (30 BC); an event popularly regarded as the official foundation-date of the Roman Empire.

However, calendars, this time connected with the life and epoch of Alexander himself, were also known and employed in Byzantium. One of these was the Era of the Seleucids, which began in 312 BC. This counted time according to the establishment of the Seleucid kingdom upon the ruins of Alexander's Empire, and was the one employed, for example, in the Hebrew Book of Maccabees, where it is known as the era of the Kingdom of the Greeks. Another and related Era was the Philippian, named after Philip Arrhidaeus, which began a few months prior to Alexander's death. Both these calendars were employed at Constantinople, and were connected, in the public mind, with

240

the Age of Alexander. The Philippian Era in particular was closely linked to the death of Alexander (323 BC) and began almost 300 hundred years – actually 293 – ahead of the Alexandrine Era, which, remember, was established by the Emperor Augustus. This latter Era, we are told, was "the most widespread occurring Era," and was "long in use in the Orient."[365]

It will be immediately observed that one of these two similarly-named calendars dates almost from the birth of Christ (Christians were aware that Christ was born sometime in the reign of Augustus), whilst another, roughly three hundred years longer, dates from the death of Alexander. Since both calendars were actually used at Constantinople, it seems obvious that the scholars who accompanied Theophanou to Germany would have been well-acquainted with each. In the words of Illig, "We have therefore two eras which are very similarly named. One could indeed very well speak of two Alexandrian Eras. The difference between the Era after Alexander's Death and the Alexandrian Era amounts to 294 years."[366] Thus, in the latter years of the seventh century, which is – according to Illig – when Otto III and Theophanou really lived, by the calendar of the Alexandrine Era (counting from the time of Augustus and therefore also the time of Christ) it would have been the latter years of the seventh century. But by the calendar of the Era after Alexander's death (the Seleucid and Philippian calendars), it would have been the latter years of the tenth century.

With such confusion, both in the East and in the West, it would have been the easiest thing in the world for the apocalyptically-minded Otto III to have declared himself reigning in the latter years of the tenth century, which would simultaneously have been declared the latter years of the sixth millennium.

This then, according to Illig, is how the 300-year error could have, or rather did, come about. We need not accept his every word to concede, I feel, that he has put forward a very plausible argument. And we would be remiss if we proceeded without mentioning the fact that his thesis has a very powerful astronomical, or rather calendrical, support. This concerns the Gregorian Calendar and the circumstances surrounding its introduction in 1582. The latter was intended to replace the old Julian Calendar, introduced by Julius Caesar in

---

[365] "Ära", *Brockhaus Enzyklopädie in zwanzig Bänden* (Wiesbaden, 1966)
[366] Illig, *Wer hat and der Uhr gedreht?* p. 179

APPENDIX: A MYTHICAL DARK AGE?

45 BC, a necessary reform owing to the inaccuracy of the Julian system. The Julian Calendar treated the year as exactly 365.25 days long – an extra day was added every fourth year, or Leap Year. But the year is not exactly 365.25 days; it is more precisely 365.2422 days, which means that, following the Julian system, about eleven minutes are added every year; and this, in the 1,627 years that had apparently elapsed between Caesar's reform and Pope Gregory's, should have produced an error of roughly thirteen days. In fact, the astronomers and mathematicians working for the Pope found that the civil calendar needed to be adjusted by only ten days, and it thus appears that the calendar counted roughly three centuries which never existed. The normal explanation for this discrepancy is that the Julian calendar must have been "updated" and two or three days removed at the Council of Nicea in AD 325, when the date for Easter was set. Yet there is no evidence in documents dealing with the Council that this occurred.

Possible Objections

Accepting then that a German Emperor, in co-operation with the Pope, could have declared his own reign as marking the millennium, this still leaves us with a number apparently very serious problems. (a) Scores, or perhaps even hundreds of medieval documents and chronicles, many of them claiming to have been written during the "dark centuries" (seventh to early tenth), describe the events of this period in great detail. Often the chronicles and annals of one country provide detailed confirmation of those of another. Thus the Anglo-Saxon Chronicle, for example, will mention the visit of an English monarch to the Continent, and the visit will also be noted in the corresponding chronicles of Gaul, or whichever country he was said to have visited. How is this to be explained, without recourse to a vast conspiracy taking in the scribes – invariably monks – of all the nations of Western Europe? And (b): The chronicles and records of the Byzantine and Islamic worlds also agree – generally speaking – with the Western documents. We can scarcely believe that the Byzantines, and certainly not the Muslims, would have co-operated with the Latins of Western Europe in a deliberate falsification of history. How is this to be explained?

HOLY WARRIORS

Let us deal first with point (a): There can be no doubt that the chronicles of Western Europe do provide a wealth of detail about events during the dark centuries; and the details provided in the various manuscripts are indeed internally consistent. According to Illig, all of these documents were composed in the eleventh, twelfth and thirteenth centuries, and none of them date from the periods they claim. Now, there is no question that the high Middle Ages was a period noted for document forgery. The best-known example of this was the so-called Donation of Constantine, supposedly written in the eighth century, but now widely recognized as originating at a later date. Purportedly issued by the Emperor Constantine, the *Donation* grants Pope Sylvester I and his successors, as inheritors of St. Peter, dominion over lands in Judea, Greece, Asia, Thrace, Africa, as well as the city of Rome, with Italy and the entire Western Roman Empire, while Constantine would retain imperial authority in the Eastern Roman Empire from his new imperial capital of Constantinople. The text claims that the *Donation* was Constantine's gift to Sylvester for instructing him in the Christian faith, baptizing him and miraculously curing him of leprosy.

Another famous, or rather infamous, example of this *genre* are the so-called Pseudo-Isidorean Decretals. These constitute the most extensive and influential set of forgeries in medieval Canon Law. Some collections of them included, for good measure, copies of the Donation of Constantine. These works, supposedly produced during the mid-ninth century, but probably a good deal later, in north-eastern France, have been universally recognized as forgeries for well over a century. We should note that "Immense labor and erudition went into creating this work, and a wide range of genuine sources were employed."[367] Like the Donation of Constantine, the forgers' main object was to empower the Church, or more accurately, church officials; in this case bishops, who were thereby emancipated not only from the secular power, but also from the influence of archbishops and synods. This was achieved partly by exalting papal power. The uses made of the forgeries form a historical study in themselves.

Document forgery then was something of an industry during the Middle Ages. These, as noted above, were not produced by amateurs, but by men of immense erudition, who employed, to make matters worse, a wide range of

---

[367] http://en.wikipedia.org/wiki/Pseudo-Isidore

genuine sources. All deceptions are more difficult to detect if they are mixed with truths.

Aside from those recognized forgeries, Illig and his colleague Nimitz have noted that a great many of the Early Medieval documents which are still regarded as genuine have an "anticipatory" nature. In other words, they framed laws which, at the supposed time of writing, was useless or redundant, but which later, during the twelfth, thirteenth and fourteenth centuries, became very useful indeed to the temporal and ecclesiastical authorities. I have already, in Chapter 5, cited the documents of the Councils of Toledo, of the seventh and eighth centuries, as prime examples of these. These texts set legal and moral precedents for the treatment of Jews which, during the thirteenth, fourteenth and fifteenth centuries, were in fact enacted against that people. And it should be noted that the documents of the Council of Toledo deal with a period of time very close to the life of Isidore of Seville, whose epoch is also the setting for the forged Pseudo-Decretals.

What then of the various chronicles and annals of the seventh, eighth and ninth centuries, which provide a detailed record of the kings, princes and churchmen of Western Europe in those centuries? These, according to Illig's thesis, had to be created in the years after Otto III, since, following his calendar reform, there existed on paper three centuries which never existed in fact and which had, therefore, no history. The three hundred years had to be filled with something. Illig speaks of an enormous project, carried out in the eleventh and twelfth centuries, by the monks of various monasteries throughout the West, to provide a history for those three hundred years. He has drawn attention to the fact that modern textual criticism and forensic science has proven and is in the process of proving more and more of these "Dark Age" documents to be forgeries. This is the case, for example, with up to 60% of the documents purporting to derive from the Merovingian Age and a great majority of the documents dealing with the Langobard or Lombard monarchy.[368]

Because the centuries between 614 and 911 never existed, neither, according to Illig, did the characters said to have lived in them. Thus most of the historical figures of this period, including some of the most famous, such as Charlemagne and Alfred the Great, are fictitious. Illig has now modified this

---

[368] Illig, *Wer hat an der Uhr gedreht?* pp. 228-235

somewhat extreme position, and has suggested that these persons probably did exist; only they didn't live when the chronicles said they did. A King Alfred of Wessex probably did fight the Danes, but he would have done so in the early seventh century, not in the ninth. In the same way, it could be that the entire Carolingian Dynasty, of the seventh, eighth and ninth centuries, is little more than a replication or duplication of the Merovingian Dynasty (both dynasties were Frankish) of the fifth, sixth and seventh centuries. Kings in early times regularly had several names, and it would have been the easiest thing in the world to present a Merovingian king, such a Clovis I, who was without question a "Carl" or warrior, as an entirely separate character named Carl the Great. It should be noted in this regard that the life of Charlemagne displays striking parallels with that of Clovis, and the two men, significantly enough, are placed almost precisely 300 years apart. If Charlemagne is identical to Clovis, this would explain why he is never credited with fighting the Muslims: Islam didn't exist in his time.

As well as duplications, other characters and events, which were actually contemporaneous, were placed in sequence and the therefore made to "fill-in" a lot of time. This would not have been difficult to do, as the previous century (ie before 1000, or, in Illig's scheme, before 700) was rich in events, with continual military action against Muslims, Vikings and Magyars. Since there was so little accurate record-keeping (thanks to the severing of the papyrus-supply from Egypt), people's memory of these events, and their sequence, would have been hazy at best. In such circumstances, they could easily have been "drawn-out" and made to fill a couple of centuries. In this way the Viking raids, for example, would actually have commenced around the middle of the seventh century, say close to 640. Since they are well-known to have continued till just after 1050 (ie 750), this would have made the real epoch of the Vikings fall between roughly 640 and 750. Thus one hundred years of raiding would have been stretched out to make it look like two hundred and fifty years.

Undoubtedly straightforward invention also took place, as the Pseudo-Isidorean Decretals make clear, but these are not easy to identify – with the possible exception of certain obviously fabulous events said to have marked the lives of Charlemagne and the Byzantine Emperor Heraclius.

There remains problem (b). How is it that the Christian calendar apparently agrees with the Muslim calendar, which dates, or claims to date, from the flight of Muhammad (*hijra* or *hegira*) from Mecca to Medina? To this there are a couple of possible solutions. On the one hand, it is possible that the Muslim Calendar (Age of Hijra or Hegira) is correct and keeps an accurate record of Muhammad's flight to Medina. In this scenario, the prophet of Islam would have lived three hundred years earlier than is commonly believed vis a vis the Christian calendar. In other words, he would have lived between 270 and 332 rather than 570 and 632. This is not impossible since, as Illig mentions, Muhammad was evidently influenced by the ideas of the heretical Ebionite Church, a group that was condemned at the Council of Nicea in 325, and which around 400 went into exile in Arabia.

This solution however seems to be unlikely, for reasons we shall now explore.

There is in fact good evidence to show that the Arabs did not keep an accurate record of the years since Muhammad's lifetime, and they simply borrowed the idea of a calendar reaching back to Muhammad from the Christians and their *anno domini*. The evidence suggests indeed that they copied the Christian calendar, along with its errors and anomalies. This is made fairly clear by the fact that the earliest Arab coins which give AH dates also give, side by side, the AD date. The earliest of these date to the eleventh century. Furthermore, Muslim historiography contains the same anomalies and enigmas as we find in the Christian. Thus we saw that Mahmud of Ghazni, who conquers Northern India in the early eleventh century, is virtually identical, in terms of deeds and name, to Muhammad bin Qasim, who conquers Northern India in the early eighth century. That both these are one and the same person is made highly likely by the fact that Mahmud of Ghazni is said to have lived only four generations after Muhammad the Prophet: Thus his father Sebektagin was described as "the slave of the slave of the slave of the commander of the faithful [Muhammad]."[369] Thus four generations only (about one hundred years) separate Mahmud of Ghazni from the foundation of the Islamic faith; which means, in essence, that Mahmud of Ghani must have flourished around 700 AD, and he must, therefore, be one and the same as Muhammad bin Qasim.

---

[369] See Gibbon, Ch. 57.

The Muslims then simply copied the Christian idea of a calendar dating back to the lifetime of their founder and, basing their own system on that of the Christians, repeated the chronological mistakes of the latter.

Consequences

Accepting that Illig is correct has dramatic consequences. Most obviously, if the years between 614 and 911 did not exist, this means that all years post-911 must be reduced by almost three centuries. Thus for example the Norman Conquest of England did not occur in 1066 but in 766, or, more precisely, 769. In the same way, the First Crusade would not have been launched in 1095, but in 795 or shortly thereafter. The widespread feeling among historians therefore that the Crusades represented the Christian response to the Islamic conquests is stunningly confirmed. Historians have long been puzzled by the fact that the Christian riposte had to wait four centuries to materialize. Remove the three hundred years of the Dark Age however and the Crusades, at last, make perfect sense.

No area of European history can escape the consequences of such a chronological shift. The Viking expansion, for example, currently seen as a final thrust of the great Germanic migrations, or *Völkerwanderung*, though almost three centuries removed from the rest of these, now takes its rightful place at the tail end of those migrations. Thus the Vikings would have commenced their marauding and piracy not circa 800 AD, but closer to 640 AD, shortly after the Lombard invasion of Italy and only about two centuries or so after the migration to Britain of their Angle cousins from Jutland. Yet the onset of Viking slave-trading, we have seen, was also intimately connected with the rise of Islam, and the Muslim demand for European slaves only really appeared after the conquest of Spain. Thus the Islamic invasion of Spain must also be back-dated, and indeed appears to have occurred early in the seventh century – perhaps up to 75 years before the date (711) given in the textbooks. And this redating is confirmed by the archaeology. As we have seen, Spain is virtually devoid of Islamic remains before the middle of the tenth century. There is almost nothing that can be dated to the eighth and ninth centuries – supposedly the most glorious epoch of Islamic Iberia. Indeed, as Illig emphasizes, Islamic remains only make a real appearance during the second quarter of the tenth century. And here archaeology does correspond with written history; for, in Illig's words: "It is just in the 10th century that we find the struggle between Christians and Muslims raging throughout the land. A stronghold like Toledo was conquered and lost more than once. Abd er-Rahman III is the first notable character. During his reign (916-961) for the first time, the dominion of the Omayyads was secured (renewed?). As the title of Caliph indicated, he united in himself both temporal and spiritual authority. His possessions in Spain consisted of much more than Andalusia. His defeat at the Battle of Simancas in 939, best demonstrates the extent of his influence. Simancas lay between Salamanca and Valladolid on the Duoro, marking therefore the most northerly position of the Arab troops. In spite of this defeat, the Omayyad State reaches its apogee in the middle of the 10th century. Reflecting this is the fact that the Christian king of Leon could only hold the throne with Omayyad help. In 980 there emerged once again in Al-Mansur a conqueror in the grand style. He burned Leon, Barcelona and Santiago de Compostela, and advanced even over the Pyrenees. His progress was only halted with his death in the year 1002."[370]

Illig goes on to note that this tenth-century Islamic expansion, the only one attested by archaeology, has striking parallels with the eighth-century Islamic expansion of the textbooks, whilst the *Reconquista*, which reputedly commenced with the victory of Don Pelayo at Covadonga around 720, looks very like the real *Reconquista*, which began in the 1020s with the campaigns of the Norman Baron Roger de Tony. But if Iberia first came under Islamic rule during the time of Abd er-Rahman III (912-961), this means, in Illig's revision, that Spain really came under Islamic rule in the early seventh century. Thus Abd er-Rahman III would properly be dated to circa 612-661. (We should note here too that Abd er-Rahman III's life and career offers remarkable parallels with that of his supposed ancestor Abd er-Rahman I, who is placed almost exactly two centuries earlier, and who completed the conquest of Spain begun by Tarik the Berber).

Clearly then the Muslim conquest of Spain must have occurred about a century, or at least three-quarters of a century, before the date given in the textbooks. Yet if Spain was Islamicized at that time, this means in turn that the

---

whole of Muslim history needs to be back-dated. If the Muslims were conquering Spain in circa 625, Muhammad can scarcely have still been alive in 632. In fact, as we have seen, Illig suggested that Muhammad might more logically be placed in the fifth or even fourth century; when a Judaising sect of Christianity, known as the Nazarites or Ebionites, were declared heretical and disappeared into the Arabian interior. It is known that Islam, as found in the Koran, has much in common with Ebionite beliefs; and there seems little doubt that Muhammad, whenever he lived, was influenced in part by the thinking of the Ebionites.

If then Muhammad lived a century or so before the date normally given, as seems likely, it means a complete revision of the narrative of Islamic expansion. Muhammad may have personally led armies and subdued the Arabian Peninsula, but his comrades certainly did not launch the great conquests which, within little more than seventy-five years, are believed to have seen Arab arms victorious from the Pyrenees to the borders of India. That Arab armies were clashing with Byzantium as early as the mid-sixth century is evident from the fact that Procopius refers to "Saracen" raiders on several occasions. These are normally believed to have been pre-Islamic Arab bandits, but it is much more likely, in view of what we have discovered above, that these Saracens were early Islamic warriors, possibly forces under the command of some of the Ommayad caliphs such as Umar or Uthman.

In any case, the last events that we can be sure of before the onset of the confusion that marks the seventh century, are the wars waged between the Byzantine Empire under Heraclius and the Persians under Chosroes II. In those years it was the Persians, and not the Arabs, who were the main power in the Near East. According to Illig, it seems probable that the Persians, whose well-attested conquest of Syria in 614 and Egypt in 616 or 617 brought shame to the Byzantines and the loss of some of Christianity's holiest relics, encountered Islam in Syria and there converted to the heretical Shiite branch, probably sometime between 610 and 620. Alternatively, it may have been that the Persians and Arabs, finding a common foe in the Eastern Roman Empire, joined forces around 615 and, overwhelming Syria, pushed then into Egypt and westwards towards Tunisia and Algeria. During this period, some members of the Persian nobility, quite possibly including Chosroes II himself, converted to Islam; and we should note that the crescent moon, which adorns the crown of

APPENDIX: A MYTHICAL DARK AGE?

Chosroes II in one famous illustration, is afterwards found as the symbol *par excellence* of Islam.

Whatever the truth, historians have noted the profoundly Persian flavor of the earliest Islam encountered archaeologically in Spain and North Africa.[371] It is admitted, of course, that a Persian or Persianizing dynasty, the Abbasids, did seize control of the Caliphate in the eighth century. Thus it is agreed that by circa 750 the real Arab impulse of the Omayyad dynasty had been superseded by the Abbasids, with whose Persian spirit an "entirely new epoch of Islam begins." Furthermore, "Islam possessed an almost exclusively Abbasid [ie Persian] historiography, which Omayyad historical literature deliberately and extraordinarily successfully suppressed. ... The entire old-Arabian historiography was, for the period until circa 400 AH/1000 AD, completely reworked on dogmatic lines."[372]

The dogmatic lines included a fictitious Arab conquest of Persia,[373] and the invention of an Arab conquest of Egypt, Babylonia, and North Africa into the bargain – a conquest achieved by little more than a few Bedouin raiders on camels. But it was the might of Sassanid Persia, with the overwhelming force of Persian cataphracts, that achieved these conquests – admittedly in alliance with the Arabs, who, however, contributed little more than a potent ideology. It was this relatively tolerant Persian, or Sassanid/Abbasid period, that saw the flowering (very briefly) of the arts and sciences. But this Golden Age was short-lived indeed.

Whatever may be the consequences of Illig's hypothesis for Islamic history, the narrative of the clash between Islam and Christianity is completely transformed. As we have seen, historians have long been puzzled by the fact that, though the Crusades represent the Christian response to the great Islamic conquests, a gap of three and a half to four centuries separates the two episodes. Fifty years ago Sidney Painter noted that early in the eleventh century the monks

---

[371] The early caliphs, it is known, ruled largely, if not completely, through a Persian bureaucracy. See Trevor-Roper, op cit., p. 142

[372] Günter Lüling. *Die Wiederentdeckung des Propheten Muhammad. Eine Kritik am "christlichen" Abendland* (Erlangen, 1981) p. 411

[373] Firdausi (or Firdowsi), the Persian chronicler-poet, who unquestionably flourished after the Islamicization of his country, makes no mention of an Arab conquest.

of Cluny called on the nobles of France to undertake expeditions against the Spanish Muslims. "One can only guess at their motives," said Painter.[374] And this comment is symptomatic of our entire view of the Crusades. Separated as they are by almost four centuries from the initial Muslim expansion, they make little sense. Even worse, they convey the impression of an unprovoked attack by barbarous Westerners against a peaceful and sedentary Muslim world. Reduce all dates by three centuries however and we see things from a different perspective. The monks of Cluny called for Frankish help because they were living not in the early eleventh century but the early eighth, and the tide of Muslim aggression had not yet begun to ebb. Europe itself was in imminent danger of conquest by a foe bent on the eventual elimination of Christianity.

Now at last that great century of the Spanish Reconquista, the eleventh, begins to make sense. But it was not the eleventh century, it was the eighth. The 1018 expedition by Roger de Tony actually took place in 718 (or 721), and the great invasion of the Burgundians was in 733, not 1033. The 1063 expedition of Gui-Geoffrey, Duke of Aquitaine, was really in 763, and the famous expedition of Burgundians in 1085, which saw the capture of Toledo, actually took place in 785.

These battles, admittedly the first Crusades, were the precursors and models for the official First Crusade of 1095 (actually 795 or 798); and it is thus nothing more than a myth that the Crusades were launched against a long-established and peacefully settled Muslim world. They were in fact a Christian counter-attack in what was still, essentially, a defensive measure. It should not be forgotten either that the First Crusade was called when Alexius Comnenus called on the Latins to assist him in defense of his realm, which was under threat by the Seljuk Turks. These newcomers from Central Asia had already occupied all of Anatolia and Asia Minor and now threatened Constantinople itself. In every respect, the First Crusade was defensive. Why Urban II chose to instruct the Crusaders to go on from Anatolia to Jerusalem is unclear, though he may have felt that by establishing a Christian presence in Palestine, right in the middle of the Muslim world, he could have fatally weakened Islam and helped precipitate its downfall.

---

[374] Painter, op cit., p. 193

APPENDIX: A MYTHICAL DARK AGE?

Whatever the motive, the central fact remains indisputable: the First Crusade, like those of the previous seventy-five years in Spain, was a defensive war launched to stop ongoing Muslim aggression. Later Crusades sought simply to retain what was held, though by the thirteenth (ie tenth) century the Muslims were again advancing into Christian territory; this time under the aegis of the Ottoman Turks, who crossed from Anatolia and began the conquest of South East Europe.

Perhaps the most important consequence of Illig's redating is that it renders the notion of a four-century long Islamic Golden Age, during which the Muslim world was intellectually and technically superior to the Christian world, untenable. If the kings and prelates of tenth-century Europe, who occupied Roman-style villas and palaces, were actually living in the seventh century, then there was no European Dark Age, in the sense of an epoch during which all civilized life came to an end, and the Muslims cannot be blamed for creating what did not exist. Yet there most definitely was a Medieval Age, an age which, properly speaking, began in that selfsame tenth (actually seventh) century; an age which was markedly inferior, in terms of humane ethics, learning, culture in general, science and economy. This Islam most certainly did create. By the end of the tenth (seventh) century Europe – both East and West – was markedly inferior to the world of Islam, at least in terms of science and technology; and Christians began to emulate what they found in the Saracen kingdoms. Over the next century or century-and-a-half the Arab world remained ahead of the European, in scientific terms; but by the middle of the twelfth (ninth) century that lead had vanished. That it lasted such a short time speaks volumes. In Egypt, in Babylonia, in Persia, and, a little later, in India, Islam came to control the most ancient, most opulent, and most enlightened civilizations on earth. What did she do with this overwhelming advantage? By the twelfth century (ie the ninth), these territories began to show unmistakable signs of a stagnation, a cultural impoverishment, and a general decline that left all of them (with the exception of the non-Islamic parts of India) within a couple of centuries, virtual economic wastelands. The period which elapsed from the Islamicization of these regions to their economic and cultural ruin was therefore no more than a century or two at the very most.

This is an astonishing indictment: In spite of having inherited in the seventh century all the territories of the ancient Near Eastern civilizations – with

252

their wealth, learning and technologies – and in spite of being first in line, through Persia, in receiving such vital Chinese inventions as the compass, gunpowder, paper, printing, etc, and such Indian discoveries as the decenary numerical system, by 800 (ie 1100 in conventional chronology) backward and impoverished Europe had caught up, and by 900 (1200 in the conventional system) she had taken the lead, a lead she would never again relinquish. We need only recall here the Muslim world's ignorance of firearms manufacture during and after the thirteenth and fourteenth (in Illig's system tenth and eleventh) centuries. And by the fifteenth (ie twelfth) century it was Europeans, in European ships, who began the great age of exploration.

The squandering by the Muslim world of its massive head-start is explained entirely by Islam. A system which sanctifies war and plunder can only produce the kleptocracy which in the end destroyed commerce and all kinds of innovation. Formerly prosperous provinces were reduced to poverty, and by the twelfth century (ie the ninth) the populations of Egypt, Syria, Mesopotamia and North Africa had begun a long and catastrophic decline. Large regions, which had, until the seventh century, been cultivated and productive, were reduced to wasteland, whilst banditry made life outside the protective walls of cities a virtual impossibility throughout vast areas of the Near and Middle East. And this situation prevailed until the coming of the Europeans in the nineteenth century. In his 2001 book *What went Wrong?* Bernard Lewis asked the question: What went wrong with a civilization which – he believes – showed such promise at the start, only to be mired in poverty and backwardness from the 12th-13th century onwards? Lewis concludes his volume without arriving at an answer. Yet at one point in the book he makes a telling observation: Wheeled vehicles were virtually unknown, up until modern times, throughout the Muslim lands. This was all the more strange given the fact that the wheel was invented in the Middle East (in Babylonia) and had been commonly used in earlier ages. The conclusion he comes to is startling: "A cart is large and, for a peasant, relatively costly. It is difficult to conceal and easy for requisition. At a time and place where neither law nor custom restricted the powers of even local authorities, visible and mobile assets were a poor investment. The same fear of predatory authority – or neighbors – may be seen in the structure of traditional houses and quarters: the high, windowless walls, the almost hidden entrances in narrow alleyways, the careful avoidance of any visible sign of wealth."[375] In the kleptocracy that was the Caliphate, it seems, not even Muslims – far less Christians and Jews – were "free to prosper materially."

Finally, if the Islamic Golden Age did not exist, then neither did the supposed Islamic Age of Tolerance. The slaughter of the Jews of Morocco and Spain for example did not occur in 1011, 1033 and 1066, but in 711, 733 and 766, and thus forms a continuum with the killings of Jews by Muhammad in Arabia in the early seventh century. Islam was *never* tolerant and it was never enlightened!

---

[375] Lewis, *What Went Wrong?* p. 158

INDEX

INDEX

41, 43, 52, 54, 57,
64, 93, 94, 99, 118,
162, 171, 172, 238,
244, 245

Mohammed, (see
Muhammad)

Monasteries, 21, 49,
79, 81, 82, 87, 98,
102, 108, 166, 198,
216, 244

Monks, 10, 32, 49, 62,
64, 65, 77, 79, 80-
82, 85-88, 102,
113, 147, 206, 222,
242, 244, 250, 251

Monophysite(s), 71

Monte Cassino, 80, 81,
103, 198

Moors, 10, 177, 208,
215

Mousa, 147, 227

Mozarabs, 127

Muawiyah, 102

Mughal(s), 145

Muhammad, 96, 128,
129, 131, 142, 144,
145, 150-58, 162,
170, 186, 192,
203n., 246, 249,
254

Muhammed bin Qasim,
170

Muslim(s)

Nazarites, 249

Nestorian(s), 137, 214

Nicephorus II, Emperor,
108

Nika riots, 67

North Africa, 7, 11, 13,
23, 25, 28, 49, 65,
67, 94, 96, 99, 101,
106, 107, 115, 116,
124, 125, 127, 128,
145, 157, 163, 172,
178, 186, 192, 193,
204, 208, 211, 212,
214, 220, 250, 253

Northumbria, 89

Olybrius, Emperor, 27

Olympiodorus, 73

Omar Khayyam, 138

Ommayad(s), 249. (see
also Ummayads)

Ostrogoth(s), 25, 26,
29, 31, 32, 44, 48,
53, 67

Oswald, 89

Otto I, 173, 201, 202

Otto II, 240

Otto III, 14, 174, 229,
237, 239-41, 244

Otto the Great, 200,
238, 239. (see also
Otto I)

Ottonian(s), 39, 54,
172, 173, 201, 202,
226, 238, 239

Ovid, 81

pagans, paganism, 47,
48, 50, 56, 70-76,

84, 89, 91, 114,
149, 150, 189, 205,
207, 208, 235

paper, 9, 10, 50, 135,
152, 253

papyrus, 3, 6, 36, 98,
99, 100, 106, 113,
207, 210, 223, 245

parchment, 36, 98-100

Parthians, 75

Persepolis, 138

Persia, Persians, 9-11,
13, 57, 68, 72-78,
105, 107, 133-40,
153, 170, 181, 183,
192, 193, 197, 203,
212, 149, 250, 252,
253

Peter the Hermit, 183

piracy, pirates, 3, 89,
104, 108, 109, 111,
115, 120, 145, 178,
195, 198, 211, 212,
220, 247

Pirenne, Henri, 3-5, 8,
12, 15, 22-41, 44,
55, 93, 95, 97-101,
103-07, 109, 112,
113, 115, 118, 121,
123, 125, 132, 134,
171, 187, 201, 207,
233

Plato, 236

Pliny, 81, 98

Poitiers, Battle of, 102

INDEX

261

Lightning Source UK Ltd.
Milton Keynes UK
02 February 2010

149473UK00001B/86/P